MAJOR EUROPEAN

JAROSLAV H

BOOKS IN THIS SERIES

Other studies in preparation

Hašek aged nineteen

JAROSLAV HAŠEK

A STUDY OF *ŠVEJK* AND THE SHORT STORIES

Cecil Parrott

CAMBRIDGE UNIVERSITY PRESS

Cambridge

London   New York   New Rochelle

Melbourne   Sydney

CAMBRIDGE UNIVERSITY PRESS
Cambridge, New York, Melbourne, Madrid, Cape Town, Singapore,
São Paulo, Delhi, Dubai, Tokyo

Cambridge University Press
The Edinburgh Building, Cambridge CB2 8RU, UK

Published in the United States of America by Cambridge University Press, New York

www.cambridge.org
Information on this title: www.cambridge.org/9780521136778

© Cambridge University Press 1982

First published 1982
This digitally printed version 2010

A catalogue record for this publication is available from the British Library

ISBN 978-0-521-24352-0 Hardback
ISBN 978-0-521-13677-8 Paperback

To Ellen

CONTENTS

ILLUSTRATIONS

Hašek aged nineteen (*frontispiece*)

GENERAL PREFACE TO THE SERIES

This series was initiated within the Cambridge University Press as an at first untitled collection of general studies. For convenience it was referred to inside the Press as 'the Major European Authors series'; and once the initial prejudice against the useful word 'major' was overcome, the phrase became the official title.

The series was always meant to be informal and flexible, and no very strict guidelines are imposed on the authors. The aim is to provide books which can justifiably be given a title which starts simply with the name of the author studied: therefore to be general, introductory and accessible. When the series started, in the 1960s, there was an assumption that a biographical approach or an approach via historical background was old-fashioned, and it is still relatively hard to find books which address themselves directly to the works as literature and try to give a direct sense of the general intention, or particular structure or effect. The aim is principally to give a critical introduction to a whole *œuvre*, or to the most important works; to help the reader to form or order his own impressions by liberal quotation and judicious analysis; to assume little prior knowledge, and in most cases to quote in English, or to translate quotations given in the original.

It is hoped that the series will help to keep some classics of European literature alive and active in the minds of present-day readers: both students working for a formal examination in literature and educated general readers – a class which still exists – who wish to gain access to the best in European culture.

Sir Cecil Parrott's study of Hašek is conceived within the general framework of the series; but it deals with an author whose work is so much a reflection of his own experience and times that it is essential to have a grasp of Hašek's life and of the setting of Czech history and politics. Sir Cecil's full-scale biography is the standard reference, but it is still most useful to have in this volume his briefer account of Hašek's life, and the interesting survey of the historical background, before proceeding to the works themselves.

AUTHOR'S NOTE

Page numbers in the text refer to the author's translation of *The Good Soldier Švejk* (Heinemann and Penguin Books, London, 1973, Robert and Thomas Y. Crowell, New York, 1973). This is the only complete edition available in English.

Some of the stories discussed in this book have been translated by the author in *The Red Commissar* (Lester and Orpen Dennys, Toronto, Heinemann, London and Dial, New York 1981); and further details about Hašek's adventurous life can be found in the author's biography *The Bad Bohemian* (The Bodley Head, London 1978).

I

THE INDIVIDUAL AND
THE GIANT POWER

'Human existence, humbly report, sir, is so complicated that the
life of a single individual is nothing more than a bit of rubbish in
comparison.' (Švejk)

The distinguished Czech critic František Šalda found *The Good
Soldier Švejk* for all its comedy 'a desperately sad book'. If he
was right, then its tragedy lies as much in the personal disappointments of the author as in the frustrated hopes of the Czechs.
Šalda went on to say that in the book 'the individual fights
against...a giant power'. This could be applied not only to
Švejk, but to his creator, Jaroslav Hašek himself. He was always
trying to come to terms with life and no doubt in his imagination
saw himself 'fighting against a giant power'. He certainly portrayed Švejk in this rôle and there is much of Hašek in Švejk –
but not all of him, because he deliberately avoided creating Švejk
in his own image.[1]

Hašek's life was in many respects a picaresque novel itself.[2]
Born in Prague in 1883, there was nothing in his ancestry to
suggest inherited literary talent. The Hašeks had been fairly
prosperous farmers in Southern Bohemia for many generations
and one of them, it is claimed, had been a parliamentary deputy.
Hašek's father was an impoverished schoolmaster and alcoholic
who died when the writer was only thirteen. His maternal grandfather had been a water bailiff on one of the famous Bohemian
fishponds on the Schwarzenberg estate. He himself was brought
up by his mother, who seems to have had no outstanding
characteristics except her inability to control her wayward
son.

Although the family were poor, they had well-placed relations
and patrons. Hašek's paternal uncle was a master-printer on the
largest Czech daily *National Policy* and later helped him to
become a contributor to it. After his father's death Hašek was

Jaroslav Hašek

fortunate enough to have as his guardian Jakub Škarda, an alderman of the City of Prague and founder of the then influential Young Czech Party.

Even though the Hašeks lived in straitened circumstances and changed their address many times, they always managed to find accommodation in one of the best quarters of Prague among the academic institutions in the New Town, even if the accommodation itself was not of the best. It was this quarter of Prague which Hašek knew best and which is most often mentioned in *The Good Soldier Švejk* and his stories. In some of the churches in the neighbourhood he earned a little pocket money by acting as a server, which taught him a good deal about the Catholic liturgy. He made good use of this knowledge in *The Good Soldier Švejk* and his anti-clerical stories.

At school he was intelligent, but headstrong and rebellious. According to his brother Bohuslav, complaint followed complaint, and he was often made to stand in the corner or sent to the bottom of the class. He had little respect for authority, whether in the shape of his schoolmasters or the police, and took a leading part in fights with rival bands of youths, especially Germans. When posters were put up proclaiming a state of emergency, he and others of his gang went around pulling down all they could find and setting fire to them. When armed dragoons with drawn swords chased the adult demonstrators, he succeeded in escaping by climbing over walls and hiding away in the gardens of some of the academic institutions, but not before he had thrown a large paving stone through the window of the German Institute on the other side of the road. Official complaints arising out of these escapades and excesses were too much for the school and Hašek was finally expelled. However, thanks to the help of his guardian, he managed to obtain a job at a chemist's store, from which he was soon sacked for playing a joke on his stupid and fussy employer. He was then taken on by another more discerning chemist who came to recognise his talents and recommend that he should complete his education at the Czechoslavonic Commercial Academy. This institution, contrary to what its name implies, was in fact a general secondary school of high repute, and had on its staff some very distinguished literary men of the time, including V. A. Jung, one of the editors of the standard large

2

Anglo-Czech dictionary, who was far-seeing enough to prophesy that Hašek would eventually become a second Mark Twain.

Hašek spent three years at the Commercial Academy and passed his final examinations with distinction. He showed from an early age that he had many qualities which could be assets to him as a writer. He was not only observant and imaginative, but full of mischief too, and soon revealed an unusual capacity for creating absurd situations, which lent themselves readily to literary exploitation. At the age of fourteen, while still employed at the chemist's, he had already started writing – an occupation which he continued after finally leaving school. But it was the walking tours which he undertook in Moravia, Slovakia and Hungary during his vacation which kindled in him a literary flame that was never quenched. They also provided him with the material for many of his early stories.

His first trip, undertaken in the summer of 1900, when he was seventeen, led to the publication of his first newspaper story, 'Gypsies at Their Feast', which was accepted by the largest Prague daily, *The National Paper*. By the time he left the Commercial Academy at the age of nineteen, he had succeeded in placing eleven stories in various leading newspapers. Meanwhile he was developing a taste for a vagabond life and spending more and more time exploring the Czechoslovak and other Austrian lands.

In October 1902 he obtained a post in a Prague bank but soon put his career in jeopardy by his unruly conduct. Bohuslav described how his brother came to part company with the bank in the spring of 1903: 'One day Jaroslav had a special errand to perform at Vyšehrad. On the way he stopped at a pub and took a decision. He packed up his ledger, put his visiting card inside it and sent it by messenger to the bank. The message on the card was short and sweet:

'I'm not baking today!*
Jaroslav Hašek.'

His employers at first treated his truancy with indulgence for the sake of his widowed mother, but, when he repeated the offence, they could tolerate it no longer and he was finally dismissed in the spring of 1903.

* 'I'm downing tools!'

3

Jaroslav Hašek

A few months earlier he had published a volume of poems called *Cries of May* in collaboration with his best friend at the Academy, another budding writer, Ladislav Hájek. By 1904 he had contributed fifty articles to the press, a respectable quantity for a beginner of twenty-one, but not nearly enough to pay for his keep or contribute to the family funds.

An important development in Hašek's career at this time was his recruitment by the Anarchist movement. It is not quite certain how this came about, but it is known that in Prague in 1904 the Anarchist and Social Democrat youth tried to break up a service of prayers for Russia's victory in her war with Japan which had just broken out. Hašek was among the young and noisy demonstrators who were arrested and held for questioning. In the process he made friends with one of the group, who persuaded him to help compose a radical pamphlet attacking the 'reformist policy' of the Social Democrat Party, which placed its hopes on universal suffrage rather than revolution. Later he got to know Bedřich Kalina, editor of the Anarchist paper *Progressive Youth*.

It should be remembered that at this time there was no Communist Party in Bohemia, and the only Left parties were the Social Democrats and the National Socials. Neither of these were radical enough for some of the Czech youth, but the National Socials, who were Socialists of nationalist persuasion as against the traditionally international Social Democrat Party, had links with the Anarchists, and Hašek had some friends among them.

Partly to escape trouble with the police, in which his drunken escapades were increasingly involving him, and partly out of genuine enthusiasm for the Anarchist cause, Hašek left Prague shortly afterwards in Kalina's company to work in the editorial offices of *Progressive Youth* in Lom (Bruch) in Northern Bohemia, where the Anarchists had strong support among the miners. After contributing a number of articles to the paper and taking part in the distribution of propaganda, he had a disagreement with the editor and threw up his job. Feeling that it might be risky for him to reappear in Prague, he went on a tramp round Bavaria and Switzerland, in the course of which he found plenty of material for many new stories. But when funds ran out, he returned to his mother's home in Prague, where during 1905 he got into further minor scrapes with the police. Having quarrelled with

4

the Anarchists, he published no more articles in their press for the time being, but concentrated on the more remunerative and more respectable conventional newspapers and reviews, where he had considerable success.

Probably at the end of 1905 he made the acquaintance of Jarmila Mayerová, a student of the Women's Manufacturing Association, a girls' commercial school, and the daughter of a well-to-do partner in a firm of plasterers and sculptors. She was not pretty; freckled, snub-nosed and pince-nezed, she had all the appearance of a bluestocking, except that she was elegantly and fashionably dressed. But there was something appealing and tantalising in her sensitive and piquant little face, and her timid look seemed to call for his protection. As an 'emancipated woman' she admired him for his bold views, even if she did not always approve his unconventional behaviour. At this time one of Jarmila's friends described Hašek as 'not at all romantic looking, but very handsome. His eyes were grey and his hair wavy and chestnut colour. His face was like a girl's, with a silky, pink complexion. He looked healthy, well-nourished and level-headed.' (He had obviously not suffered physically from the straitened circumstances in which he was brought up, or from the effect of his exhausting and penniless hiking trips all over Austria-Hungary.)

But Jarmila's father not unexpectedly looked with disfavour on his daughter's friendship with the impecunious young Anarchist. He had been born the son of a mill-hand, who had worked up to a position of respectability and means. After a family quarrel in the autumn of 1906, Jarmila was forbidden to see Hašek for half a year. The frustrations of a winter of separation, broken only occasionally by clandestine meetings, drove Hašek back to the Anarchist fold. He started to contribute to their Prague publication, *Commune*, which he later edited, and to its supplement *Pauper*. On 13 April 1907 he spoke at one of their rallies in Northern Bohemia and on the following day led a demonstration to break up a Catholic Party meeting. Three days later the police ordered him to be placed under regular surveillance.

In the meantime Jarmila had become quite ill from the effects of their separation and the Mayers had to relent and agree that the lovers should go on meeting, provided Hašek promised to quit

5

the Anarchist movement for good. He glibly gave this undertaking, and they were allowed to go about together. This permission was given on May Day 1907 – an unfortunate date, because on that very day the Anarchists had arranged a mass meeting in Prague. Hašek attended it only as a reporter (or so he claimed) and was arrested by the police for 'inflicting serious bodily injury on a policeman and inciting the public to similar assaults'. He was remanded until 14 May, and Jarmila tried her best to keep from her parents the news of his detention and the ensuing trial. He was finally sentenced to a month's imprisonment which he served in the gaol of the New Town Hall in Prague.

When Mr Mayer finally got to know what had happened, he refused to allow them to meet any more and warned Hašek that his only hope of marrying Jarmila lay in his solemnly promising to reform. He must really stick to his promise and never again have anything to do with the Anarchist movement, and he must go about respectably dressed and try to find a steady job. In a serious endeavour to make good, Hašek renewed his efforts to achieve literary success and secure permanent employment on one of the papers he contributed to.

Meanwhile, until Hašek could satisfy Mr Mayer, the lovers had once more to go on meeting in secret and communicating through friends. Worried by the effect this was having on Jarmila's nerves, Hašek determined to take the bull by the horns and go and see Mr Mayer. So one day he went to his front door and calmly knocked at it. But his characteristically jocular and jaunty approach did not pay off. Menger, one of Hašek's biographers, tells us: 'When Jarmila's father opened the door and asked him what he wanted, Hašek replied: "I'm coming to ask you for Jarmila's hand, my dear respected father-in-law. I thought for a long time beforehand whether I should clean my shoes or put on a clean collar, and finally I plumped for a clean collar. It means less work." But he had no time to finish. Mr Mayer froze him with a withering look and slammed the door in his face.'

Hašek's efforts to find a job were unsuccessful, because they were not seriously meant, as a letter which he addressed to the Director of the Library of the National Museum shows very well:

Gentlemen,
I offer you my services.

6

The individual and the giant power

I have practical experience behind me.
I have edited the journals *Commune* and *Pauper* and although I
am not an outright Anarchist I edited them in an anarchist way.
Would someone of the age of twenty-five suit you?

One day Hašek waylaid his would-be-father-in-law in the street
and tried to appeal to his better nature. Mr Mayer, who was a
tender-hearted man, was moved by his pleading. Finally he gave
way and said, 'Come for her, when you've got a job. I'll gladly
give her to you.' But Hašek's chances of getting a job were not at
all promising. He had alienated editors and Party leaders not only
by his Anarchist activities but by his erratic conduct. A friendly
Prague Police Commissioner allegedly advised him as follows:
'If you want to join a party where they shout a lot, join the
National Socials. If you've still got revolutionary ideas, join the
Social Democrats.'

Hašek tried to do both. With his usual optimism he wrote to
Jarmila on 10 January that he had been in touch with Social
Democrat leaders and they had allegedly promised him a job on
their main daily *The People's Right*. Discouraged by what he
believed to be their failure to keep their promise, he stupidly
resorted to blackmail. One day he brought them an article guying
the National Social leaders. When they hesitated to accept it, he
sat down, crossed out the original names and substituted those of
the Social Democrat leaders instead. After making a few further
alterations, he sent it to the National Social press, who published
it. He then started to make fun of both parties, offering articles to
People's Right (Social Democrat) and *Czech Word* (National
Social) and even carrying on polemics between the two papers by
writing anonymously both sets of articles himself.

Hašek had been too strongly associated with the Anarchists'
campaign against the Social Democrats to be wholly trusted by
their leaders. His relations with the National Socials were rather
better. At the by-elections in the Vinohrady district of Prague in
1908 he was given charge of their offices in their campaign
against the Young Czechs. But he turned the whole proceedings
into a farce and alienated not only the Young Czechs, the party of
his former guardian, but also the National Socials who employed
him.

After his electioneering escapade Hašek found himself on the

7

rocks once more. Fortunately his friend Hájek took pity on him and found him a job on the magazine, *Animal World*, of which he was editor. By a coincidence it happened that shortly afterwards Hájek quarrelled with the owner and resigned, which enabled Hašek to take over his post. It was the first offer of a salaried job he had received since he left the bank. He immediately wrote enthusiastically to Jarmila's mother that he had a job at last and that the proprietor had promised to increase his pay as soon as he was married. The Mayers now felt that they could no longer oppose the marriage and gave permission for the wedding on condition that it was in church. It took place on 23 May 1910 in the huge pseudo-Gothic brick basilica of St Ludmila, which stood opposite a leading Prague theatre – not inappropriately perhaps, because the ceremony had an air of comedy about it. Hašek had typically tried to 'fix' his return to the Catholic fold by attempting to bribe the sexton to give him a false certificate of attendance at confession.

After a brief honeymoon in the environs of Prague and not far from the editorial offices of *Animal World*, the young couple installed themselves in a flat in a new building in the neighbourhood, which Mr Mayer had provided for them. Hašek not only ran *Animal World*, but looked after the proprietor's kennels and his pet monkey as well. He was genuinely fond of animals, and his experiences provided him with the material for many of his stories about pets.

One would have thought that this kind of life would have suited him down to the ground. He was at last united with Jarmila and had a job which was to his taste. Indeed at first he seemed to have become a reformed character, staying at home with Jarmila in the evenings and sending to the local inn for beer instead of going out to drink with his cynical and pleasure-loving bohemian companions.

Unfortunately this hallowed period did not last long. He soon became bored with the editorial routine and made as much of a farce of editing the paper as he had of running the electioneering offices for the National Social Party. He had an irresistible penchant for hoaxing, and nothing lent itself better to it than *Animal World*. Perhaps his best piece of spoof was to advertise a couple of 'thoroughbred werewolves' for sale, and, when the proprietor was flooded with applications and nearly went off his head, Hašek consoled him by saying, 'It's quite simple, Mr Fuchs, I'll send them the following circular: "We are unfortunately out of stock of thoroughbred werewolves. Be assured that as soon as a new consignment arrives we shall pick out a nice pair for you!"'

But soon some incredible articles which he wrote about animals which never existed began to arouse the suspicions of the readers. Mr Fuchs became alarmed and secretly persuaded Hájek to return and take over the editorship from him. The story is told by Marek in *The Good Soldier Švejk* (pp. 323–8).

And so the 'ideal' job was lost to Hašek, and after two months he had left the offices of *Animal World* for good. Hájek, pitying his condition, tried to get him a job as editor of a paper at the provincial town of Poděbrady, but Hašek drank too much before the interview and offended the selection board. As a last resort he and Jarmila set up a dog business on their own at the end of 1910, which Hašek pretentiously called their 'Cynological Institute'. He secured the services of a certain Čížek, who, like Švejk, dyed and trimmed the dogs and made forged pedigrees for them. But as a result of Hašek's questionable business methods they soon found themselves in court. However, the adventure ended happily, because, thanks to a lawyer friend, they were finally acquitted on appeal.

Hašek's dismissal from *Animal World* greatly distressed the Mayers. He was now without a job again and the young couple had no money. Family relations were strained and for the time being the parents took Jarmila home to live with them. They wanted to persuade her to make a final break with her husband, and for a time she gave in. Later she rebelled and went to live with Hašek once more.

At the beginning of December 1911 Hašek succeeded at last in obtaining a staff appointment as a local reporter on *Czech Word* (National Social). He did not hold the job long but just before he was sacked there occurred a mysterious episode in his life which has never been satisfactorily explained. On 9 February 1911 at 1.45 a.m., according to a newspaper report, he was seen climbing over the parapet of the Charles Bridge with the apparent intention of throwing himself into the river. He was allegedly only prevented from doing so by a theatrical hairdresser who happened to be passing that way. The hairdresser handed him over to the police, who took him off to the lunatic asylum.

He remained there eighteen days, and in the meantime Jarmila and her father came to visit him. Afterwards Hašek wrote a comic story called 'A Psychiatric Enigma', which described the episode as having occurred to an elderly man who was on his way back from a meeting of total abstainers. He had bent over the parapet, because he thought he heard a cry for help from the river, and was furious when his rescuer (also a hairdresser) insisted to the police that he had been trying to throw himself in the river. In the end, like Hašek, the total abstainer was taken off to the lunatic asylum 'where he has already been kept for one and a half years because the doctors have not yet been able to detect in him an awareness of his mental illness, which, according to the rules of psychiatry, is a sign of an improvement in mental condition'.

One can only suppose that Hašek had had some scene with Jarmila and threatened to leave her or do himself harm, because he left the flat at 5 p.m. and the very same evening she was enquiring about him at the police station. And in his first statement to the police he said he hated the world and wanted to drown himself. Later he withdrew this, but it is unlikely that Jarmila and her father would have allowed him to stay in the asylum for so long unless they had reason to believe that he was suffering from a temporary mental disturbance.

On leaving the asylum Hašek went to stay for a time with his mother, but when Jarmila's parents learned that she was expecting a baby they agreed that she and Hašek should move into a flat which the father had taken for them and be reunited. It was probably here that Hašek first conceived the idea of writing about the Good Soldier Švejk (as will be told in Chapter 4). In 1911 he published for the first time five stories about the Good Soldier in *Caricatures*, a fortnightly published by Lada, the future illustrator of the final book. At the end of the same year the stories were republished in book form.

Hašek now planned his biggest hoax yet. He and his friends had founded a mock political 'party' called 'The Party of Moderate Progress within the Bounds of the Law', and he thought it would be a great joke to stand as its candidate at the parliamentary elections of 1911. The name of the 'party' and its manifesto had been Hašek's own invention. Its programme comprised among other aims the nationalisation of house porters and sextons and the rehabilitation of animals. (No one in future would be allowed to insult the animal species by calling anyone a pig or a dog). The whole idea was a gigantic spoof. Hašek had not even officially registered his candidature and those few ballot papers which bore crosses against his name were declared invalid. However the result was celebrated by him and his supporters as a gigantic victory.

František Langer, the Czech playwright, was a member of the 'party' and has described Hašek's antics at election meetings:

> We listened to speeches about various saints, about the war on alcohol, the genuineness of the manuscripts,* the usefulness of missionaries and other phenomena of contemporary life. He pilloried nuisances supported or tolerated by the state, such as the obligatory charge of twenty hellers levied by house-porters for opening the outer doors at night and the entrance fees for public lavatories, which forced needy citizens, who cared for their health and could not afford the payment, to use more public places and be fined by the police for doing so. He thought up grandiose promises, likely to attract voters of the most varied occupations and the most contradictory interests, and with mysterious allusions to the next evening's performance, promised various revelations about rival candidates, hinting at crime and the murder of their grandmothers.

As soon as the elections were over, he set about writing what he called 'The Political and Social History of the Party', which he completed in 1911, although it it could not be published until 1963 for various reasons, mainly because of its libellous contents. Then he returned to his bohemian existence, while his wife who with good reason felt deserted, remained at home, expecting a baby. After the birth of a son, Richard, in 1912, the marriage finally broke up. The story goes that the Mayers came to the flat on a visit. Hašek welcomed them joyfully, although obviously in some embarrassment over his misspent life. He volunteered to go out and fetch some beer – and never returned. The parents waited for him in vain and then took Jarmila and the baby, first to their home in Vinohrady, and later to a villa they owned in Dejvice.

* This referred to the notorious 'newly discovered' mediaeval manuscripts, which at that time were the centre of a heated controversy. Many had been taken in by them, including Goethe, but they were eventually exposed by T. G. Masaryk as an ingenious forgery.

Jaroslav Hašek

Jarmila's explanation of the event was as follows: 'After leaving *Czech Word* Jaroslav was without a job. He felt that he could no longer maintain a family, especially after the birth of little Ríša [Richard]. He knew too that if he went away his father-in-law would look after his wife, and this is in fact what happened.' It was as terse as an official communiqué.

After the breach with Jarmila, Hašek together with his 'party' comrades wrote, produced and acted in various cabaret shows. Until he was called up in January 1915, he spent an anonymous vagabond existence, sponging on his friends Lada, Hájek and Longen, tramping around and writing more sketches and *feuilletons*. Since he began writing, he had published over 800 short stories – an average of nearly 60 a year. This was a by no means unsuccessful achievement in terms of freelance activity, but the proceeds of it were quite inadequate to maintain himself, let alone a family.

Hašek had by now become a regular down-and-out and, although he was anti-militarist, his call-up probably came as a relief to him. Certainly he does not appear to have resisted it. He enrolled as a one-year volunteer and was drafted into the 91st Infantry Regiment at České Budějovice in Southern Bohemia in February or March 1915. On 30 April his photograph appeared in an illustrated paper among a group of soldiers in an army hospital. He had grown a moustache and looked miserable and forlorn. In view of his poor physical condition due to his irregular life it was surprising that he was passed as fit. He stayed at České Budějovice until 30 June, when on its long journey to the front his regiment left for Királyhida, a town lying 25 miles south-east of Vienna on the then frontier between Austria and Hungary and known in Austria as Bruck an der Leitha. But during the two months he spent at Budějovice he got up to all sorts of escapades, was thrown out of the Volunteer School and sat for much of the time 'locked up in the barracks', as he himself claims. Hašek did not make these adventures part of Švejk's experiences, but of Marek's, who tells Švejk about them when they are in gaol together (pp. 287–8).

It was in Királyhida that the eleventh company was formed and Hašek enrolled in it. Oberleutnant Rudolf Lukas – the one officer whom he respected and liked – was to be its commander

and it would form part of a new 'march battalion' (re-inforce-
ment battalion) under Captain Sagner. In this Hungarian town
the Czechs were cooped up in a long wooden hut with several
bays of beds. They spent their time in performing front exercises
in the daytime and making visits to restaurants in the evening.
Isolated in the hated Hungarian environment, the men were bored
and were bound sooner or later to come to blows with the population. No doubt it was at this stage that Hašek thought up Vodička
and his hate campaign against the Hungarians. He himself is
alleged to have got out of the front exercises by feigning sickness,
and to have been assigned instead to Quartermaster Sergeant
Major Vaněk, who managed to make life easy for him during the
period of great disorder prevailing in the company before Lukas'
arrival. However Hašek's 'dodging' and sickness record brought
him before a 'superarbitration commission' on 25 May, which
was to decide whether he should be cashiered or not. The verdict
was that he was incapable of performing the duties of an ordinary
soldier in the trenches at the front, but fit enough to perform
'guard duties or similar tasks'. If Hašek hoped to 'dodge' the
front altogether, he must have been disappointed. He was signed
up on the next 'march battalion' and allowed to keep his
volunteer's rank. On 30 June he left Királyhida for the Galician
front. The night before, in defiance of strict orders, he left the
camp to have a last fling, and only returned within hours of the
scheduled departure. He was disciplined for the offence, but
escaped punishment because the battalion was about to entrain.

During the whole of the summer months of 1915 the Russian
troops steadily retreated before the German and Austrian troops
after fierce fighting and at terrible cost. It was the frightful
destruction in the wake of this withdrawal which Hašek describes
in the chapter 'From Hatvan Towards the Galician Frontier'.
'The train went slowly over the freshly built embankments *so
that the whole battalion could take in and thoroughly savour the
delights of war*' (p. 592).

Eventually his battalion reached Sanok. Hašek describes the
scene as he must himself have seen it. 'Everything was in a great
muddle. The Russians were retreating very hastily in the north
east tip of Galicia so that some Austrian detachments got mixed
up with each other and in some places units of the German army

drove wedges into them. The chaos was completed by the arrival of new march battalions and other military detachments.' (p. 619).

Soon the battalion had to face its biggest test yet. It was moved to the important railway junction of Sokal – a vital Austrian bridgehead on the eastern bank of the river Bug. From 20–31 July the battles to gain and regain this bridgehead were intensive and bloody, with heavy casualties on both sides. Hašek took part in them and the casualties of his regiment alone (dead, wounded and missing) amounted to 1,314 officers and men.

These eleven days of fighting were the only taste of the real horror of war which Hašek had during his service in the Austrian army. For the whole of August the regiment was inactive and the time of rest was used to decorate the deserving. (Hašek was awarded a silver medal of the 2nd class and promoted lance-corporal.) But at this point the Russians made a sudden counter-attack, which took the battalion by surprise and led to Hašek's subsequent capture. Whether he let himself be taken prisoner by the Russians or was just caught napping by them cannot be confirmed. Lukas afterwards attributed Hašek's good mood during the last stages of the march to his pleasant anticipation that he would soon be out of it. If Hašek had in fact planned to cross over to the other side, the reasons for his doing so may well have been the terrible sight of the ravages of war in the aftermath of the Russian retreat, his final taste of what modern warfare was like in the battle of Sokal and a long period of inactivity which gave him time to reflect on the war and its meaning. But it seems odd that he should have chosen to defect immediately after having been decorated for bravery and promoted. Also there is no record of Hašek having subsequently admitted to having deserted. One would have thought that if he had intended to do so all along, he would have boasted about it afterwards.

According to Lukas the Russian armies suddenly broke through the front in the sector defended by the 91st Regiment. As the men were running away in confusion he caught a glimpse of Hašek climbing laboriously out of the trench, slowly doing up his puttees and putting on his boots. He told him impatiently to hurry up, but Hašek only replied that he had a swollen foot and would have to tighten his puttees to run better. After that Lukas lost sight of him.

The individual and the giant power

In the morning of 24 September Hašek took final leave of the Austrian army. On the battlefield 135 of the 91st Regiment were left dead, 285 wounded and 509 missing.

Conditions in the Russian prisoner-of-war camps at that time were terrible, not least for the Czechs. The Russians regarded their fellow Slavs as the least privileged category among the prisoners and considered them devoted enough to Mother Russia to be proud to undergo the worst suffering and take upon themselves the most arduous labours. Hašek was sent first to a camp near Kiev and later to another one at Totskoye near the southernmost point of the Urals. Here he was fortunate enough to be able to escape the worst rigours of the camp by working in the very comfortable office of one of the camp commanders. Like most of the other prisoners he caught spotted typhus but the attack was not a serious one.

One day the news reached him that a military volunteer unit composed of Czechs and Slovaks in Russia was about to be formed. It was to be the nucleus of the future Czech Legion, and he at once applied to serve in it. He was accepted and immediately employed as a recruiting officer. His literary gifts predisposed him for journalistic and propaganda work and it was natural that he should be employed in this capacity. In his spare time he worked on a journal, *Čechoslovan*, which was published by the Czech colony in Kiev, and it was here that he began to write a second series of stories about Švejk which bore the title *The Good Soldier Švejk in Captivity*. It was published in Kiev in book form in 1917. But it was not long before Hašek started to annoy the Czech authorities in Russia by his independent stand and the insubordinate tone of some of his articles, just as he had done in Austria. It was odd that as a former anarchist he should have fallen so quickly under the influence of, of all people, the most reactionary Czechs in Russia – a group at Kiev who were the staunchest defenders of the Tsarist régime. Already, on 4 September 1916, he had written an article in fulsome praise of the members of the old Czech colony, the Russian Czechs, who were the first to take up the cause of Czechoslovak independence. Without them there would have been no resistance abroad, he argued. Two months later in an article 'The Ruler Who Will Sit down on Czech Bayonets' he stated unequivocally, 'We raised the

15

revolution to call to the Czech throne a member of the great Slav family of the Romanovs.' By March 1917, however, after the February Revolution, in an article 'Dark Forces' he was already attacking Rasputin, the Empress and the members of the Tsarist régime.

On 24 April, he pilloried several leading members of the Czech National Council in Russia in an article called 'The Club of the Czech Pickwicks'. For his insubordination and impertinence he was brought before a military court of honour and made to print a humiliating apology. Furthermore, he was taken off the paper and sent to the front line. In June he distinguished himself in the famous battle at Zborów and was decorated with a silver medal for valour. A week after the outbreak of the October Revolution he was reinstated as a member of the editorial staff.

Here he fell under the influence of a Communist on the staff named Hůla, and from then on his articles revealed growing traces of Bolshevist propaganda. He was now giving priority to the social revolution over the national one and strongly opposed the Czech National Council's plan to send the Legion away from Russia to fight on the Western Front. Its place was at the side of the Red Army, he maintained. On 24 February, he took part in an attempted *coup* against the leadership of the Czech National Council in Russia and a few days later finally burnt his boats. In company with Hůla he left the Legion to join the Bolsheviks in Moscow. The Legion proclaimed him a traitor and issued an order for his arrest. Later he was sent to the town of Samara to act as recruiting officer for the Bolsheviks, but when the Legionaries were about to capture it he had hastily to disappear into the Central Asian provinces of Russia disguised as the half-witted son of a German colonist. When the Red Army established control in Russia and the Legion was gradually withdrawn Hašek started to make a career for himself in the Russian Bolshevik Party organisation – to become in fact an *apparatchik*. In December 1918 he was appointed Deputy Commandant of the town of Bugulma. The Czech Red Army man became the Soviet Commissar Gashek (the Russians, having no 'h' in their alphabet, spell and pronounce his name in this way). In 1919 he was appointed Secretary of the Committee of Foreign Communists in the Russian town of Ufa, in the same year Secretary of the Party Cell of the printing office of *The Red Arrow*, and a year later Head of the International Section of the Political Department of the 5th Army. He was enthusiastic for the cause and his job of editing newspapers and writing propaganda articles came easily to him. Finally in his work with foreign Communists and ex-prisoners-of-war he found full scope for his love of languages. He even edited a paper in the Bashkir language and learned to speak 'pidgin Chinese'. It was a new experience for him to feel that he was making himself useful and that his talents were appreciated.

For the first time in his life he began to exhibit a sense of responsibility and dedication, combining it with an unexpected asceticism. Not only did he renounce alcohol for two years and a half, but became a fanatical crusader for temperance, carrying the campaign to extreme lengths. He even openly pilloried his own chief for coming drunk to a meeting, which was the equivalent of pasing a death sentence on him – an example of the surprising ruthlessness which Hašek could and did display throughout his life. But he was happy. He had found a companion too. He had gone through a form of marriage with a Russian woman, Shura Lvova.

It seems improbable that Hašek – bohemian and anarchist as he was – would have been able to adapt himself to the rigidities of the Soviet system for any length of time, but fortunately he did not have to, for when a visiting Czechoslovak Social Democrat delegation invited him to come back and help the Party in his own country, he agreed, if somewhat half-heartedly to do so. His assignment was to help set up a Bolshevik republic in Czechoslovakia after the model of Béla Kun's Soviet Republic in Hungary. Plans had been laid for a *putsch* by the left wing of the Social Democrat Party. But unfortunately for him the whole conspiracy was nipped in the bud by President Masaryk acting through the Minister of the Interior with the help of the right wing of the Social Democrat Party.

Shura has described how Hašek received the news of the failure of the Communist *coup* soon after his arrival in Prague in December 1920.

'He looked depressed and banged his cap on the bed. "And so we've lost everything, Shura. We've come too late. The people I was supposed to be in touch with have all been rounded up and put in gaol. And those who are still free don't seem to trust me any more." '

One can understand his dilemma. What was he to do now? He would have liked to return to Jarmila who was still his wife in the eyes of the law, and his nine-year-old son, but he could not do so because he had brought with him another wife. None the less he was anxious to re-establish contact with her, not only because he loved her, but because he wanted to enlist her help in finding permanent employment. But this was no simple task. In the new Republic Hašek was badly thought of nationally, politically and socially. He was branded as a traitor, a Bolshevik and finally a bigamist. He published a number of articles and stories in the press of the Left, but, unable to secure a steady job, he drifted back into the drunken vagabond existence of the pre-war years. However, he had to maintain himself and Shura, and this spurred him to try his hand at a complete novel for the first time. Early in 1921 he started writing *The Good Soldier Švejk* and in the summer of the same year moved to Lipnice on the Sázava which lies some hundred miles to the east of Prague, where in beautiful surroundings he hoped to be able to concentrate on his writing with least disturbance. Because initially no publisher would handle it, he was forced to publish the first volume privately and distribute it himself together with a friend, Franta Sauer. But after the success of the initial volume a publisher was found who was ready to take over the remaining parts. Although Hašek did not make much money out of the first volume he earned enough to buy a cottage at Lipnice, where he could begin to dictate the subsequent volumes.

But his renewed irregular life coming on top of his hard existence in Russia had taken a severe toll of his health. After the abstemiousness of thirty months his system could ill support a return to the orgies and excesses of his youth. He fell seriously ill and died on 3 January 1923. The only mourners at his funeral were his little son, Richard, and a few friends. He had completed three volumes of the novel but the fourth volume remained unfinished.

'After all, by and large, every soldier's stolen from his home', Švejk says consolingly to himself, as he contemplates the dog he has just stolen for his lieutenant (p. 199). Hašek looks particularly miserable on the photographs taken of him soon after his call-up in 1915 (see Plate 2). But he was worse off than any soldier or any dog, because he had no home to be stolen from and none to return to, once the war was over.

At heart he was a deeply unhappy man. Contrary to what most people thought, the basic trait of his character was not gaiety, cynicism or high spirits. 'Life paid him back all the kicks he gave and he pined for thunderous applause to deaden the cries and groans within him', Jarmila wrote of him. 'Why did so many of his stories have a bitter undertone? Because it was his own grief he was laughing at...His smile was not the smile of a naïve and good-natured man, who smiles because he is happy. It said, "I am smiling so as not to weep!"' And one of his bohemian companions, the novelist Eduard Bass, spoke of another Hašek, 'whom very few managed to look in the eyes, but who saw with frightening certainty the futility of human existence and, having apprehended it, tried to muzzle it, escape from it or beguile it with jokes...' 'His magnificent comedy', he said, 'was in fact tragedy.'

His wife, who knew him best and certainly loved him most, blamed his failures on his irresponsibility. This was the inevitable price, she said, which had to be paid for his originality. And most people would have agreed that his main fault was that he could not take the world seriously but made fun of everything. He hoaxed his way through life.

Hašek knew only too well that his misfortunes were due to his own rashness and thoughtlessness. His many promises to Jarmila that he would improve are in themselves a confession of guilt, as were his apologies and excuses for breaking them. On the very threshold of his career, at the age of twenty, he had written a poem in which he said:

> And I recalled how in my life I too
> Had trampled down all sorts of things
> ...Spring was singing,
> But I was sad and cheerless.
>
> (*Cries of May*)

And within a year or two of his death he was writing, 'I always want to put something right, to do good, but nothing ever comes out of it except trouble for me and all around' (p. 172). He put these words into Švejk's mouth but were they not a cry from his own soul?

His alcoholism was undoubtedly one of the factors which ruined his life. We do not know whether it was hereditary, although the fact that his father and brother died from it would seem to suggest so. After he joined the Bolsheviks he succeeded for thirty months in denying himself alcohol, which shows that he could have overcome the habit earlier if he had made the effort. That he was successful in doing so when working for the Soviet may have been due to his feeling that he had at last found an identity. But it may also have been the grisly prospect which faced Soviet Commissars who were found drunk: the Revolutionary Tribunal and the firing squad. Discipline was one of the qualities which Hašek lacked and which no one could apparently instil in him. Perhaps only the threat of the firing squad could achieve this.

His attempt to commit suicide by throwing himself off the Charles Bridge in 1911 may have been a hoax – an irresistible urge to draw attention to himself, which was one of his besetting sins – but it may have been a genuine act of despair. The ensuing period which he spent in a mental home with Jarmila's consent indicates suspected psychiatric disturbance. Many people who knew Hašek would have said that he was mad anyway. Who else but a lunatic would set up kennels when he had no dogs, and register it under the pretentious title of a 'Cynological Institute'? Although he made a joke of the suicide episode in a story he wrote later, the title he gave to it, 'A Psychiatric Enigma', is revealing.

Hašek never talked about himself and seldom wrote in a serious vein. The exception are his letters to Jarmila and the poems he wrote during the War for himself and his lieutenant. His verses express wistfulness and nostalgia – but for what? Did he have anything to go back for? They show that he had not forgotten Jarmila and longed for her to write to him, although he could not bring himself to write to her. They also bring out poignantly the effect of the sight of the havoc of war on the individual. They are indeed the letters of a creature 'stolen from home'.

One day he made the following bitter remark to his friend Mareš: 'In this world you can only be free if you're an idiot.'

Perhaps this was why he tried to assuage his bitterness by writing a book about an idiot in a futile war, fortifying himself with liberal draughts of alcohol as he did so. But it was all in vain for 'the giant power' was really within himself.

2

THE OPPRESSOR'S SHAME

'Oh dear,' Švejk answered, 'before we get any food I'd have time
to tell you the whole history of the Czech nation, sir.' (p. 163)

The great historian of Bohemia, František Palacký, believed that
in Czech history the tragic element prevailed over the epic. He
saw it as dominated by two issues – the national struggle between
Czech and German, and the spiritual conflict between Rome and
the Reformation.

It is undoubtedly true that Bohemian history is composed of
two strands – the Czech strand and the German strand – and they
are so intertwined that at times it is difficult for those who do not
know the country to disentangle them. But to the inhabitants of
Bohemia itself these strands have always been as clear and easy to
identify as the coloured leads of an electric circuit. Each race has
always seen its history as a lead of one colour in isolation from or
in conflict with the other.

F. X. Šalda called *The Good Soldier Švejk* a 'monument of
shame': not the shame of the Czechs, as the Catholic writer
Durych had said, but rather of the shame of their oppressors.
For centuries the Czechs had had their fate settled for them in a
foreign city (Vienna) by foreigners who looked on them with contempt. And, in spite of all their efforts, nothing they could do
could change the situation.

Josef Švejk was a citizen of Prague, the capital of Bohemia, that
country whose name is dear to us because Shakespeare clothed it
with such magic in *The Winter's Tale*. In the first English history
of Bohemia, written probably by John Harrison in the seventeenth
century (who happened to be the Winter Queen's groom),
Bohemia is described as 'one of the richest, civilest and strongest
nations of Europe...'[1]

It had indeed once been a proud, independent kingdom. But by
the time Švejk was living in it, it had fallen on hard times and

sunk to the position of a mere province of Austria. The 'Historic Provinces of the Bohemian Crown', as they were proudly called, had once comprised the Kingdom of Bohemia, the neighbouring Margraviate of Moravia and the Duchy of Southern Silesia. The Czech name for Bohemia was *Čechy*, which explains the connection between Czechs (*Češi*) and their name for the lands they inhabit. The small provinve of Southern Silesia, which is today a part of Moravia, had in Hašek's day a mixed population of Czechs, Germans and Poles.

For the Germans, Bohemia has always been *Böhmen*, originally *Boiheim* or the home of the Boii, a Celtic tribe who are known to have inhabited the Bohemian lands from the fourth century B.C. In the first century B.C. they were displaced by German tribes, the Marcomanni and the Quadri. According to Czech historians all these German tribes had evacuated Bohemia before the arrival of the Czechs in the sixth century A.D. German historians, however, liked to believe that some of them had continued to live there. One of the great political debates between Czechs and Germans, which was still going on in Hašek's life-time, was which of them had the 'primogeniture'. The Germans believed that their ancestors had been living in Bohemia and Moravia without interruption since a century before the birth of Christ. The Czechs were insistent that the Germans appeared in Bohemia for the first time as invited colonists from the twelfth century A.D. onward. This controversy, once white hot, is now cold and dead, if only because there are few Germans left in Czechoslovakia, and certainly no German lobby, to fight about it.

The Czechs are Western Slavs and came to the Historic Provinces in the sixth century A.D. From then until the twelfth century they had these lands to themselves, but after that they had to share them with a minority of Germans. With time this minority multiplied so considerably that by 1910 in Bohemia the proportion of them to Czechs was 36.7 per cent to 63.1 per cent and in Moravia 27.6 per cent to 71.7 per cent.[2] Broadly speaking, the German settlements lay in the frontier districts of Bohemia and Moravia, in most of the larger towns, and throughout Silesia.

This eventually numerous and powerful alien element, living among the Czechs in what the Czechs had always regarded as their own homeland and considering themselves to be its co-heirs,

Jaroslav Hašek

enjoyed the protection and favour of successive Kings of Bohemia
– Czech and foreign. For the Czech nation they posed the gravest
problem which it had to face throughout its troubled history until
1946, when almost all of them were summarily evicted. The
Czechs then heaved a sigh of relief in the fond belief that they
had attained that blessed state where 'the wicked cease from
troubling and the weary are at rest'.

In an article called 'What Every Czech Should Know about
His Country', which appeared in a pocket calendar published by
Čechoslovan in Russia in 1918, Hašek describes this historical
process as many Czechs of his time saw it: 'The German element
pushed its way into Bohemia with the help of bad kings...
The Czech kings...brought the German nobility to Bohemia.
They bestowed on them numberless favours by robbing the
peasants of their land and incorporating it into the estates of a
nobility created by privilege.'

Throughout the nineteenth century it was the main political
aim of the Czechs to secure from the Emperor recognition of the
unity of their three Historic Provinces and of the historic rights
of the Bohemian Crown, and to have that recognition ratified by
his coronation in Prague as King of Bohemia. The aim of the
Germans was to prevent this at all cost. The unity of the Czech
lands under Czech majority rule would have reduced their status
within the Historic Provinces to one of a national minority,
whereas in Austria as a whole they were in a majority over the
Czechs (although not over the Slavs as a whole). And so they
stubbornly resisted any form of decentralisation which might give
the Czechs increased power within the Historic Provinces. In consequence, thanks to German hostility, supported by Vienna, the
Czechs never achieved the autonomy they sought until the defeat
and break-up of Austria in 1918. Nor, in spite of all his promises,
did the Emperor ever consent to have himself crowned in Prague
as his predecessors had done. What the Czechs thought of this is
well conveyed in *The Good Soldier Švejk* (p. 248). 'There's no
enthusiasm for the War because he wouldn't have himself
crowned...When you promised you'd be crowned, you should
have kept your word, you old bastard.'

At the time when Hašek was writing, many Czechs still recalled
with justifiable pride and excusable nostalgia for past greatness

24

their once powerful native dynasty – the House of Přemysl – which had ruled Bohemia in unbroken succession almost from the dawn of history until 1306. One of these early Přemysls had been Prince Václav I, whom the English-speaking world commemorates as 'Good King Wenceslas' and whom the Czechs long revered as their national saint and protector. It was he who built the church in Prague, which became famous as his shrine, and which a later dynasty transformed into the Cathedral. The Bohemian Crown was known for generations as 'The Crown of Saint Wenceslas'.

By the thirteenth century Bohemia had become one of the most important member states of the Holy Roman Empire. Its king was *ex officio* Cup-Bearer to the Emperor and the most powerful of the seven Electors – indeed the only one to have the title of King. Přemysl Otakar II, King of Bohemia from 1253 to 1278, who had immensely increased his power by marrying the rich Austrian Babenberg heiress, gave Europe a foretaste of the later Austro-Hungarian Empire when he created and held together for a time a Czech–Austrian–South Slav dominion, to which he hoped in time to add Hungary and Poland. But when he decided to stand as candidate for the Imperial Crown, the other Electors, who were jealous of him and afraid of his power, resorted to dubious means to exclude him and elect in his place Rudolf of Habsburg. This then little known and far from powerful count, with the help of the Hungarians, decisively defeated King Otakar in battle and overran Bohemia.[3] But the Czechs recovered surprisingly quickly from this disaster, and by the time Otakar's son, Václav II, had died in 1305, not only Bohemia's Crown, but those of Hungary and Poland were in Přemysl hands.

In 1306 the male Přemysl line died out and was succeeded by the Luxembourg dynasty, King John, the first Luxembourg ruler of Bohemia, had obtained the Crown by marrying a Přemysl, the sister of the last king. His son Charles IV became both King of Bohemia and Holy Roman Emperor, with Prague as the Imperial capital. This outstanding ruler was half Czech and very conscious of it. In his autobiography he wrote that he loved Bohemia and 'spoke and understood Czech like any other Czech'. Under his reign the Charles University was founded and the wonderful Gothic architecture of Prague created.

25

But this time of civilisation and prosperity was swiftly followed by one of fanaticism verging on barbarism. Bohemia was torn by the Hussite Wars – for most Czechs their country's finest hour, when they victoriously defended against foreign oppressors the teachings of their great religious reformer, Jan Hus. Later, Czechs were to look back on it as a struggle to safeguard freedom of conscience against blind obedience and dogma. Although a great moral victory, it was something of a Pyrrhic one, because the wars devastated Bohemia and brought about her political and cultural isolation. If it filled Czech hearts with pride, it also earned for the nation the stigma of being 'Europe's heretics'.[4]

With time the power of the Czech kings waned while that of the nobles grew. Eventually the Crown of Bohemia – the Crown of St Wenceslas – became the symbol of the Czech 'nation' rather than of its rulers. The nobles, now called 'The Estates' and claiming to be the voice of that 'nation', made the crown elective and imposed conditions on its wearers. In the turbulent times that were to follow, a small country had little hope of preserving its independence without a powerful dynasty behind it. A foreign ruler could more easily provide military and financial backing than a native one. More particularly, he could provide a shield against the great peril of the time, the Turkish threat from the east. It was with these considerations in mind that in 1526, in spite of their Protestant beliefs, the Czech Estates took the fateful decision of electing as their King the ardent Catholic, Ferdinand of Habsburg, brother of the Emperor Charles V.

The Habsburgs were the most powerful ruling house of the time. Before becoming Emperor, Maximillian I (1439–1510), son of the Emperor Frederic III, had by his marriage with Marie of Burgundy acquired Holland, Belgium and Luxembourg (afterwards to be called the Spanish Netherlands) as well as a great part of France. His son, Philip, added to the Habsburg possessions the kingdom of Spain, the joint kingdoms of Naples, Sicily and Sardinia as well as vast territories across the ocean in the Americas and Indies. And the whole of this mighty empire eventually passed to Philip's son, Charles (Charles V), who added to them by conquering the Duchy of Milan.

When Charles V was elected Emperor, he wisely decided that his patrimony was too large for one ruler, and ceded the Austrian lands to his brother Ferdinand. He also passed to him his claim to the Crowns of Bohemia and Hungary.

Although in his discussions with the Czech Estates Ferdinand I agreed to be the 'elected' King of Bohemia, he argued that through his wife, Anna Jagellon, the sister of the last King, he had an unassailable claim to the Crown in his own right. Being a self-willed man, he stuck to this opinion throughout his reign.

Repeated violations of their promises and infringements of the privileges of the Estates by the Habsburg rulers in the sixteenth and seventeenth centuries finally drove the Bohemian nobles to revolt. In 1618 they unceremoniously bundled the royal commissioners out of the window at the famous Defenestration of Prague. This was no sudden fit of temper or flash in the pan. The plan was deeply laid. The Estates were resolved once and for all to assert their rights and depose a King who did not abide by their rules. It was a test case. Who was to have the final say, the Monarch or the Estates? The Monarch, Ferdinand II, believed that he held the throne by right of descent. The Estates claimed that he held it by election only and that, as he was not of their religion and did not abide by his agreements with them, they were entitled to depose him and elect in his place a Protestant King. Their candidate was Frederic, the Calvinist Elector of the Palatinate and son-in-law of James I of England.

The issue was finally fought out in 1620 at the Battle of the White Mountain just outside Prague, where Ferdinand's army was victorious. As a result of this historic defeat the Bohemian Estates, and thus the Czech 'nation', lost their say in the government of the country, their freedom to practise their religion, and finally even the use of their native tongue.

After their victory the Habsburgs ruled Bohemia and Moravia as absolute Monarchs. Twenty-four of the rebellious nobles were executed in the Old Town Square in Prague. The rest were exiled and their estates confiscated and handed over to the Emperor's followers and foreigners. The period of the Counter-Reformation followed, during which the 'Czech heresy' was ruthlessly suppressed and Bohemia subjected to alien centralist rule. For some 200 years the Czechs were a forgotten people – anonymous Imperial or Austrian subjects. Germans and other foreigners, whom the Habsburgs favoured, changed the face and spirit of

Prague, and reclothed it in sumptuous baroque. To the Czechs
it seemed no longer their own city. The reign of the enlightened
Emperor Josef II brought some alleviations at the end of the eighteenth century. The power of the Church was broken, religious
freedom introduced and serfdom abolished. But the Emperor's
policy of germanisation proved a blow to the survival of the
struggling Czech language, and his measures of centralisation
violated Czech historic rights.[5]

Czech national feelings began to revive only at the beginning
of the nineteenth century after the French Revolution and the
Napoleonic Wars. The revival took the form of a rebirth of the
Czech language, which until then had been facing extinction, and
a renewed interest in Czech national history and literature. But
soon demands for greater political independence began to be
heard too, although not much progress could be made under the
repressive and reactionary government of Metternich.[6]

The success of the February Revolution in Paris in 1848 threw
Austria into a ferment and inspired radicals in Vienna to demand
the end of absolutism and Metternich's resignation. Hard pressed
by demonstrations and riots, the incapable Emperor, Ferdinand V,
gave in and promised the insurgents a constitution for the whole
Monarchy. Metternich resigned and fled to London.

In Prague young radicals and students, roused by what had
happened in Vienna and fired by feelings of Slav solidarity
generated at a Slav Congress held in their city, soon fell foul of
the Austrian military commander and his garrison. Prince
Windischgraetz upset the inhabitants (who at this time were
behaving in a normal, orderly fashion and whose leaders were
indeed engaged in discussions with the government) by ostenta-
tiously addressing his troops as if it were the eve of a great battle,
and, in an already tense atmosphere, demonstratively moving
men and guns from one side of Prague to the other. There was
a sudden flare-up on 12 June and barricades were set up. This
gave Windischgraetz the excuse he needed. He bombarded a
shocked Prague and restored 'law and order'.

In July a constituent assembly, in which there was a Slav
majority, met in Vienna to draft a new constitution which was
to reorganise Austria on federal lines. On 6 October there was
another outbreak of rioting in Vienna, when the radicals tried to

stop troops leaving the city to march against the rebellious Hungarians. It ended disastrously. The Austrian Minister of War was lynched by the crowd. The frightened Emperor fled to Olomouc in Moravia, Windischgraetz was ordered to intervene in the capital with his troops, and the radicals were quickly forced to capitulate. The assembly moved to Kroměříž (Kremsier) in Moravia, where it hoped to be able to work on without interruption.

Alarmed by these disturbances, the ruling circles in Vienna resorted to radical measures. A new government was installed under Prince Felix Schwarzenberg, and the Emperor was persuaded to abdicate in favour of his nephew, Francis Joseph. In March 1849 the assembly was dissolved and a new absolutist constitution imposed on the country. The situation was more dangerous in Hungary, where the national forces had succeeded in driving out the Austrians, but the new Emperor called on the Tsar to help crush the rebels. Caught in the Austro-Russian pincers, the Hungarian forces surrendered. In Italy, Field Marshal Radetsky reduced Italian insurgents to submission, and in Germany the movement to exclude Austria from the Federation was temporarily halted. Austria could breathe again. The *status quo* had been re-established.

By now we have reached a point in Czech history which has some direct relevance to the author of *The Good Soldier Švejk*, because Hašek's grandfather František is said to have been a member of the Bohemian diet or *Landtag*, to have fought on the barricades in Prague in 1848 and to have been a member of the Kroměříž assembly. If this was so, one can imagine the bitterness he must have felt at this arbitrary and unexpected blow to Czech hopes, a resentment which was no doubt passed down to his son and grandson.

For the Czechs this was not to be the last of their disappointments. Optimists among them continued to believe that they would still achieve autonomy, if only in a diluted form, once things had settled down and the Hungarian rising had been quelled. They little realised that they would have to undergo ten years of oppressive despotic rule before there was even a glimmer of light on the horizon. In the immediate aftermath of the Rising, Prague was to have a taste of the cold terror which was to be re-enacted far more brutally under the Nazis in the Second World War and under Stalinist rule in the nineteen-fifties. In 1849 the Czech leader Palacký found that if he showed himself on the streets of Prague, his friends would quickly cross to the other side. (Many Czechs experienced something of a similar kind after the Prague *coup* of 1948.) His faithful follower, the outstanding journalist and fighter for reform, Karel Havlíček, in spite of his acquittal by a jury, was shamefully arrested and exiled to the Tyrol, where he spent four and a half years in banishment. He was only allowed to return to Bohemia when his wife was dying. Even so, he arrived late. He himself died a year later, but, before he did so he was to undergo the same experience as Palacký and be shunned when he appeared on the streets. This was not concentration camp treatment, but, until the Czechs experienced at German hands much worse indignities, Havlíček's fate remained for them a monument to Austrian injustice and brutality, which had brought about the death at the age of only 35 of a high-minded Czech patriot and gifted writer – 'the monument of shame'.

But at length, after ten years of seeming darkness, some light appeared. In 1859 Austria, while attempting to secure her hold in Italy, suffered two serious military reverses. The battles of Magenta and Solferino, which she fought against the Piedmontese and the French, cost her the loss of Lombardy and indeed of all her footholds in Italy except Venetia. At the same time she was experiencing serious financial difficulties at home. Faced with these setbacks, the Emperor was driven in 1860 to issue the *October Diploma*, which contained a solemn promise for the second time to renounce absolutism and allow the various nationalities of the Monarchy the self-government they had been calling for. But when the promised new measures were promulgated a year later in the so-called *February Constitution*, they proved a disappointment because, while granting Hungary a special position, they still left the Austrian half of the Monarchy, including Bohemia and Moravia, under strong central control.

The rivalry between the Hohenzollern dynasty of Prussia and the Habsburgs of Austria had been of long standing, but in 1862, when Bismarck became Prussia's Prime Minister, it took a sharp turn for the worse. Prussia's object was to isolate Austria and exclude her from the German Federation, which was later to be turned into the German Empire with the Hohenzollern King as Emperor. Bismarck sought to weaken Austria by holding out support for the discontented Italians and Hungarians in the Monarchy.

On 15 June 1866 Prussia and Italy declared war on Austria, and 18 days later the Austrian army was disastrously defeated at Königgrätz (Hradec Králové) in Bohemia. The victorious Prussian forces went on to occupy Prague. But Bismarck let Austria off lightly, demanding no territorial concessions and soon withdrawing the Prussian occupying forces.

Already on the eve of the war the Czechs had demonstrated their loyalty to the Monarchy by offering to send a Czech national defence guard to help protect the frontiers, but the Emperor, always distrustful of the Czechs, declined the offer. He had no reason to question their loyalty.[7] On occupying Prague, the Prussian troops set up posters at all street corners, appealing for the support of 'the inhabitants of the glorious Kingdom of Bohemia'. The Prussians, so the proclamation read, had come not as enemies but full of respect for the historical and national rights of the Czechs. 'If the righteous Prussian cause triumphed, the Czechs and Moravians would perhaps again have the opportunity of freely deciding their future.'

The Czech leaders saw through the Prussian advances and decisively rejected them. Not so the Hungarians who were ready to consider them. In agreement with the Prussians a legion of Hungarian volunteers and prisoners was raised and held ready for action on the Austrian frontier. At one stage it actually moved on Bratislava side by side with Prussian troops.

The effect on Vienna of this totally unexpected defeat at the hands of 'little' Prussia was disastrous for the future hopes of the Czechs. Fear that Bismarck's malign influence might induce the Germans in Bohemia to join up with Prussia and the Hungarians to secede, drove the Emperor to make far-reaching concessions to Hungary without conferring comparable favours on the Czechs. By the *Ausgleich* (or Compromise) of 1867 (officially known as the *December Constitution*) which the government concluded with the Hungarians (without consulting the Czechs) Austria was to be divided into two separate halves, joined administratively at

31

its apex. From now on Hungary would be Austria's partner in ruling the Empire, which was to be 'Austro-Hungarian' rather than 'Austrian'. The various nationalities whom the Hungarians ruled over and oppressed – Serbs, Croats, Slovaks and Romanians – who had previously looked to Vienna for protection as Hungary's overlord, would now be abandoned to the far from tender mercies of Budapest.

When the news of the *Ausgleich* broke, the Czech leaders Palacký and his son-in-law Rieger manifested their disgust by going off to St Petersburg and Moscow in a huge party of eighty-four to attend a Slav ethnographical exhibition, at which they gave open expression to their pro-Slav sympathies. The climax of the pilgrimage was their reception by the Tsar Alexander II. Before leaving, Palacký and Rieger had gone to France in the hope of winning the support of the Emperor Napoléon III. Their efforts led to a visit to Prague the following year by the Emperor's nephew, Prince Jérome Napoléon, and Rieger's audience with the Emperor himself in 1869, which took place in strict privacy without the knowledge of the Austrian Ambassador. But Prince Jérome was pro-Polish and pro-Hungarian and therefore not well disposed to the Czechs; and the French Emperor, in the year before the Franco-Prussian War, was far too anxious not to offend Austria to take any helpful action.

In a memorandum which he handed to the Emperor, Rieger wrote *inter alia*: 'A Germanised Bohemia would most certainly fall a prey to Prussia, but a Slav Bohemia never to Russia, because it is too jealous of its historic character and its national independence.' But Napoléon played the Czechs an underhand trick by sending a copy of the document to the Austrian government. The French Ambassador in Vienna, when consulted, warned the Emperor that the Czech nation scarcely merited French sympathy.

However, the persuasive efforts of the Czechs to enlist French support were not without effect. The Austrian Prime Minister was told by one of his special emissaries in France, 'Austria has many friends here...and all wish its consolidation. More than once I have been asked the naive question, "Why does Austria not grant the Kingdom of Bohemia what it has just granted to the Kingdom of Hungary?" '[8]

The oppressor's shame

What is remarkable about this diplomatic activity is the evidence it showed of a precocious Czech interest in foreign politics. From it emerges the first outline of a Czech foreign policy – a reorientation of Austrian policy towards France and Russia (the future Entente) and away from Germany (the future Triple Alliance). But the future Entente powers were unreceptive. The Russian Tsar was distrustful of any movement for autonomy anywhere, and the British Foreign Secretary Lord Clarendon is reported to have told an Austrian diplomat that Vienna was right to suppress the disturbances in Bohemia. 'It should not pay too much attention to the ridiculous aims of a people of whose existence Europe knows nothing.'[9]

An opportunity for the Czechs to manifest their faith in their 'Historic Rights' occurred on 20 August 1867 on the occasion of the return of the Czech Crown jewels to Prague from Vienna, where they had been taken for safety before the Prussian invasion. Although the Austrian authorities arranged for the transport to take place by night, Czechs stayed up at all hours to wait for the train. All the stations it passed through were brightly illuminated and beacon fires were lit on the surrounding hills.

In the spring of 1868 the ceremony of the laying of the foundation-stone for the Czech National Theatre in Prague, which the Emperor had declined to attend, became a solemn national political event, with music specially composed for it by Smetana himself. This was followed a month later by a great manifestation on Palacký's seventieth birthday. There was also a pilgrimage to Constance, the place of the martyrdom of Jan Hus, and in Prague people flocked to the battlefields of the White Mountain, where their nation had lost its independence nearly 250 years before.

But these were nothing more than manifestations. The only political weapon available to the Czechs was the strike, or in parliamentary terms, obstruction. From now on they resolved to make the task of running the Monarchy as difficult as possible.

In August Rieger made the Czechs' most powerful and uncompromising policy statement, known as the *Czech Declaration*. He proclaimed that they would boycott the then existing *Landtag*, because the *December Constitution* had no validity in the lands

33

of the Bohemian Crown, which were joined to Austria solely through the dynasty. The existing disagreement could be removed only by a compact between the Monarch as King of Bohemia and the politico-historical Czech nation. A slightly more moderate declaration in the same sense was made by the Moravian Czechs in their own *Landtag*.

The Czech population took the opportunity of demonstrating their disgust during the Emperor's visit to Prague in June. Most people pointedly left the city on summer excursions. Some of those who stayed behind demonstrated in support of language equality and tore German flags to shreds. Some laid wreaths on the spot where the leaders of the Czech Rising of 1618 had been beheaded. There was no one to line the streets except schoolchildren who were there on orders.

When the Emperor opened the new city bridge, the press published a picture of him over the caption: 'Walk on the Bridge'. As the Czech for 'walk' is *procházka*, which happens also to be a common surname like our 'Walker', the Czechs soon began to joke about the Monarch, referring to him among themselves as 'Mr Procházka'. Hašek, who always depicts the Emperor as slightly gaga, recalls that his comment on this occasion was: 'How interesting! This bridge leads from one side [of the river] to the other!' ('In the Tracks of the State Police in Prague').

But the most striking and original feature of this and the following year were the vast protest meetings which were held all over the countryside and later in Prague itself. The cry was for the renewal of 'National Historic Rights...which mean nothing less than the freedom, autonomy and independence of the glorious Kingdom of Bohemia.' But there were also more radical demands for universal suffrage. The demonstrations merged with commemoration ceremonies for Hus, and the black Hussite flag with the white chalice in the centre was much in evidence. Even the name given to each of these meetings – Tábor – the spot in Southern Bohemia where Hus preached to crowds of Czechs and where the most famous Hussite city of that name still stands, recalled the Taborites, and the period of their history when the Czechs offered the fiercest resistance to the oppressors.

In Prague itself demonstrations were violent. Everywhere, in the newspapers, at the theatre, in public places, there were protests at the way the Czechs had been betrayed and demands for the same rights as those enjoyed by the Hungarians. Even the Bohemian nobility joined in and Count Thun, who was no longer Governor and had sympathies for the Czechs, announced his intention of boycotting the Upper House of the *Reichsrat*. Windows were broken in the German Club, the German Church and the Jesuit Church of St Ignatius – events which seriously alarmed the Governor and the Austrian authorities.

When protest meetings persisted the state police and military were ordered to suppress them. Shots were fired, and there were many prosecutions and sentences of long imprisonment. There were rumours too, emanating from Prussia, that Prussian troops might cross the frontier and restore order. The Monarch and the government were scared to death of Bismarck, and their reaction was one of panic. When the Prague Police Chief reported to the Governor that Bohemia was on the brink of revolution, martial law was proclaimed and the Governor, von Kellersperg, who had some understanding of Czech grievances, was dismissed and replaced by Field Marshal Baron Koller, a 'hawk', who as the Czechs well knew, had been appointed to punish them. Retribution was swift. Czech newspapers were confiscated and their editors prosecuted. Protest meetings were dispersed by troops. Actors and actresses were punished for 'extemporisations' and anyone caught singing the Russian national anthem was charged. According to Hašek a bookseller at a *tábor* at Kutná Hora 'spoke disrespectfully of the Emperor Ferdinand I of the sixteenth Century who has long since turned to dust, and got six months for it'. ('The Cause of the Oppressed'). But all these measures only stiffened Czech opposition.

But how far were Czech grievances justified? What was their position in Austria after the passing of the *Ausgleich*? And how did it really compare with that of the Hungarians?

The new constitution cut the old Monarchy clean in half like an apple. This division had existed before, of course, the river Leitha having long been the boundary line between the Austrian and Hungarian lands, which were in consequence referred to as Cisleithania and Transleithania. But whereas until 1867 Hungary had been subject to Austria, she was now her equal partner, joined to her by three institutions only – the Monarch, the 'joint' ministers appointed by him to deal with 'joint' affairs (Foreign Affairs, Defence and Finance) and the *Delegations* (which will be explained later). 'Joint' affairs were to be dignified by a special title. They were no longer Austrian but 'Imperial and Royal' (*Kaiserlich und Königlich*) or more familiarly K. and K. ('*Ka und Ka*').

The name 'Austria' was no longer to be used officially. Its place would be taken by the cumbrous phrase 'The Kingdom and Lands Represented in the *Reichsrat*'. Bohemia and Moravia fell into this category, while Hungary did not. She had no desire to; she had a parliament of her own. This was the discrimination which outraged the Czechs, who had nothing but their provincial *Landtag*.

The Emperor continued to appoint the ministers, as he had always done, but under the new constitution they would now be responsible to a parliament and have to obtain its support for their policies. For the western half of the Austro-Hungarian Empire – Cisleithania – the *Reichsrat* would be that parliament. It would have an upper house, the members of which would be appointed by the Emperor mainly from the nobility and higher clergy, and a lower one, which would be elected, albeit by a very retrograde and heavily biassed indirect voting system, which enabled only about 6% of the population to vote. The *Landtag* in each *Land* would elect from its own ranks deputies to attend the lower house of the *Reichsrat*. A simple majority was required, and if the Germans had more than 50% of the seats in any individual *Landtag* (as in many places they had), they could ensure the return to the *Reichsrat* of all their own candidates.

Clearly the system of electing the members of the *Landtag* was all-important, as this would be the corner-stone of Cisleithania's 'democracy', and a very rickety corner-stone it was. There was no direct universal suffrage yet and those who were privileged to have the franchise could only vote through *curiae* or electoral colleges. In Bohemia and Moravia there were four such. The first and most important one was the *curia* for wealthy landowners. There were only a handful of them and yet they elected seventy deputies. Next came the *curiae* for the towns and the country districts. To be eligible to vote, voters here had to have special financial qualifications. Those qualified in the towns

The oppressor's shame

returned seventy-two deputies and those in the country seventy-nine. The system was heavily biassed against the Czechs, because the towns, where the Germans preponderated, returned one deputy for every eleven thousand inhabitants, while the countryside, which was mainly Czech, returned one for every forty-nine thousand. In addition fifteen deputies were returned by the business community, which could not vote individually but only through the Chambers of Commerce, where the Germans were strongly entrenched. In general the process was both nationally and socially discriminatory, because the wealthy conservative landowners, who were pillars of the Monarchy, and the Germans, who spoke the same language as their rulers and shared many of their interests, had all the electoral muscle. In these conditions it was not to be wondered at that the Czechs had little faith in the *Reichsrat* and increasingly tended to boycott it in the years to follow. As for the Hungarians, they had no intention of attending it at all, and had expressly excluded themselves from it under the *Ausgleich*, because it would have meant their being answerable for Hungarian affairs to a body which was not composed exclusively of Hungarians.

Of course the 'joint' ministers had to be nominally responsible to some higher body, and this could only be the *Reichsrat*. But some of these 'joint' ministers were Hungarians. To get round the refusal of this nation to sit in a common parliament with any other nation, the system of *Delegations* was thought up, which enabled them to voice their opinions on 'joint' affairs without compromising their sovereignty. There were two such *Delegations*. One consisted of deputies from the Hungarian parliament and the other of those from the *Reichsrat* – in each case twenty from the upper house and forty from the lower. The two *Delegations* met separately, but in the same place and at the same time, and discussed the same agenda. Thus when Masaryk wished to make an interpellation on Foreign Affairs, which lay in the competence of a 'joint' ministry, he could not do so in the *Reichsrat* itself, but only in its (Cisleithanian) *Delegation*. Similarly if a Hungarian deputy wished to do the same he would only do it in his own Transleithanian (Hungarian) *Delegation*. The two *Delegations*, sitting apart, had to agree, and only in the case of total failure to do so could they meet together, in which case they were only

37

permitted to vote and under no circumstances to debate. If they failed to agree, the Monarch had the casting vote.

It has been necessary to recount all this in detail to explain how ramshackle the Monarchy appeared in Hašek's eyes, and how justified was the resentment the Czechs felt against the Emperor. Their bitter hostility to Hungarians and Germans was understandable too. The Czechs felt that whereas in the past they had shown great restraint and behaved loyally to the Emperor, the Hungarians had led a military insurrection against the Crown and continued to be an unreliable factor still – a threat to the unity of the Monarchy. But instead of being rewarded for their loyal attitude, the Czechs had been assigned a status inferior to the Hungarians. They resented this all the more because the Hungarians, while complaining bitterly of Austrian oppression in the past, were themselves even more oppressive to the Slav minorities – Slovaks, Croats and Serbs – whom the *Ausgleich* had abandoned to their mercies.

The totally unexpected victory of the Prussians over the French in 1870 brought about a momentary change in the otherwise rigid political climate. It shook the Emperor, who had been secretly hoping to embark on a war of revenge against Prussia. He realised that this would now be out of the question, and fearing the effects in Austria of the Prussian victory came to the conclusion that he must do something to keep his own German liberals in check, who were far too cock-a-hoop over the Prussian success. And so the following year he invited a German Catholic, Count Hohenwart, to form a government to breathe new life into the conversations with the Czechs which had been only half-heartedly conducted by his predecessors. To secure Czech co-operation the Czechs must be offered the hope of concluding a Czech *Ausgleich* on the lines of the Hungarian one.

With a view to encouraging the Czechs, the Emperor issued an *Imperial Rescript* on 12 September 1871, which contained memorable words which rekindled hope in their breasts: 'Mindful of the constitutional position of the Bohemian Crown, conscious of the glory and power which this crown conferred on us and our forefathers and remembering the unshakable loyalty with which the inhabitants of the Czech lands have supported our throne at all times, we gladly acknowledge the rights of this

Bohemian Kingdom and are ready to renew our recognition of it with our coronation oath.' The *Rescript* urged the Bohemian *Landtag* to put forward proposals in the spirit of the Monarch's proclamation.

The Czechs, who knew of this in advance, had their proposals ready and tabled them in the *Landtag* two days later, after having had them previously sanctioned by the Emperor. They were known as the *Fundamental Articles* and proved to contain quite radical constitutional changes. Under them the Czechs would be asked to accept and join the *Ausgleich*, although still on less favourable terms than those secured by the Hungarians. In future all questions relating to Bohemia and Moravia, which were not of common interest to the other *Länder* in Cisleithania (such as defence, finance, trade and communications), would be conducted by a Bohemian provincial *government*, headed by the Governor and responsible to the Bohemian *Landtag*.

Questions common to Cisleithania would be handled by a special Cisleithanian government, in which the various *Länder* would be represented by their own ministers. This would not be answerable to the *Reichsrat* but to a special Cisleithanian parliament to be called *The Congress of Delegates*. In the case of Bohemia and Moravia their minister, who would bear the revived historical title of *Bohemian Court Chancellor*, would also hold a watching brief over Bohemian and Moravian interests when 'joint' questions were discussed in the *Delegations* (to which the Bohemian *Landtag* would send delegates).

Agreement to these proposals by the Czechs represented a major concession on their part. Rieger had only three years previously made a solemn declaration that they would accept nothing short of a constitutional position equal to that of Hungary. The new measures would still leave the Czechs at a disadvantage, because the Hungarians had a government of their own which was not subject to any Austrian control, whereas their government would still be subject to the future *Congress of Delegates*. Further, whereas the Hungarians had a whole *Delegation* to themselves, the Czechs had to take their places in the Cisleithanian *Delegation* with all the other *Länder* and share their quota of places with the Germans in Bohemia. The Czechs also made a considerable concession in agreeing to the division of Bohemia and Moravia into German and Czech districts – a solution they had hitherto adamantly opposed. But in return they received from the Emperor and the Hohenwart government other concessions which, if put into practice, would have considerably changed the nature of the Monarchy to their benefit and to the benefit of other of the nationalities.

When the German members of the Bohemian *Landtag* read the *Fundamental Articles*, they were outraged, but as they were now in a minority they could do little but storm out of the session. In their absence the measures were carried unanimously. The Moravian *Landtag* also passed them, while reserving its position in regard to the historic rights of the Margraviate of Moravia.

But a storm was brewing among the Germans all over Austria. The Viennese press, which was partly under the control of the German Liberals, was vigorous in its onslaughts. Nationalist German students took to the streets and demonstrated vociferously. Every *Landtag* with a German majority joined in the protests. The changes, it was claimed, would destroy the century-old German culture in Austria and reduce the country to barbarism. All this was designed to intimidate the Emperor, and it succeeded. Anxieties about safeguarding the rights of the Bohemian Germans were expressed by no less a personality than Bismarck himself and a hint was even dropped by the King of Prussia, who had recently become German Emperor, that he did not want to have these Germans in Austria turning to him for help. The Austrian chancellor, Beust, who had originally favoured a Czech *Ausgleich*, was now scared too and rapidly convinced himself that a change of course would be prudent. In this he was backed by the Hungarian ministers. Finally the Emperor, afraid that the *Fundamental Articles* might precipitate the very situation he had wanted to avoid – a joint German–Hungarian agitation to break away from the Empire – went back on his word, not for the first or last time. At a Crown Council attended only by Austrian, German and Hungarian ministers, he bowed to the majority opinion and agreed to have the controversial articles watered down out of all recognition. Count Hohenwart then handed in his resignation.

The Emperor's emasculation of the *Fundamental Articles* and his refusal to restore justice to the Czechs was fatal for Austria's future. It consolidated the predominant influence of the Germans and Hungarians on the domestic and foreign policies of the Monarchy – an influence which was to prove calamitous. Not only the Czechs but all the nationalities came more and more to believe that only the break-up of the Monarchy would bring them the liberty they sought, and the rulers' fear and distrust of the nationalities and the Slavs in particular drove them on a headlong course towards war with their Slav neighbours – the Serbs and the Russians – and increasing dependence on Germany.

After a brief interregnum, Hohenwart's government was succeeded by the opposition – a government of German Liberals. The most powerful figure in it was the new Joint Foreign Minister, the Hungarian Andrássy – fiercely anti-Slav and pro-German. The angry reaction of the Czechs was to boycott the *Reichsrat*, but the new government was determined to break Czech opposition by the most ruthless measures. The Governor of Bohemia, a Czech noble, who under the *Fundamental Articles* was to have been the *Bohemian Court Chancellor*, was dismissed and replaced by the hated Baron Koller, who was brought back from Vienna with instructions to crush Czech resistance in two years. There was a renewed harsh drive against the Czech press, editors were fined or imprisoned, Koller unconstitutionally making use of all-German anti-Czech juries to secure the verdicts he wanted. Freedom of assembly was suspended, some Czech clubs and societies disbanded and others kept under strict surveillance. Typical of the situation in Austria at that time was that it was even forbidden to possess or publish the Emperor's *Rescript*! The opening words of it became a favourite tag for the Czechs ('Mindful of the constitutional position of the Bohemian crown...') and were much quoted. Hašek suggests that the police were so stupid that they did not know what a 'Rescript' was. They had orders to search the houses of people who had copies and asked them if they had the 'prescription'! ('The School for State Police').

In the Bohemian *Landtag* the Germans managed to increase their representation by the so-called *Chabrus* fiddle, which permitted them to purchase estates, buy themselves into the nobility and thus secure stronger representation in the overwhelmingly important first electoral *curia*. Outraged by this, the Czechs now boycotted the Bohemian and the Moravian *Landtag* as well as the *Reichsrat*. So, with a strong German majority in the *Reichsrat*, the new government was able to introduce constitutional changes with stronger centralist tendencies. For the next eight years it was able to govern unchallenged.

It was at this unhappy time that Hašek's father came to Prague to take up a teaching post at a German school. He would have to wait 13 years before he could afford to marry.

In 1878 the Austro-Hungarian government, under an agreement with the Turks, decided to occupy the Turkish provinces of Bosnia and Hercegovina with a view eventually to annexing them. The Germans in Austria opposed this decision, because the two provinces were populated by Serbs and Croats and annexation would inevitably lead to an increase in the already existing Slav majority in the Monarchy. This cost the German Liberals the Emperor's favour and in 1879 he dismissed the government and appointed a new one, led by Count Taaffe, a school friend of his, and including one Moravian Czech.

Taaffe's first aim was to try to persuade the Czechs to return to the *Landtag* and *Reichsrat*. In this he was helped by the Young Czech Party, the new bourgeois Czech party, which believed that the Old Czech Party (the nobility and *haute bourgeoisie*) had made a mistake in overstressing the importance of Bohemia's Historic State Rights. The Czechs should, in their opinion, base their claims rather on National Democratic Rights. They would also do more for the Czech cause if they abandoned their policy of abstention and took part in the debates of the *Landtag* and *Reichsrat*. The death in 1876 of Palacký, who had originally initiated the policy of abstention, opened the way to a reappraisal of tactics and renewed active participation of all Czech parties.

In 1879, as a result of the return of the Czechs to active political life, the combination of Slavs of all political views and conservative opponents of German liberalism produced a majority in the *Reichsrat*, while in the Bohemian *Landtag* the Czech majority was increased. In the Moravian, however, the Germans were still in the lead.

Most historians have criticised the Czech leaders of the Old

The oppressor's shame

Czech Party – Palacký and his son-in-law Rieger – for persisting in a policy of abstention and obstruction. But, as with all boycotts, such a course demanded considerable self-abnegation and moral courage. It deprived the Czech politicians of many material advantages in political, industrial and commercial life and even threatened their livelihood. But the Czech 'abstainers' were motivated by principle and regarded those who did not follow them as opportunists or 'collaborators'. In any case this same policy continued to be pursued by fits and starts by both Germans and Czechs until the end of the Monarchy. There was no doubt too that by boycotting the *Reichsrat* and *Landtag* the Czechs caused great anxiety to the Emperor and his advisers, who were desperate to find a solution to the breakdown in 'parliamentary government' which obstruction brought about. In particular it gravely embarrassed them in trying to get the budgets passed or the *Ausgleich* renewed. In the long term it forced on them the decision to introduce universal suffrage. On the other hand, Czech abstention undoubtedly left the field open to the Germans, who did not hesitate to seize for themselves what the Czechs abandoned. The Young Czechs believed that this was damaging to the Czech cause in the short run.

As a *quid pro quo* for this return to 'activism' Taaffe had promised the Czechs to grant their language the same official status as German. This he did in 1880. From now on every Czech would be entitled to deal with officials in his own tongue. Although this only legalised what had gradually become the existing practice, it infuriated the Germans who immediately pressed for the splitting of Bohemia into two regions – one Czech–German and the other German only (which they called a 'closed' area). When in 1886 the *Landtag* rejected their proposals they walked out in a fury. They never gave up the idea of splitting off those areas of Bohemia where there were denser German settlements. They reverted to it in 1918, when the Monarchy was breaking up, and it was the basis of Henlein's demands under Hitler.

Continuing a policy of appeasing the Czechs, Taaffe amended the electoral laws slightly in their favour. Another concession to them was the division of the Charles University into two sections – a Czech and a German one. During this long period of

Jaroslav Hašek

'sausaging along' (as Taaffe's policy was jokingly described), there was another positive event in Prague. In 1883 Jaroslav Hašek was born.

In 1890 the government and the majority of the Old Czechs in the *Landtag* discussed a new set of language laws, called the *Punctations*. But, unfortunately for Taaffe, in the elections the Young Czechs swept the board. From now on they replaced the Old Czechs as the spokesmen of the Czech nation. The *Punctations*, which had been discussed before the elections without their participation, were not nearly radical enough for them, now they had emerged in strength. Consequently they rejected them and brought about Taaffe's fall in 1893.

Language laws may seem hardly the stuff of which serious politics are made, although we know what a contentious problem language can still be today in Belgium and Yugoslavia. In Bohemia it was a very sensitive issue indeed, one which dominated the domestic political situation in Austria-Hungary until its collapse.

The nub of the question was this. With two nationalities living in Bohemia, there were of course two languages. The Germans wanted to entrench themselves in their language and ignore the existence of Czech, which they were still reluctant to learn after some 700 years of existence in the Historic Provinces. Indeed they cherished the hope that the Czechs would one day become germanised. The Czechs knew German, because they were obliged to learn it. The language dispute affected mainly teaching in schools and the language of administration. The Germans not only opposed the use and spread of Czech in what they regarded as their own areas, but tried to preserve the predominance of German even in the Czech areas. Apart from the important questions as to what language school instruction should be given in (reading German books meant imbibing German views) and what language should be used in the law courts, the disdainful attitude of the Germans to the Czech language was deeply insulting to the Czechs.

It was the public outcry on the language question which had led to the defeat of the Old Czechs at the polls, the overwhelming victory of the Young Czechs, and the adoption of a far more militant and radical attitude by the Czech opposition in their

44

struggle for their rights. The nobles and *haute bourgeoisie* passed into the background, and the nation's aspirations were henceforth to be put forward more stridently by the middle class – professors, journalists, teachers, some of whom were politically and socially radical. This was the time when Thomas Masaryk entered active politics. As one of a group of three he helped to found a new 'Realist Party'. He was still in favour of preserving the Monarchy, but many of the more radical elements among the Young Czechs were beginning to contemplate its break-up or destruction.

And so the 1890s began in an atmosphere of sharpened conflict. The government increased its repressive measures against the press and freedom of assembly and tried to carry out the *Punctations* in a diluted form by means of governmental decrees. The mood was well shown by the episode of the Jubilee Bohemian *Land* Exhibition which was held in Prague from June to October 1891. The Germans boycotted arrangements for it and did all they could publicly and privately to discredit it. Hašek was only eight at the time but frequently mentions it in his stories.

It became a major political factor when plans were made for the Emperor to visit it. He should have come in June, soon after the opening, but the Governor fell ill with typhoid and the Prime Minister accordingly advised the Emperor to postpone his visit. The Germans made good use of the opportunity to persuade the Emperor that the exhibition was panslavist and treasonable, and as such injurious to the Monarchy's foreign policy. In this way they tried to make the question of the exhibition a matter of 'joint' concern, which should be within the competence of the 'joint' Minister for Foreign Affairs, and therefore subject to the agreement of the Hungarians.

The leading German Liberal, Plener, who came from Bohemia, was strongly anti-Slav and anti-Czech. He had served in the diplomatic service and was a close friend of the Foreign Minister, the Hungarian Kálnoky. It was he who urged on Kálnoky that the presence in Prague of French and Slav guests – particularly Russians – could make difficulties for the Triple Alliance.

The governor did his best to explain to the Emperor that the Czechs were after all Slavs and that if the exhibition had become

45

a Slav one it was partly the fault of the Germans, who had refused to let it become what it was originally intended to be – a Czech and German one.

Nonetheless the Emperor, drawing his information from malicious and untrue reports in the German press, remained unmoved and refused to confirm that he would patronise it. Meanwhile he was outraged to learn that delegations from Galicia had arrived in Polish costume, and gave orders that the authorities should do everything possible to reduce to a minimum any official receptions planned for further Slav visitors and clamp down on any sign of a popular ovation for them. He viewed with alarm even expressions of solidarity among Slavs within the Monarchy and personally telegraphed to the Prime Minister that the Governor must 'force obedience [on the Czechs] by repression and penal measures'. Czech schoolchildren travelling to Prague from Liberec (Reichenberg) had their flags taken away from them, and a school-mistress accompanying them, who instructed them in harmless Czech 'national' songs, was rebuked by the school inspectors on orders from above. The Governor solemnly impressed on all Czech party leaders and newspaper editors that the national and Slav note must be silenced, otherwise the Emperor would not come.

In the end he did attend it (albeit reluctantly) and everything passed off without incident, although according to Hašek, Praguers were gaoled for three months for singing in front of the fountain *Hej, Slované* (a song in favour of the Slav languages) and shouting 'Death!' as they passed the German Club. ('On Reading Through Old Newspapers'). But, possibly out of a misguided endeavour to be 'impartial' and against the Governor's advice, he insisted on visiting Liberec (Reichenberg) too, the stronghold of the Germans in Bohemia, and decorating its mayor as well as the Czech mayor of Prague, although on the governor's insistence he was given a less high decoration than the Emperor had originally proposed.[10] (Hašek instances as an example of the pro-German prejudices of the government, 'the Prague municipality had to use German in communication with the Germans but the Reichenberg City Council were not obliged to use Czech with Czechs' ('The Cause of the Oppressed').)

From that moment on, each camp seemed to be provoking

the other. The Prague City Council (now Czech) authorised the removal of all the German street signs and notices in order to 'emphasise the Czech character of the capital'. The visit of a Czech Sokol delegation to a sports festival at Nancy in 1892 was seen by the government as a political gesture, in view of the conclusion the previous year of the military convention between France and Russia – a belated reply to the German Triple Alliance of Austria, Germany and Italy of 1883. In the same year the Austrian government forbade Czech primary and secondary schools to celebrate the 300th anniversary of Comenius.

In May 1893 the police found a hangman's noose round the neck of the statute of the Emperor Francis I on the Francis Embankment in Prague. In the following August, the eve of the Emperor's birthday, military music was interrupted by demonstrators and subversive leaflets distributed. Taaffe intervened to impose martial law in Prague, but this did not stop violent disturbances between Czechs and Germans on the streets, which even extended to the youth of both nationalities. Among those caught tearing down the posters proclaiming martial law was the author of *The Good Soldier Švejk*, then ten years old. Accused of having stones in his pocket for throwing at the police or at the windows of the German academic institutions, which were close to where he lived, he is reputed to have defended himself by saying innocently that they belonged to the school mineralogical collection.

Further demonstrations in Prague against the Monarchy gave Taaffe the excuse to take reprisals against the Czechs. This took the form of the imposition of martial law and the trial of members of the Progressive Youth movement (*Omladina*) in 1894. On false evidence manufactured by a police informer sixty-eight young people were sentenced to terms of imprisonment varying from seven months to eight years. Among them were the future Finance Minister of the Czechoslovak Republic, Alois Rašín, and the future poet, S. K. Neumann. If Hašek had been older, he might well have been involved too.

At the end of 1893 the Taaffe government had fallen and been replaced by two successive governments formed by the German opposition. They took even stronger measures against Czech radicalism, which only led to further obstruction. According to Hašek there followed 'times of spiteful persecution and ruthless rape of everything Czech' ('On Reading Through Old Newspapers'). When the situation became too tense in 1895 the Emperor asked Count Badeni, a Pole from Galicia, to form a government and try once more to conciliate the Czechs. Martial law in Prague was withdrawn and the sentences on those convicted in the *Omladina* trial reduced. Badeni tried to negotiate with the Czech leaders more acceptable language laws, from which emerged the *Badeni Language Ordinances* of 1897. These laid down that in all state offices in Bohemia and Moravia both German and Czech must be used according to requirements. This would mean that all state employees appointed after 1 July 1901 would have to have a knowledge of both languages, even though the official 'inner' language of the bureaucracy would remain, as in the army, German.

These proposals, not unexpectedly, caused an outcry from the Germans, who saw them not only as a threat to their jobs in government and municipal service but as cutting across their plans for the division of Bohemia and Moravia into Czech and German districts. They were particularly incensed that they had been enacted without parliamentary approval and imposed by decree (even though the Austrian Fundamental Law of 1867 had long ago established the principle of linguistic equality.) There were rowdy scenes in the *Reichsrat* as well as on the streets. In the *Landtag*, the President's tribunal was stormed and there were demands for impeachment of the Cabinet. The well-known Berlin historian of Ancient Rome, Theodore Mommsen, published a message to the Germans in Austria, calling on them to fight against the Slav 'apostles of barbarism'. His notorious reference to the Czechs as a nation 'whose skulls are not susceptible to reason but only to blows of a club' has deservedly never been forgotten. Not unexpectedly Badeni resigned in 1897, but not before he had brought about a liberalisation of the franchise by adding a fifth *curia* to the existing four, which would return seventy-two deputies to the *Reichsrat* by universal suffrage. This brought the first representatives of the working class – Social Democrats – into the Austrian parliament.

On Badeni's fall the Emperor sent for Baron Gautsch and asked him to form a government. According to Hašek he said 'Badeni must go. He is a Slav and favours the Czechs.' ('Twenty Years Ago'). Baron Gautsch then immediately renewed martial law in Prague. There were further riots in Bohemia between Germans and Czechs, and the army was brought in to quell them. The Germans organised monster processions, let off fireworks and finally set on fire Czech houses at the hop centre at Žatec (Saaz), where there was a large German majority. They also destroyed furniture in Czech houses in other towns.

By 1898 Gautsch had brought in new language ordinances under which Bohemia and Moravia were to be divided into three language zones – Czech, German and 'mixed', but the day after promulgating these he too had to resign, to be succeeded by Count Franz Thun, who included a Czech as his Minister of Finance. But unrelenting German opposition forced Thun's resignation too as well as the repeal of Gautsch's language ordinances, so that in this respect the situation went back to what it had been before 1896. It was once more a bad year for the Czechs, who found that all their gains of the previous year had been lost and so resumed their policy of obstruction.

By this time the ruling circles in Austria had at last come to the conclusion that the nationalism of the Czechs and Germans could only be curbed by a process of democratisation. In 1907 a new Prime Minister, Baron Beck, introduced a bill for universal suffrage which had been in preparation for some years. It was to be implemented all over Cisleithania – but not in Hungary. The Hungarians would not hear of it.

The new measures partly fulfilled their object, at least initially. As a result of the elections the large Czech and German nationalist parties came off badly and those representing sectional interests (the Agrarian Party, representing peasants and farmers, and the Social Democrats, urban workers) emerged greatly strengthened. The Young Czechs, who had been the most powerful party, were now relatively weak and the Old Czechs were practically eliminated. The future was to lie with a coalition of Social Democrats and Agrarians, and indeed this would be the determining factor in the first years of the Republic when it was founded. But in 1907 the distance between the two parties was too great to allow co-operation.

Jaroslav Hašek

Unfortunately the electoral results did not eliminate the national disputes or stop obstruction, because thanks to their increased numbers the smaller parties were enabled to tip the balance and block legislation. This obstruction extended to the *Landtag* too, whenever two nationalities or more were ranged against each other. And for the Czech cause it had the disadvantage that henceforward ten political parties would be fighting against each other in an often unseemly struggle of words in which the national interests seemed to be submerged. In 1908 the Bohemian *Landtag* ceased activity altogether and the government had to set up an administrative commission to approve the necessary credits. From now on succeeding governments had to govern by means of the notorious Paragraph 14, which gave the government power in emergencies to enact legislation independent of the *Reichsrat*. In *The Good Soldier Švejk* Hašek describes in Dickensian terms how: '...all logic mostly disappeared and the paragraph triumphed. *The paragraph* strangled, went mad, frowned, laughed, threatened, murdered and gave no quarter' (p. 24).

In his article 'The Republican Programme in Bohemia', published in *Čechoslovan* on 29 March 1917, he draws a vivid picture of the state of Prague in 1908 on the occasion of the Emperor's Jubilee. 'Great demonstrations. Shouts of "Down with Austria! Long Live the Republic!" Students at the university burnt the black and yellow flag. There is a sound of drums on Příkopě and martial law is proclaimed.'

On 26 July 1913 the Prime Minister, Baron Stürgkh, dissolved the Bohemian *Landtag*. Eight months later he prorogued the *Reichsrat* indefinitely. Thus on the eve of World War I, when Austria sorely needed inner unity, it was torn apart more than ever by the feuding of nationalities, mainly Czech and German.

To sum up what many of the Czechs thought about the Monarch and the Monarchy, one need only quote what Hašek wrote during the war.

> We were forced to conduct our politics in Vienna, on foreign soil, in a foreign, hostile milieu, where we came up against difficulties at every step.
> Vienna was the birthplace of those notorious cabinets of Bach, Schmerling, Beust, Hohenwart...Windischgraetz, Gautsch, Thun, Körber and Heinerle – And then came Stürgkh and Aehrental.

The oppressor's shame

And all those cabinets [...] violated our language rights, prohibited the display of the emblem of the triple lands of the Bohemian Crown and hung out instead the Great German Tricolour [black, white and red], honoured the Germans and ruled us with hostility. They always went the same way. Ministries came and went. New ones were made and each one of them had the same goal...

And if ever we succeeded in overthrowing a ministry, then the new one was worse than the one before and we always brought back with us from Vienna the impression that every government was the worst there had ever been [...].

In these dismal times we wrote a vast number of articles and made fiery speeches. We drafted many sharp resolutions and after our political conferences we drank a great number of enthusiastic toasts.

Count Stürgkh once said to the Czech representatives: 'Just go on, gentlemen. You know how to make fine speeches – but we have the power!' And by that he meant the whole system of state police, gendarmerie, district police officers, governors, judges on the bench, gaolers' keys.

Parliaments were dissolved and deputies enjoying immunity were sent home and investigated by the police. The authorities confronted the Czech people with Paragraph 14. And all interpellations, by which we tried to convince Vienna of the thousands of wrongs and violations which it committed against us, disappeared into volumes of printed stenographic reports of the proceedings of the *Reichsrat*. The paper is yellow with all the pages of our complaints and grievances, just as old parchments become yellow. So it is with the Emperor's *Rescript* and the old *Diploma* of 20 October 1860, which once confirmed our Historic Rights. They have turned yellow too!

('The Cause of the Oppressed')

The assassination of the heir to the Austrian throne in Sarajevo on 28 June 1914 offered the war party in Vienna the opportunity they had long been waiting for. The annexation of Bosnia and Hercegovina in 1908 had dangerously increased the number of potential disaffected Serbs and Croats in the Monarchy, and Serbia, which had become after the Balkan Wars the most powerful military force in the Balkans, had long aimed to bring about the unification of all the Southern Slavs. When the Archduke's assassin turned out to be a Bosnian Serb, Austria accused Serbia of complicity and declared war. The danger of Russian intervention was foreseen, but the calculation was that before the cumbrous Russian war machine had had time to mobilise Serbia would have been decisively defeated.

51

The outbreak of the war took the Czechs by surprise and placed them in a dilemma. To most of them the idea of killing their Slav brothers and their friends, the French, was anathema. And they knew only too well that a German victory would make their existence even harsher and put an end to their hopes of autonomy. But the increased repression, the hopelessness of resistance to it and the widely-held belief in a German victory cowed them into passivity. They waited to see how the war went. Fortunately the suspension of the *Landtag* and the *Reichsrat* robbed their deputies of the necessity of taking a public stand. Mobilisation in Bohemia passed off without friction in spite of a few isolated demonstrations.

But then the fortunes of the war suddenly turned. By the end of 1914 the Austrian troops had been repulsed and driven out of Serbia, while the Russians had conquered the whole of Galicia and reduced the fortress of Przemyśl to a beleaguered island in a Russian sea. The enormous losses suffered by the Austrian troops necessitated a new round of call-ups and among those summoned at the beginning of 1915 were Jaroslav Hašek – and Josef Švejk.

> At the time when the forests on the river Rabe in Galicia saw the Austrian armies fleeing across the river and when down in Serbia one after the other of the Austrian divisions were taken with their pants down and got the walloping they had long deserved, the Austrian Ministry of War suddenly remembered Švejk. Why, even he might help to get the Monarchy out of the mess. (p. 55)

The Russians were now poised to cross the Carpathian mountains and invade Slovakia. In Bohemia Hašek had been impudently telling Austrian officers that 'Russian was being spoken in Náchod' (a Bohemian frontier town) and, according to Masaryk, the market-women were keeping their best geese for the Russians. Czechs at the front let themselves be taken prisoner by the 'enemy' or openly deserted. As Hašek tells us, two whole battalions with their officers went over to the Russians, although not 'to the strains of their regimental band', as he picturesquely described it. This was partly prompted by the intensified persecution at home, where the military had for all practical purposes taken control: Czech newspapers were suppressed, journalists and politicians arrested, including the National Social Party leader

Klofáč, and death sentences were passed at the slightest hint of treason.

But Czech hopes were dashed when in the spring of 1915 the German General Mackensen launched a combined Austro-German assault on the weak sector in the Russian lines and forced the Russians to make a massive withdrawal. During the whole of the summer months of 1915 they went on retreating, leaving in their wake terrible losses and unbelievable havoc. By June they were back at the point where they had started. In the autumn combined Austrian, German and Bulgarian forces routed the Serbs and drove them out of their country. But there was a ray of hope still: in May Italy had declared war on the Central Powers and Austria was once again forced to fight a war on two fronts. Some of the best Austrian troops had to be withdrawn from the Eastern Front and sent to the Trentino. Knowing that the Austrian lines were depleted, General Brusilov launched a new offensive in the spring of 1916 and the Russian steamroller was soon on the way to the Carpathians again; but this time the Austrian forces, reinforced by German, were able to check its advance.

If Czech politicians at home under Austrian pressure publicly rejected the Allied promise to liberate the Czechs and Slovaks from foreign domination, their compatriots abroad were of different mettle and formed foreign legions to fight the Germans and Austrians on the French and Italian fronts. The largest Czech emigré force was the *Družina* in Russia, later to become the Czech Legion and to comprise some 200,000 men. But successive Russian governments, distrustful of Czech loyalty, refused to allow the volunteers to undertake more than reconnaissance duties, where they risked hanging if caught by the Austrians.

But the main Czech political resistance abroad was led by Masaryk and Beneš, who had left Bohemia to form a National Committee, leaving behind them at home an intelligence network called 'The Mafia'. Making Britain his base, Masaryk travelled to America and Russia in a successful effort to win support for Czech independence and rally his countrymen abroad behind the movement.

The assassination of the Austrian Prime Minister, Baron Stürgkh by the Prague German Friedrich Adler, son of Victor

Adler, the Austrian Social Democrat leader, led to an intensification of Austrian oppression. More journalists were imprisoned, and influential political leaders like Kramář and Rašín sentenced to death. The cumbersome name 'Kingdom and Lands represented in the *Reichsrat*' was abolished and changed to 'Austrian lands', while the Crown of St Wenceslas and the title of King of Bohemia disappeared from the Emperor's coat of arms and style. Meanwhile the Germans planned constitutional changes, which would establish their supremacy over the Czechs. Bohemia was garrisoned more and more by Hungarian troops, while Czech troops were banished to Hungary.

On 21 November 1916 the aged Emperor died and was succeeded by his great-nephew Charles, who immediately made attempts to liberalise the régime and put out peace-feelers to the West. But Russia, the ally on whom the Czech hopes were most centred, was soon in a crisis, her military effectiveness having been undermined by the February Revolution of 1917. Fortunately this was compensated by American entry into the war on the Allied side. Kerensky, who was to become Prime Minister of the Russian Provisional Government, was still opposed to the use of the Czech *Družina*, but Masary's visit and Russian desertions finally persuaded him to allow the Czechs to hold a sector of the line at Zborów, where they earned high praise for breaking through the Austrian defence. Their success, which was published throughout the world, helped Masaryk in his plans for the attainment of Czech independence, which had been gravely embarrassed by the negative attitude of the Czechs at home, and jeopardised by the reluctance of the Allies to agree to the eventual break-up of the Monarchy. But Czech writers at home showed a more resilient attitude in May 1917, when they issued a manifesto calling upon the deputies to 'act like independent men'. At the reopening of the *Reichsrat* at the end of the month the deputies responded by calling for a federated monarchy with equality for all its components.

The Bolshevik Revolution in October 1917 took Russia finally out of the war and the treaty of Brest Litovsk between the Soviet régime and the Central Powers was signed on 13 March 1918. The *Družina* or Czech Legion was now isolated and had to fight its way across Russia in the teeth of Soviet resistance to reach

Vladivostok, from where it was to be transported to France to fight on the Western Front. Its military successes amazed the world but the war was over before it could reach its destination.

At home on 16 October 1918 the new Emperor offered the nationalities a federated Austria, but it was too late. The German army was collapsing and its leaders were already suing for peace. The Czech National Council, now a provisional government, proclaimed Czech independence. Twelve days later a Czech National Committee which had been formed at home took over power in Prague.

Who was to lead the new Czechoslovak state? There were two principal contenders – Masaryk who had led the movement for independence abroad, and Kramář, who had been the leading figure in the resistance at home, and who had only been saved from a martyr's death by the new Emperor's amnesty. Masaryk looked to the West and distrusted Russia. Although no Socialist, he shared many Socialist aims. Kramář was a man of the Right. His Russian wife, his villa in the Crimea and his close connections with Russian politicians of Tsarist times had prompted him to look Eastwards and Slavwards. But the rivalry between these men, one speaking for the Czechs abroad and the other for those at home, had been settled for them once and for all by the Bolshevik revolution, which cut the ground from the feet of Kramář. The new state could not now be a kingdom ruled by a Russian prince; it would be a republic modelled on Western parliamentary democracy. Masaryk was the obvious choice as president. Kramář had to be content with the premiership (which he was unable to retain long, because after the war his party lost considerable ground).

Now the young republic's problems began – where to draw the frontiers, whether or not to include Sub-Carpathian Russia, how to deal with the Germans, the Slovaks and Polish claims to Teschen, and above all, how to resist a Communist take-over on the lines of what had happened in Hungary under Béla Kun. Only the last of these concerned Hašek, who had stayed on in Siberia. After serving the Bolsheviks in various posts as a propagandist he was at length sent to Prague to help to carry out a planned Bolshevik Revolution. But by the time he arrived there it had been foiled. And so the new Czechoslovak state emerged as a bourgeois, not a Soviet, republic, a solution approved by most Czechs but deplored by Hašek, who had hoped for a more radical solution. Coming on top of all his personal difficulties it was his crowning disillusionment.

3
HAŠEK AS A JOURNALIST AND SHORT STORY WRITER

> I was originally editor of *Animal World*...From *Animal World* I slipped down easily into *Czech Word*. My friends said that I didn't change my political views at all. I simply exchanged bulldogs for the National Social Party. The only difference was that, whereas I used to feed bulldogs, now it was the Party which fed me. ('How I Left the National Social Party')

In addition to *The Good Soldier Švejk* Hašek wrote some verses, a few short dramatic sketches or revues, a number of political articles and some 1200 short stories and *feuilletons*.

Few of his verses have come down to us. They are of little literary merit and are only interesting for the light they throw on the author himself and his reaction to the days he spent in the Austrian army. Apart from some youthful efforts published before the war when he was only 20 (*Cries of May*), they were obviously composed to kill time and please his company commander, Lieutenant Lukas, the only person in his entourage likely to appreciate them. Lukas carefully kept them all after the war, but after his death some of them disappeared.

Hašek's dramatic sketches are mere fragments. We cannot always be certain whether he wrote them himself or merely shared their authorship with other members of 'The Party of Moderate Progress within the Bounds of the Law'.

His political articles are mostly war propaganda – composed in Russia either for the Czech Legion or the Bolsheviks – and as such ephemeral productions. Those for the Legion are well argued, although Hašek had had little political experience in this kind of writing. Before he started working as a war correspondent for the Czech Legion in Kiev, he had never tried his hand at serious polemical articles. His talent had lain rather in parodying them. But he certainly wrote them with conviction. His effectiveness as a propagandist for the Legion is well described

Jaroslav Hašek

by the playwright František Langer, who heard one of the speeches he made in the course of a recruiting drive.

It was the first public speech I had heard on the struggle against Austria-Hungary for Czechoslovak national independence which was not broken up by the police. And I couldn't help marvelling at the irony of fate in putting it into the mouth of Hašek of all people, from whom I had been accustomed to hear political orations only in 'The Party of Moderate Progress'. He delivered this speech with unaffected solemnity. It contained all the stock historical references from the Battle of the White Mountain onwards, and like all such recruiting addresses was designed to appeal to patriotic feelings [. . .] But in contrast to most such speeches, his did not sound like a tirade or a schoolmaster's lecture. He observed the required moderation and controlled himself so as not to be guilty of what he once used to parody in others. Moreover, he seemed to have unlearned all the tricks by which he had tried to beguile his listeners in the old days; there were no little jokes, no clowning, no covert grins [. . .]
Altogether it was an entirely different Hašek from the one I had known. He, who had always been against militarism and patriotism, in fact always against something, was now for the first time speaking *for* something. And this something was nothing less than honest and consistent patriotism, the volunteer army and its fight for national independence. I listened to him and had the feeling that, although he had probably repeated them God knows how many times, these were not just empty phrases, but came direct from his heart.[1]

Hašek's *feuilletons* are mostly light-weight pieces. He himself amusingly describes a *feuilleton* as 'Something which can be read in the morning at breakfast when a man is still yawning and in the afternoon when after lunch he lies agreeably stretched out on a soft sofa. A kind of writing in which one can skip half a column without missing it.' ('How My Wife Writes *Feuilletons*')

His numerous stories cover a wide range of subjects. They are almost all of them very short – averaging three or four pages (some little more than a thousand words) – because they had to fit the dimensions of a daily *feuilleton*. Their length affects their style: they had to catch the reader's attention in the opening paragraph and the plot is revealed in simple and unadorned sentences, bare of description or other literary adornment. If the beginning is promising, the ending is often predictable and sometimes disappointing. The author found himself too cramped to introduce a surprise factor. Either it was beyond his ingenuity or he did not bother. A frequent solution to the dénouement is the lunatic asylum or suicide.

58

Hašek had a natural gift for writing and wrote easily and lucidly. He began at an early age, publishing his first story in the much-read *National Paper* when he was only eighteen. For a number of years he experimented with various literary forms and at one time seemed likely to develop into a descriptive or character writer. But he soon settled down to a fixed pattern of style and produced a stream of stories and articles of varying merit. Their tone tended to be cynical and abrasive. He was always 'bashing' someone or something. He seems to have been wary of trying his hand at longer narrative, and *The Good Soldier Švejk in Captivity* which he published in Kiev during the War, though short too, was the first novel or novelette he attempted, except perhaps for a fifty-page short story, 'The Tribulations of Mr That-Time'. As he always had trouble in finding suitable endings to his short stories, it is not surprising that when he finally decided to embark on a full-scale novel he planned to make it run into six volumes and died before the final three were completed.

For his earliest stories Hašek drew on the material provided by the walking tours he made with his friends. These excursions proved to be voyages of revelation for him – especially his visit to Slovakia, then under Hungary. His discovery of a country whose inhabitants spoke a kindred tongue but whose rulers were quite foreign made a deep impression on him. These youthful stories reveal, in an author whose writings were to become so cynical, an infectious enthusiasm for the customs and characteristics of probably the first foreigners he had met outside Bohemia. They are surprisingly mature for one so young and unschooled, and convey something of the colour and fascination of the world of gypsies on the road, Slovaks in the mountains, Hungarians in the *puszta* and Poles beyond the Carpathians. The titles of some of these stories are eloquent of their contents – 'Oh, Dunajec, You White Water...' (the Dunajec was a river in Galicia), 'The Death of the Horal' (an inhabitant of the Polish slopes of the Carpathians), 'The Gypsy's Funeral', 'The Serbian Priest Bogumirov and the Goat of the Mufti Isrim', 'In the Mountains on the Romanian Side', 'Three Sketches from the Hungarian Plain', 'Above Lake Balaton', 'Galician Landscape with Wolves' and many others. Referring to these early stories the critic Max

Jaroslav Hašek

Brod wrote, 'Hašek's short stories. . .set in the Carpathians among Hucul [Sub-Carpathian] thieves, Romanian bandits, young and old gypsies and cunning bears aroused no attention [when they first appeared]. When we read them today we look upon them differently and could wish that their bold, yes, cruel adventures, told so laconically and wittily had found a translator.'

These promising first steps were unfortunately cut short by Hašek's two lapses into Anarchism, first in 1904 and then between 1906 and 1907. During these periods he contributed to the Anarchist press and the quality of much of his writing deteriorated: he wrote a series of cheap stories and articles which, even if they had not been provocative and libellous, would almost certainly have been rejected by more respectable papers on account of their poor literary quality. In any case they appealed to only a small minority of readers.

It was in 1904 that he first made contact with the Anarchists and started contributing to their paper *Progressive Youth*, which was published in Lom in Northern Bohemia, their stronghold in the mining community there; but his relations with them were brought to a temporary halt by his quarrel with the editor and his subsequent disappearance into Bavaria. His adventures there inspired him to compose some amusing stories, ironical but not unkind, about the inhabitants of that part of Germany.

Hašek's return to the Anarchist fold in 1906 and his association with their Prague paper *New Progressive Youth*, had a further injurious effect on his writing, because instead of developing his *črty* (sketches), he wasted more time turning out cheap political squibs, many of which were anyhow truncated or even suppressed by the censors. And so we can be grateful to his future father-in-law for insisting that he must finally leave the movement, which resulted in his making his last contribution to the Anarchist press in May 1907, though not alas in his prostituting his literary talents for the last time.

In 1908 he published in *Merry Prague* a series of stories called *Stories from a Water-Bailiff's Watchtower,*[2] which were not merry, as the title of the magazine might lead one to expect, but were based on the experiences of Hašek's maternal grandfather, who had been a water-bailiff on one of the fishponds on the Schwarzenberg estate in Southern Bohemia. The stories are of no great merit, but they give an indication of the sort of writer Hašek might have become if fate had not confined him mainly to Prague and driven him to write political articles. They are in the vein of Turgenev's *A Sportsman's Sketches*, and show that at this time Hašek certainly knew how to convey to his readers the charm of the Czech countryside and to draw convincing character studies of the people who inhabited it. The fishponds of Southern Bohemia, where there are a multitude of interconnected 'ponds' (really 'lakes', the largest of which extends to 1,800 acres and has a dam over 10,000 feet long) are a fascinating terrain, and the life of the water-bailiff with his struggles either with crafty poachers or tyrannical superiors is a subject which Hašek – at that time still only twenty-five and relatively inexperienced in the craft – treats well. The story, 'Director Behalt', in which he depicts a land-agent who is the embodiment of corruption and gluttony, is the most effective of the series.

The following year Hašek attempted a more ambitious group of stories called 'From the Old Pharmacy',[3] which were also accepted by *Merry Prague*. They are based on his own experiences when he was apprenticed at the age of thirteen to chemist's shops. In the stories the author describes well the comings and goings in an old pharmacy, which combines the functions of a chemist's and an ironmongery – the hen-pecked proprietor, his martinet of a wife, her father who tyrannises over him too, the clerk and the messenger as well as many of the customers. Hašek's realism is much in evidence. He depicts in elaborate detail every activity of the pharmacy including the appearance and contents of the cellar, the loft and the shop. He goes on to recount the petty vices of those who work in or patronise the pharmacy. Everyone is trying to get his rake-off and succeeds. It is like life in the army as portrayed in *The Good Soldier Švejk*. The proprietor tells the young apprentice that he must lie to the customer but never lie to him. The vibrant wife of the proprietor and her sudden sally into the shop lay dramatically bare the pitiful home-life of the down-trodden proprietor. Not all the stories are of the same quality. The chapter on the customers, for instance, falls short of expectation, but the study of the messenger and his adored trolley, which he trusts so implicitly but which lets him down in the end, is most affecting.

61

Jaroslav Hašek

In 1909 the National Social Party started to publish a popular 'comic' called *Caricatures*. The illustrator Lada, who was then only twenty-one years old, was put in charge of it under the responsible editorship of Stříbrný, a leading politician of the party, and invited his friend Hašek to contribute to it. The following year it was supplemented by a large coloured edition with higher literary and artistic pretensions. Lada concentrated most of his attention on this, leaving the small popular edition to Hašek's almost unsupervised care.

The freedom to write what he liked without submitting to editorial control was of course a bonanza for Hašek and he made full use of it. Why the authorities did not prosecute him but confined themselves to blacking various articles or banning some whole numbers is hard to explain. It was symptomatic of the very indulgent attitude they took to him during the whole of his bohemian existence. No doubt they did not take too seriously a little four-page rag which was quickly read, thrown away and forgotten.

So Hašek had his journalistic fling, even if it did not do his future any good. He pilloried the leaders of *all* the parties, including Klofáč of the National Social Party which owned *Caricatures*, accusing him of travelling to Russia and Serbia, ostensibly to raise funds for the party, but in fact to transfer some of those funds to a bank in London, 'where he intends to run to, when he has received the due reward for his services'. Such 'services', according to Hašek, included selling to the Russians all his knowledge of the Austrian army, and working out a war-plan for the Russian army, which was responsible for their defeat by the Japanese ('Where Deputy Klofáč Gets His Money').

Hašek was equally hard on Dr Kramář, the leader of the Young Czechs, but he reserved most of his venom for the Social Democrat leaders, probably because, as he wrote to Jarmila in 1908, he thought that one of them, Dr Soukup, had promised him a job on the party daily *The People's Right*, and nothing had come of it. Consequently he writes of Dr Soukup that his name means in German *Unterhändler*, which, 'when translated back into Czech means "jobber" and will be found in the encyclopaedia under the heading of "Bourse" or "Agent" '. After this highly unflattering beginning, Hašek suggests that in his violent speeches and political articles Soukup uses the language of the countryside, where he was born – or rather of the farm-yard. Dr Soukup's particular worry however was, according to Hašek, that having campaigned very energetically for universal suffrage and having been elected a member of the *Reichsrat* he was now unable to draw his allowance, because of the obstruction in parliament which had led to sessions being suspended (the suggestion being that those who oppose obstruction only do so because it means financial loss for them) ('Dr Fr. Soukup').

Hašek's description of a Social Democrat Party meeting in 'The Sad Fate of Peter Hříbal' is scarcely more flattering. It resembles Švejk's lunatic asylum. 'They wrung their hands, sang whole sentences – according to the latest fashion – spat into the spittoon specially provided for them, bawled, waved their arms, clasped their hands, beat their heads as though in a trance, and spoke of cripples, widows, orphans, suicides, cattle and animals, ending to deafening applause with the call: "We have not lived in vain and so let all come under the red flags of Social Democracy." ' A favourite theme is the drunkenness of deputies. 'On February 8th Deputy Folber proclaimed in parliament that but for the Social Democrat deputies alcoholism would spread all over Austria. If they drank spirits, it was only to reduce state supplies.' ('About the Activities of the Social Democrat Deputies Folber, Klička, Biňovec, Remeš and Jaroš in the *Reichsrat*, in the *Couloirs* and Outside.').

In another of his articles, 'The Commercial Academy', he libels its Rector, to whom he had taken a hearty dislike. His article, if remotely true, throws a revealing light on the snobbish way the Rector ran that institution, of which Hašek was a former pupil. This is how Hašek describes him:

His watchword is: 'No one is to be let off school fees. They are 120 guilders a year, and anyone who is unable to pay that sum is a pauper and can be of no benefit whatsoever to the Czech nation as a businessman...' It often happened that if anyone was let off school fees, he was told by the Rector on various occasions: 'Now, then remember. You have been let off school fees, and therefore you must tell us the name of the culprit.' [In other words, you are expected to become an informer.] But there is nothing dishonourable in using various means of compulsion in the course of an interrogation.

Jaroslav Hašek

> The [Rector who is a] government counsellor spent a long time in
> Russia – and that's the long and short of it.

Hašek laughed at the way the Rector apparently insisted that the students of the Academy should greet him from a distance. Woe betide anyone who failed to notice him! The culprit was given a dressing down before the whole class and his crime was recorded in the class register. His marks for good behaviour were slashed and he was led off to the Rector's office, where he got a second dressing-down and his parents were informed of his unheard-of behaviour. Hašek must have been thinking of him when he described Colonel Kraus von Zillergut in *The Good Soldier Švejk* (pp. 201–6). Nor did Hašek ever forget the way they taught him to write business letters at the Academy, or so he claimed: 'With your esteemed letter to hand I beg to inform you that your esteemed sack of coffee reached us in good order.'

The issue of *Caricatures* carrying Hašek's defamatory article was a great success, especially with the pupils and ex-pupils of the Commercial Academy, and quickly sold out. But Stříbrný, as responsible editor, was soon sued for libel and summoned to appear in court together with Hašek. When the judge asked Hašek what he had against the Academy, he replied defiantly that he was against all schools of any kind. After hearing this, Stříbrný decided to abandon his defence and publish an apology. The task of drafting it devolved on Hašek, who formulated it so ambiguously and ironically that the Rector can have had little satisfaction from winning his case.

In May 1912 the great idea came to Hašek of inventing the character of the Good Soldier Švejk and writing five stories about him in *Caricatures* (as will be told in the next chapter). Soon after this he had great success with his performances as candidate for the mock 'Party of Moderate Progress within the Bounds of the Law' and, to preserve something of this charade for posterity he resolved to write its history (*The History of the Party of Moderate Progress within the Bounds of the Law*). It was not a very practical idea, because the discreditable anecdotes he invented and retailed, not only about public figures, who might have sued him for libel, but also about his relatives and friends, some of whom would have had nothing more to do with him if they had seen the book in print, made it risky if not impossible to

64

publish it. In the event the editors of the last edition of Hašek's works were only able to publish a text in 1964, after experiencing great difficulty in locating all the missing parts. Indeed even now it is not absolutely complete.

In this highly original and ingenious book Hašek ridiculed political life in Prague in the same brash way in which he would later lampoon the Austro-Hungarian army. But of course his novel was written after the fall of the Monarchy, whereas 'The History' was recorded while it was still powerful and vindictive.

It is divided into four sections: (1) From the Annals of the Party, (2) The Apostolic Activity of Three of Its Members, (3) The Party's Espionage Scandals and (4) The Party Goes to the Polls.

But it is of course one glorious leg-pull from start to finish. Space does not permit an analysis of it in detail.[4] The 'Party' consists in fact of Hašek's bohemian companions, who met together at various taverns in Prague about 1904 – at 'The Golden Litre' (The Party Headquarters), 'Blaha's', 'The Slav Café' and 'Svíček's' (branch offices). Just as Dickens presents the members of the Pickwick Club as people of stature whose acts are notable and deserve recording so Hašek introduces his characters – the members of the Party – as heroic types, although their stupid ideas and unscrupulous actions naturally belie it at every turn.

Unlike *The Pickwick Papers* there is no connected story. Most of the book consists of humorous portraits of various contemporary personalities whom Hašek knew or came into contact with – writers, poets, painters, actors, translators, pianists, critics, editors, architects and members of literary groups. They include three of Jarmila's brothers, several of her girlhood friends, as well as most of Hašek's own boon companions.

The 'Apostolic Activities of the Party' is a euphemistic description of the attempts of its members to carry their campaign into the country, or to spy out what the other political parties are doing (mainly directed against the National Social Party). The trials of its members, who continually meet with failure, are likened by the author to those of the early Christians. The joke lies in the great earnestness with which the members of the Party embark on their 'worthy' activities when contrasted with the ridiculous and undignified scrapes they get into. Their visit to

Vienna has the avowed object of sponging on Czechs living there and 'touching' them for money, but it is presented as a favour they are doing to Czechs abroad, who will be delighted to give hospitality to their countrymen and have news of Prague.

The book ends with some chapters on the Party's electoral activities (held at 'The Cowshed' tavern), the Party's programme, Hašek's electoral speeches and an account of polling day.

From 1912 to 1915, when he was called up, Hašek published between 200 and 300 stories. Some were published in book form: *The Good Soldier Švejk and Other Strange Stories* (1912), *The Tribulations of Mr That-Time* (1912), *Kalamajka*, a book for children partly written and illustrated by Lada (1913) and *The Tourists' Guide and Other Satires* (1913). In 1915 there appeared another book of his short stories: *My Dog Business and Other Humorous Sketches*.

During his short period of service with the Austrian army we know that he wrote a number of poems. Whether he also made notes for future use in his novel we do not know. In any case, if he had done so, it is unlikely that he would have been able to take the material with him when he crossed to the other side.

During his two years with the Czech Legion in Russia he published some fifty or more contributions but not more than ten of them were short stories. He also wrote the second version of the Švejk mythos – *The Good Soldier Švejk in Captivity*. All his writings of this period were designed to serve propaganda aims – to stir up enthusiasm for the Czechoslovak national struggle and pillory those Czechs who were unwilling to take an active part in it. In tales like 'The Fortunes of Mr Hurt' or 'The Story of a Guarantee' he ridicules those of his fellow-countrymen who wanted a comfortable life and who, once having laid down their arms, were not prepared to take them up again for the national cause without some material benefit or promise of compensation. Two tales foreshadow *The Good Soldier Švejk*. One, 'The Tale of the Portrait of the Emperor Francis Joseph I' makes a whole story out of what was later to appear as an episode in the novel (pp. 7–8). Another, 'The Sum Total of the War Campaign of Captain Alserbach' describes the revenge taken by the Czech rank and file on a bullying Austrian German officer after they have all of them been taken prisoner by the Russians. The political articles fulminate against the shameful situation at home, Austrian maltreatment of the Czechs, the rottenness of the Monarchy, its approaching collapse and the idiocy of the reigning house.

One cannot claim that Hašek's literary output during the first two and a half years of his stay in Russia was in any way distinguished, nor could one expect it to be. After a year in the Austrian army, when he could write little, he had spent another year in prisoner-of-war camps. Once free, he needed time to fall into his literary stride again, and his new role as recruiting officer and war correspondent did not encourage the production of humorous stories in his own inimitable vein. None the less there are a few which recapture it.

In one, which satirises the oppression in Bohemia in wartime, the district Head of Police issues an order for the editor of the local newspaper to be brought before him at 10 a.m. the following day ('The Hořice District Police Chief'). In consequence gendarmes drag the unfortunate man out of bed in the early hours and take him to the police station. 'His trousers were falling down because they had taken away his braces to prevent him hanging himself. He was without a collar because in the night they had not allowed him to put one on.'

The police chief accuses him of deliberately recommending in his column 'Hints for Householders' fruit from the countries of the Entente rather than of the Central Powers. Why did he not recommend Tyrolean apples? Perhaps because the Tyroleans were so loyal to the dynasty? And why not Cassel rennet apples? Perhaps because Cassel was a town in Germany? And why did he ignore Gravensteins? Perhaps because the motto of the Gravenstein Hussars was 'For God, Emperor and Fatherland?'

Or there is a ridiculous story about the Emperor Charles ('Charles Was in Prague') who, while still an Archduke and when living at the Prague Castle had tried to learn a few disjointed sentences in Czech. In order to practise them during an early morning walk, he fires them suddenly at one of the policemen on duty, who is taken completely off his guard. The last one is, 'The sparrow jumped on the tree and the cat ate it up.' When confronted with this statement, the policeman begins to sweat, because he thinks he is being blamed for something he did wrong and replies, 'Yes, Your Royal Highness, it did, but I wasn't here at the time, so it must have happened early in the morning.' The Archduke cannot understand what he says and continues with his sentences. When the policeman hears them he is thrown into such a state of panic that he has to be taken off to an asylum. Or there is the Czech prisoner-of-war in 'The Fortunes of Mr Hurt' who does not want to have to take up arms again because he has just bought a suite of furniture. If Austria wins the war, he will have to get it sent out to Russia and it will get ruined. If the Austrians learn that he is fighting against them, they will confiscate his furniture and sell it by auction. And if Austria loses in the end, he won't have anything to rest his head or hang his clothes on. Hašek is at his best when describing the tribulations of the little man who finds himself in this sort of fix.

During the same period Hašek devised several quite skilful propaganda articles on Czech history, some of which have been quoted in Chapter 2. But he also wrote some political articles which were critical of the Legion, its leaders and their policies as is told in Chapter 1.

After he had deserted to the Bolsheviks in the Spring of 1918 he started writing propaganda articles and stories in the Czech and Russian Bolshevik press including 'Why Are We Being Sent to France?'. Later he was to contribute articles in Russian to the Soviet press. These articles and stories are the least successful of his productions. Because of the limited space which he was allowed, they had to be trimmed to fit less than half the dimensions he was used to, less than 500 words. They show no originality and could have been written by any hack journalist working for the Bolsheviks. The themes of the stories are the stupidity of the Whites and corruption under the Tsarist régime, especially in the Orthodox Church. The *feuilletons* could have been copied from Soviet propaganda hand-outs and probably were. From the literary point of view they are of a low grade.

When Hašek finally left Russia he carried with him back to Prague either in manuscript or in his head some stories, which he knew he could not place in the Soviet press – the Bugulma tales, a series of nine of his best stories ('The Commandant of the Town of Bugulma' and others).[5] Barely a month after his arrival they began appearing in the Prague *Tribune*. The first of them was published on 23 January 1921, and the last on 13 March in the same year.

The unusual note of mellowness which pervades these delightful tales speaks eloquently of his nostalgia for his Siberian days. We seem to be hearing the voice of a much more tolerant Hašek. While he makes fun of Comrade Yerokhymov and the other Soviet officials, it is a gentle satire – far different from the sharp lash with which flayed the Austrian bureaucrats and some of his own countrymen. Even the Orthodox Church comes off a good deal better than the Catholic Church in Austria. The explanation is not far to seek: Hašek was a Slavophil at heart and he loved and understood these Russian characters, and could be forgiving to them. It is for this reason that in his Russian stories he shows his best and most amiable sides as a writer. And another reason perhaps is that, while writing them, he was still under the tranquillising influence of the milk of human kindness and had not yet become again addicted to strong spirits and excited and stimulated by them.

It is true that in his sketch 'Before the Revolutionary Tribunal of the Eastern Front' Hašek comes close to applying the sharp edge of his satire to Soviet conceptions of justice and Soviet legal procedure as he did to the machinery of the Austrian military court. It was because of this that on their first publication in Russian, some of the former members of the Fifth Army protested, accusing him of having disparaged the spirit of idealism in the struggle for the liberation of Siberia. Babel's realism evoked a much more violent reaction from the Cavalry General Budyonny. But all that is now changed. Bugulma is not the only Soviet town to have a street named after 'Gashek': it boasts a 'Gashek' museum as well. None the less it was lucky that the 'hero' left Russia when he did. Had he stayed there longer he might not have been so well remembered, because it was characteristic of him that he could never work under any authority for long. And he certainly would not have been able to control his pen, given so much good material for his satirical shafts.

Direct reports of Hašek's activity in Bugulma are practically non-existent. His name is mentioned in the archives, but only when he was in contact with the political organs of the 26th

Division of the 5th Army, which was operating in these regions. And so we do not know how far his stories are founded on fact.

Yerokhymov never existed, but he is a very vivid and faithfully drawn Russian character – especially a Russian at that time of anarchy. There was a certain Yerokhim, who was sentenced to death for filching property when conducting house searches. His case came before the Revolutionary Tribunal, of which Hašek was a member, and perhaps the name and the case suggested the stories.

The other short stories Hašek wrote in Prague before his death were far below the standard of the Bugulma tales. Hašek was now a much talked of personality, if not a famous writer, and he could no longer let his articles appear in the cheap press, insofar as it still existed. Most of them were published in the leading dailies, *Tribune*, *Czech Word*, *Evening Czech Word* and *Red Justice*. They were naturally not acceptable to the press of the right, and as Hašek had quarrelled with the right wing Social Democrats, he did not contribute any longer to *People's Right*. Two of his stories were even accepted by *The People's Newspaper*, the most highly regarded Czechoslovak paper, the cultural editor of which was Karel Čapek. In the course of his seven years' activity on the paper Čapek raised the Czech *feuilleton* to an art form, to which Hašek would never have been able to aspire.

On his return to Prague, Hašek was at first obsessed by his hostile reception. Even while he was still in Russia he had been infuriated by imaginary accounts of his death which had appeared in several Prague papers, coupled with obituary notices which were far from flattering. In one of his first articles published in *Tribune* he drew an imaginary picture of his ghost meeting the author of one of these obituaries and punishing him for what he had written. ('How I Met the Author of My Obituary').[6] The scene is laid partly in a wine cellar and partly in a cemetery. The various 'atrocities' of which Hašek was popularly supposed to be guilty as one of the 'Red Commissars', inspired him to write various mock confessions ('My Confession' and 'The Little Soul of Jaroslav Hašek Tells Its Story'), where he attributes to himself all the sins which can be found in Harry Graham's *Ruthless Rhymes*. From satirising public talk about himself, he went on to ridiculing the stories which were being told about the Soviet Union. In 'For Olga Fastrová', he portrays this well-known feminist writer and correspondent of *National Policy* as saying to him, 'Is it true, Jaroušek, that the Bolsheviks in Russia feed on the meat of an army of expendable Chinese rejects?' In 'Idyll from a Wine Cellar' he describes conversations which take place nightly between three Czechs gloating over atrocities in Russia. Why even the grandson of the most famous Czech writer, Božena Němcová, has now been beaten up! At this moment they are interrupted by an old man who says, 'But Gentlemen, excuse me, I am her grandson and I have just returned from Russia. We're all alive and they didn't do anything to us.'

'It's not important who you are', is the cutting reply. 'If you want to defend the Bolsheviks, you should have stayed in Russia and gone on committing those bestialities with them. You won't find any place for yourself in the Czech nation.' One feels that here Hašek is repeating what must have been said often enough to him. But his defence of Russia seemed to evaporate as time passed.

In some of his stories one can still catch a glimpse of Hašek at his best, as when he recounts in 'An Honest Finder' how a servant woman from the suburbs of Prague brings to the police station a wallet she has found. 'I congratulate you', says the policeman, when he has examined it. 'It contains 789,600 crowns and as the finder you are entitled to 10% of that sum.' But when the servant is told that a report is to be made of the affair and she will have to sign it, she begs to be allowed to go home, being convinced that she will be convicted of something. In the end, to the exasperation of the police officer, she renounces the reward (not understanding that it is a reward). But when her husband reads about it in the paper next day, he beats her half dead, so that she has to be taken to the hospital and from there to the lunatic asylum. The distinguishing feature of this tale is the graphic way the reactions of the servant are conveyed in Czech – in a language which is completely true to life. Another story, 'Money Sent by Telegram', tells of a tiny post office in a remote district, at which the author attempts to obtain 3,000 crowns telegraphed to him. He receives only 100 crowns because the postmaster has no 'cash flow' and can only pay out what is paid in over the counter. So Hašek has to wait as the postman brings him driblets of money as it comes in – seventy crowns for an insurance premium, 600 crowns for alimony and 240 crowns paid in by the Vicar for wine for the mass. What the intended recipients of these payments have to say about this arrangement is not revealed!

In his foreword to the collection of stories *Three Men and a Shark* (published in 1921) Hašek wrote:

> That the book is not dedicated to anyone is the fault of those individuals who offered me a too insignificant sum for dedicating it to them. I could not accept such shameless proposals and so I take the liberty of informing the honoured reader that henceforth I will furnish the book with my own signature and dedication for a certain consideration according to the following tariff:
> 'I dedicate this book to my dear friend' costs 50 crowns with autograph.
> 'I dedicate this book to my beloved friend' costs 100 crowns with autograph.
> 'In token of faithful friendship' costs 200 crowns with autograph.
> 'My most beloved friend in token of the most faithful friendship' with autograph executed in indian ink which will not rub out for years – costs only 500 crowns. ('Preface by the Author')

How was it possible that, after the decline in the literary quality of his work, which set in from the time he came to Russia, Hašek managed suddenly to write his one great work, *The Good Soldier Švejk*? The Czech Communist critic Fučík observed that 'the difference in value between the last Legionary *feuilletons* and the reminiscences of his repatriation home is too obvious to conceal that it is a difference caused by at least three years of intensive development and ripening maturity'. When Fučík wrote that, he had not read what Hašek had written in Soviet Russia. Moreover he seriously overestimated Hašek's reminiscences of his journey back ('And He Shook Off the Dust from His Shoes'), which are a disappointingly dull account of his return to Prague via the Baltic States. Fučík went on to say that the Russian milieu had had an important influence on Hašek's style and humour as well as on the character of Švejk. He meant of course Hašek's Soviet milieu, not the milieu at Kiev. But in fact Hašek's novel seems to have been hardly affected by his Soviet Russian experiences. It represents rather a return to the best of his pre-war humour, enriched by his experiences in the Austrian army.

Pytlík is right when he writes that Švejk's strength lies in his 'epic phlegm'.[7] Perhaps the discipline which Hašek had to accommodate himself to, while serving the Soviet authorities, instilled in him that phlegm, and he transferred it to Švejk. It was certainly not a quality in him which had been in evidence before, either when he was in Prague before the war, or serving in the Austrian army or the Czech Legion. But Švejk's other quality, which Pytlík rightly stresses too, his power of 'mystification', was one of Hašek's salient characteristics from his earliest years and emerges in the very first stories about the Good Soldier, which Hašek published in 1912.

Satire is a part of Czech literary tradition. Its earliest examples in Czech literature reach back at least to the fourteenth century, when the poem 'Satires on Artisans and Town Councillors' exposed the dishonesty of the various professions and accused their members of gambling, taking bribes or robbing customers. It was the first open expression of the grievances of the 'man in the street'.

Political satire came into its own at the time of the movement for National Revival in the nineteenth century. The greatest Czech political satirist was Karel Havlíček, who wrote numerous epigrams and three major satirical poems – *Tyrolean Elegies*, *King Lavra* and *The Baptism of St Vladimír*. In the first he described his own shameful arrest and deportation to Brixen in the Austrian Tyrol. In the second he attacked the stupidity of crowned heads, drawing the moral that a system which puts unlimited power into the hands of any mortal is a very dangerous one. Although the King who had asses' ears and tried to hide them was reminiscent of the Phrygian ruler Midas, Havlíček's story was based on an alleged old Irish legend, according to which the monarch had all the barbers in his Kingdom put to death so that none of them should reveal his secret. Ireland was a favourite symbol for Austria, used by Czechs and Hungarians when they wanted to write in riddles. The Czech radical movement for reform in 1848, of which Havlíček was a member, was called 'Repeal' after Daniel O'Connell's movement for the repeal of the union. The third satire, taken from Nestor's Russian chronicle, was a bitter attack on the Monarchy and the Church – in fact on the whole Austrian establishment. Havlíček wrote all three while he was interned in Brixen but they could not be published in their entirety until years after his death in 1856.

Nor was Hašek without rivals among his contemporaries. As satire is bred of disillusionment and frustration, the apparent hopelessness of the situation in the nineties led to a recrudescence of pessimism and cynicism among the Czechs in the last years of the century. One of the leading satirists of this period was the poet J. S. Machar, who worked in Vienna and could view affairs in Bohemia with greater detachment than those who lived in it. He also had fewer scruples about attacking established Czech political parties or favoured national beliefs.

The Czech poet, Fráňa Šrámek, a one-time anarchist like Hašek, also wrote satires on military life, but in verse. In his collection *Blue and Red*, published in 1906, he wrote: 'The lordly gentleman who's our captain is always telling us that we are swine, while we're always saying of him that he has a heart of gold.'

Another of Hašek's contemporaries, František Gellner, started as a political cartoonist and went over to writing satires on the same themes as Hašek. In one of them, 'William, the Mbret' (Albanian for 'Prince') he ridicules the Prince of Wied's acceptance of the Albanian throne, which Hašek made the subject of two of his stories ('The First Day after the Coronation' and 'The Albanian Throne'). Both authors made fun of Prince Thun, the Governor of Bohemia, and František Soukup, the Social Democrat leader.

Most Czech satirists, particularly Havlíček and Machar, were inspired by their reading of Heine and Gogol. Hašek was no doubt similarly influenced, but less directly, because he was no great reader of literature. He would certainly have been familiar with Havlíček's works, and from his occasional jocular references to Machar one may conclude that he knew his satires too. But Hašek's contemporaries had the advantage that they composed their satire in the form of rhymed epigrams, which made them more pointed and memorable.

A prose satirist such as Hašek had to face competition not only from the epigrammatist but from the cartoonist as well. In 1896 the German satirical paper *Simplicissimus* first appeared in Munich and exposed the vices of society in the Wilhelmine era – militarism, chauvinism, élitism, hypocrisy, false puritanism and so on. On its pages appeared many types familiar to the readers of Hašek in the brilliant, trenchant drawings of T. T. Heine, Olaf Gulbransson and Ferdinand von Reznicek: all ranks of the army from sergeant-major to general, the reactionary agrarian politician, the public prosecutor, judge, prison warder and hangman, the schoolmaster, the bureaucrat, the courtier and priests of either confession. *Simplicissimus* was available in Prague and Hašek was certainly an avid reader of it. He wanted to be a contributor but his articles were rejected. There is a probability that he took his idea about *The Good Soldier Švejk* from a story published in it in 1905 or a version of it reprinted in Czech translation in *The People's Right.*[8]

A caricature in a weekly had something of the effect of T.V. in the home today. It brought the satire more directly to the attention of the public than when it was wrapped up in a story or a novel. *Simplicissimus* was remarkably fearless in its onslaughts. Its incessant attacks on the inefficiency of the accident-prone German State Railways led to a total ban on its sale on platforms and trains. A special 'Palestine' number, brought out to ridicule the Kaiser's wild speech at Damascus, where he promised German protection to the whole Moslem race, led to a sentence of six months' imprisonment on the publisher, the cartoonist Heine and the playwright Franz Wedekind, whose poem on the subject was declared treasonable. Up to that time even the Kaiser himself had read *Simplicissimus* with pleasure (which the Emperor Francis Joseph would never have done in a similar situation), and those Prussian lieutenants with their monocles and inane sneering faces are said to have got up specially early on the day the satirical weekly was published, just to spot the jokes about themselves and be the first to tell them to their fellow officers. They seem to have been proud to look like their cartoons, which could hardly be said of the army officers in Austria.[9]

But it was not necessary to turn to Germany to find examples of bold satirical caricature. During one of the blackest times of oppression in Bohemia – the 1850s – the publisher J. R. Vilímek started in Prague his *Humorous Papers*, in which his cartoonists trenchantly exposed various scandals in the Monarchy – the oppression of the Slovaks by the Hungarians, the attempted domination of Prague University by the Germans and the Vienna government's alleged plan to 'swallow' Bohemia. Perhaps the most audacious cartoon came at the time of the Austro-Prussian War. It showed an Austrian general trying vainly to find the pass along which the Prussian troops had penetrated into Bohemia – on a map of North and South America. The proprietor of *Humorous Papers* paid for his boldness with eight months' incarceration with irons on his wrists and legs. A later writer commented that the cartoon could easily have cost him[9] his neck.[10]

Thus the political satirist in Austria, particularly if he belonged to one of the nationalities, was faced with great difficulties and dangers. Effective satires would certainly be truncated by the censors, perhaps even confiscated by them before they achieved wider circulation. In more serious cases the writer could be imprisoned. For this reason such works were circulated clandestinely in the fashion of the *samizdat* of today. (The parallel between conditions in Bohemia in the mid-nineteenth century and contemporary Czechoslovakia is the more striking when we recall that in the 1960s a revue appeared on the Czech stage called 'King Vavra', an adaptation of Havlíček's satire, which proved to be a scarcely-veiled attack on President Novotný.)

Another risk which the political satirist ran was breaking the ranks of national unity in the face of the enemy and oppressor. If he attacked the Austrians, none of his fellow countrymen would complain. But if he hit out at politicians and parties of his own nation, he could be accused of doing harm to the national cause. Later in the life of the Monarchy, as internal politics became more intense and ruthless, this consideration tended to be disregarded. Hašek certainly never bothered his head about the joy he undoubtedly gave the Austrians with his scurrilous attacks on the leaders of almost all Czech parties. It was unlikely that anyone would be put in prison for attacking Czechs, which partly explains why Hašek never spent more than a month in prison and was never convicted for anything he wrote, whereas Havlíček, who was unsparing in his attacks on Vienna, was outlawed to the Tyrol for over four years and had his life and that of his family destroyed as a result.

In Austria the rigour of the punitive arm of the law was tempered according to the gravity of the threat the evildoer posed. In the case of Hašek, the Austrian authorities refused to take him seriously and were right not to do so. Havlíček's influence on the mood of the Czech people was much more dangerous.

In his short stories the targets of Hašek's satire were not only Czech politics and Czech politicians. They extended to the Church, the nobility, the Bohemian Germans, the Austrians in Vienna, schoolmasters, parents, children and bureaucrats of all nationalities.

The prime butt of his invective was the Catholic Church, in whatever form it manifested itself – vicars in country parishes, abbots in monasteries and catechists in schools. The Catholic political parties (Christian Social and Christian National) were singled out for fierce onslaught, and their press (above all the newspaper *Čech*) for the bitterest invective of all. Hašek was quick to seize on any controversial incidents which discredited the Catholic Church, such as the Wahrmund Affair, in which Masaryk intervened to defend an Austrian professor who was being threatened with dismissal as a result of pressure from the Papal Nuncio, and other issues like the Church's campaign against cremation. For Hašek the word 'Catholic' was like a red rag to a bull and his malevolence extended even to the Catholic youth – the 'Young Eagles' (the gymnastic organisation set up to rival the free-thinking *Sokol*) or the pious neophytes of the Catholic Club. In his story, 'The Consecration of the Flag of the Catholic Club', Hašek writes: 'The privilege of embroidering the flag led to disputes between the maidens of the club. Only an innocent maiden is allowed to do the embroidery, but because at the age when girls are still innocent they have not yet learned how to embroider, there was great argument. Finally it was decided that the work should be done by the sisters Frýbert, and they embroidered the flag honourably, although evil tongues alleged that the younger sister had to hurry a great deal to have the flag ready in time.'

He ridiculed the saints with what can appropriately be described as fiendish joy, but also with an intimate knowledge of

77

them which presupposes that he was fascinated by them. He relished the thought of Catholic prelates screaming in purgatory, of saints being martyred, of Catholic missionaries being devoured by cannibals or of Satan triumphing all along the line.

Church prelates, monks or friars are portrayed as living in luxury, eating until they burst or drinking themselves into a torpor. They frequent brothels or cast lustful eyes on females around them. In 'Mr Gloatz, Fighter for the Rights of the People', a vicar in a parish in the Tyrol, who is at the same time a deputy of the *Reichsrat* in Vienna, squanders his subsistence allowance on his animal appetites and has no thought of his responsibilities to his constituents. He makes a disgusting exhibition of himself in the *Reichsrat* and is incapable of taking any part in the proceedings. It seems surprising that under the much maligned censorship Hašek was allowed to present the priesthood as self-seeking, self-indulgent and generally corrupt, and the monks as godless men who would not scruple to rob their own monasteries; but presumably the view taken was that the vices of churchmen had been targets of satire since time immemorial and there was nothing new or particularly dangerous in Hašek following this tradition. They were also perhaps aware that he spoiled his campaign by overplaying his hand. The papers which were ready to accept such stories were of little importance, and Hašek's own character as a vagabond, alcoholic, anarchist and atheist would certainly not win him credibility or sympathy when he appeared in the guise of a censor of morals. The reader was expected to believe that the clergy in Bohemia were as Hašek depicted them, but were they in fact like that? Such tales could be told with some truth about them in the sixteenth century, when the Prior of the Monastery of St Agnes in Prague incurred countless debts, stole the chalice from the church, sold off monastery land, was accused of incest and, wishing to escape punishment, fled, sending ahead his cook, a woman of doubtful character, with a whole cartload of monastery property. Or indeed in the seventeenth century, when the great Wallenstein presumed that the Augustinian friars spent 2,000 gulden 'on whoring and loose company'. But who could seriously believe that of Bohemia in the twentieth century? Hašek who as an atheist had little knowledge of church life, most certainly based his stories on what he had read about the bad old times, just as Soviet propaganda used to encourage the Russian people to think that things in England had not changed since Dickens' time.

Much of his satire was directed against the political arm of the Catholic Church, a subject on which he could usually be sure of avoiding trouble with the authorities, because in Bohemia the press of the different parties was permanently engaged in a running dog-fight with opponents, and for everything the Socialists wrote against the Catholics they were amply paid back by the Catholics in their journals. Otherwise one would have supposed that stories about the Christian Social Party suggesting that they bribed their voters ('The Intrepid Catholic Grandfather Šafler on Election Day') and welcomed brothel-keepers in their ranks in the hope of gaining the votes of their clientèle ('How in the Parish of Cikánov Brothel Keepers Joined the Organisation of the Christian Social Party') would have involved Hašek in legal proceedings. But no, the Catholic press was able to stand up for itself and Hašek maintained that no one could beat it for the range and pungency of its abuse.

There was however one occasion when one of Hašek's stories against Catholics was censored. It was called 'At the Divinity Lesson' and described a catechist's beating of the schoolchildren in his class. It was confiscated by the censors on the grounds that it was 'an incitement to hatred of Catholic clergy'. The case formed the subject of an interpellation by the Social Democrat deputy in the *Reichsrat* and the story was finally allowed to be published in the Social Democrat 'comic' *Stinging Nettles* in 1914. I quote some of it not for its merits but as an example of the virulence of Hašek's attacks on the Church. It begins: 'The only thing that the children of Koroupov knew about religion was that dear God in his unending goodness created the birch. And after the birch the catechist Horáček. Both these things were complementary [. . .] The children soon discovered that religious ideas were to be found not in the catechism but in that part of their breeches which they sat on.' The catechist was the priest who prepared boys and girls for communion and gave them lessons in religion. Hašek seems to have conceived a special hatred for his own catechist at school, who was said to have punished him by tying him by the leg to a chair. In the end one of the boys finds an answer to these endless beatings. He steals from the church a metal tablet and puts it inside his breeches. On it are written the words, 'Make Your Contribution for the Embellishment of the Temple of the Lord'.

If one is to believe Hašek, these catechists specialised in two things – flogging and swearing. Father Kalista in 'Punishment – Its Aim and Motive' tells his pupils with an affable smile, 'Paternal punishment must be an act not of vengeance but of mercy. The aim of punishment, boys, is the betterment of those chastised and the reason why I flog you is my love for you. I flog you, because you insult God [. . .]'

Katz's sermon in *The Good Soldier Švejk* with its mixture of quotations from the bible and words of abuse is anticipated in the address given by the catechist Heřman to his class at school in 'Spiritual Exercise with Obstacles'. 'He called us rogues and knaves in the middle of the most beautiful sentences which started poetically. By their aid and by drawing comparisons, he tried to awake in us the noblest feelings [. . .] "Glorious and magnificent is the view of the sparkling evening sky, you scoundrels [. . .]".'

One of Hašek's 'clerical' stories is perhaps more of a satire on the parishioners than on the clergy, although it implies that it is ridiculous for the church to try to convert the hardened sinner. It was included in the collection of short stories published in 1913 under the title *The Tourists' Guide and Other Satires from Travels Abroad and at Home* and was probably written about the same time, as it betrays a rather more experienced hand. It is called 'The Struggle for the Soul' and describes the problems a vicar with a parish in the valley has with the woodcutters from the mountains. It starts in Hašek's usual ironic vein: 'Vicar Michalejc was a saintly man with an income of 3,000 crowns a year, apart from other benefits derived from eight additional parishes attached to his own parish.' The woodcutters only come down to the church once a quarter. 'But to make up for this they prayed in advance for the next quarter, made their confessions, received the Body of Our Lord with an inexpressibly blessed awe and made their penitences with a solemn demeanour. Then they went to the inn behind the vicarage, where their tongues gradually began to loosen. Freed from their sins and exalted by the mystery of transubstantiation they grew wilder than the inhabitants of the parish [Svobodné dvory] could tolerate.'

Then they started fighting. It happened every time and the vicar mechanically dealt out punishments of forty paternosters to each. One was given fifty and 'was not allowed to leave out the amen'. Another got away with only fifteen *Ave Marias*.

The sins which they usually confess are that they have stolen wood from the forests on the Lord's estate, sometimes even from the vicar's own, or that they have set traps there to catch game. When one of them noticeably omits from his confession any reference to wood or traps, the vicar has great hopes that he has perhaps renounced sin, but, on enquiring further, he is told: 'Someone stole my trap wire and I had no time to go into the town to buy a new one.'

In despair the vicar asks for a chaplain to assist him. They send him a particularly energetic one. 'He was as thin as those ascetics who for the glory of God managed to stand for a whole week on a column without food.' He had been a missionary at Port Said for two years and had succeeded during that time in converting a mullah. But he finds the woodcutters too hard a nut to crack.

The woodcutters have their own views about his techniques. One tells the vicar, 'You know, Reverend, it's difficult. We're not going to let anyone rob us of our sins. Honesty – that's something for the rich. None of us were born respectable.' Another says: 'Reverend, I think that it's a hopeless case with us. After all we're only vermin.'

They complain that the new chaplain talks to them about 'damnation'. 'You know, Reverend, you used to explain to us so splendidly that the devil would make mincemeat of us and you never said anything about "damnation". That's for the wealthy. But for wretches like us those cauldrons with brimstone are good enough.'

In the end the new chaplain throws his hand in and is replaced by another one – 'a young, cheerful man – a real treasure for the Vicar, because he can play cards [tarock]'. Soon he has the reputation among the woodcutters of being an angel.

Jaroslav Hašek

One of them says to the Vicar: 'Praise be to the Lord Jesus Christ, you've just hit the mark, Reverend, with the new young gentleman. He doesn't ask us about our past sins or talk about our future ones. He knows it's useless. He's an angel. He swears at us so lovely at confession so that we sob like old women.'

After saying this he drags a sack which he had deposited outside the door into the room and says to the vicar in a friendly tone, 'Please be good enough, Reverend Sir, to give this to that young gentleman. It's a deer I caught last night in my trap. It's a fine catch, and tell him that I'm doing this out of gratitude to him, because he swore at us so splendidly and called us bandits.' Here Hašek rehearses a favourite theme which he comes back to in *The Good Soldier Švejk* – that men *like* being sworn at by their officers. (Not by German N.C.O.'s.) This is something they can understand. They only feel suspicious when they are being handled with velvet gloves.

Another good story about the clergy is 'An Idyll from the Almshouse at Žižkov',[11] which tells of a young chaplain, who on administering Extreme Unction for the first time in an almshouse, is moved by compassion to give a dying woman a gold piece. After that, of course, all the women have a sudden premonition that death is near them and ask for the chaplain to come. At length the town council puts an end to this nuisance by decreeing that 'the old women are prohibited from dying on their own initiative'.

It must be conceded that Hašek directed his satire not only against religious believers but their opponents as well. Repeatedly the leader of the Free Thinkers movement and its press are made the butt of his sarcasm.

Hašek hated all 'do-gooders'. Charity organisations, especially those run by the nobility or patronised by the upper classes come under regular attack. Probably the Total Abstinents take pride of place, not unnaturally, as Hašek was an alcoholic ('The Abstinents' New Year's Eve'). In 'The Adventures of Václav Pejs', the president of the Abstinents' Club is found drunk on New Year's morning. But he was only helping a stray drunk to get home. In 'Charity' a charitable club has only 120 crowns left and spends most of it on the consumption of drinks instead of aiding the poor. The heads of an organisation to clothe needy schoolchildren are accused of spending the charity's money on themselves ('The Clothing of Needy Schoolchildren'). The wife of a town councillor sets up a soup-kitchen for the poor, but only does it for show, watering the soup and profiting from the takings. ('The Soup Institute'). If the nobility is involved, Hašek feels all the more *Schadenfreude*. In 'The Sad Fate of the Station Mission' the innocent Countess Julia tries to rescue girls who arrive in Prague by train at night but ends by being seduced herself.

Of course crowned heads and members of royal families are a prime target for Hašek's satire, and he always depicts them as cretins. He was naturally not able to ridicule the members of the Austrian ruling house and could only do that when he had deserted to Russia ('The Reign of Francis Joseph', 'The Tale of the Portrait of the Emperor Francis Joseph I', 'The Ruler Who Will Sit Down on Czech Bayonets'). Before that he had been forced to confine himself to unimportant foreign rulers ('The King of the Romanians Goes After Bears', 'The Albanian Throne', 'The First Day after the Coronation – The Royal Albanian Tragedy') imaginary royal figures ('The Young Emperor and the Cat'), or fictitious Eastern potentates, about whom there are countless stories. However childish the humour in these stories may appear today, there is one feature of royal experience which Hašek successfully takes off and that is the banalities royal visitors are often constrained to talk to local authorities, when making their visits.

If Hašek knew little about churchmen, he knew still less about royalty and the nobility. He always portrays aristocrats as idiotic, mad or bad. They have no idea how to run their estates, they are without feeling towards their employees, and their rare attempts to be charitable are only made for show and are spoiled by their meanness. In fact many of the Bohemian aristocracy were anything but bad landlords, certainly not in the sense of knowing how to run their estates, as instanced by the richest of them, the Schwarzenbergs, of whom even today's Communists admit that they made a great contribution to the development of farming. Many such landowners went to England to learn modern scientific methods. Altogether the Bohemian aristocrats were far from incapable and the Czechs owed much to families like the Thuns and Sternbergs who favoured their cause and helped the movement for national revival in its opening stages. Count Kolovrat, who was Metternich's rival in the Emperor's cabinet, was known as 'The Czech of Czechs'. Count Karel Chotek, the grandfather of Princess Hohenberg, the morganatic wife of the Archduke Francis Ferdinand, was Burggrave of Prague (Governor of Bohemia) in 1826 and did much to help the development of trade and industry, to preserve the city's monuments and build its roads and bridges. When the Bohemian Estates lost their dominating political position, their descendants tried to make their lands commercially profitable and when the agricultural crisis hit them too hard, they went into industry and created the original base for much of Czech industrial wealth. Emil Škoda, who gave his name to Škoda cars and became a baron, started as an employee in Count Waldstein's engineering works at Pilsen (Plzeň). The Bohemian nobility were of course conservative, loyal to the Monarchy and the Church and opposed radicalism, but they had a local patriotism which made them often critical of the Vienna government and sympathetic to some Czech grievances.

Those who have laughed at the figure of Bretschneider in *The Good Soldier Švejk* will not be surprised at the number of stories Hašek wrote ridiculing the stupidity of the police in tracking criminals and crime, as for instance 'Wanted, a Murderer!' or 'Mr Kalous in the Rôle of Detective'. In another story on a similar theme, 'The School for the State Police', we are told about a policeman who has to learn provocative remarks by heart in order to catch traitors. He memorises his part aloud at home, to the consternation of his wife, who says, 'But, husband, what are you saying? You'll lose your job', while he tells her to shut up. 'You're a stupid goose and don't understand anything. Don't interfere in politics!' But his son, who is a bright boy, repeats at school what his father is memorising. When told to give three cheers for the Emperor, he remains stolidly silent. To the teacher, who remonstrates with him, he replies, 'We do not regard the Emperor as our ruler, because we Czechs have never had any good from living under the sceptre of the Habsburgs. My father says that and repeats it every night, and he must know, because he's in the police force.' But by this time the policeman himself has gone mad. He denounces his son and his wife, who are sent to prison, and is awarded brilliant marks for his success at the School for State Police. (Hašek wrote this in 1917 when he was safe in Russia.)

In 'Mr Kalous in the Rôle of Detective', the police turn away a man who confess to murder, partly because he is drunk and then want to get rid of him, and partly because he is clean-shaven and according to press reports the murderer was unshaven. This story is centred on a private detective, one of a class whom Hašek was later to ridicule in *The Good Soldier Švejk* (Messrs Stendler, Stern and Grot, p. 459). He was just as contemptuous of amateur detectives of the type of Sergeant Flanderka (p. 255).

The prize idiot, the personification of the *blb*, is 'Senior Police Commissioner Wagner' who, after making several stupid gaffes, orders himself to come to his own office to be cross-questioned in front of a mirror.

> He first asked himself what his nationality was and whether he had been previously convicted.
> 'It's good that it's your first offence, otherwise I should have to punish you with the full rigour of the law. This time I shan't fine you because, first, you have confessed your guilt and secondly, as I said, it's your first offence and there is a hope that you won't repeat it. You can now go home, Senior Commissioner Wagner.'
> He took his sabre and went on his way home. On the steps he met the Chief of Police, who told him not to forget that he must now go to a political meeting.
> Old Mr Wagner looked at him and said, 'Excuse me, but they have just now told me in the office that I can go home.' And he walked on with an odd smile on his face. They finally pensioned him for having become suddenly imbecile.

Some stories underline the risks the public run by going to the police for help. They are so stupid that it is bound to work out badly for the victim. In 'A Strange Happening' a man comes rushing to the police in great distress and in his underpants and implores their immediate help, because there is a thief in his house; but he is detained by an over-suspicious police sergeant. In 'Justice Will Prevail' the owner of a shop is arrested on leaving his premises at night and accused of robbing his own safe.

There is a good story ('Old Man Jančar') in which a cripple wants to get himself gaoled, because it is less trouble than sitting outside and begging. To ensure himself a long enough sentence – six months at least – he must say something particularly insulting about the Emperor and he is taught exactly what to say. He dismisses the idea of committing a theft, because that would be 'immoral'. This story appeared, astonishingly enough, in 1908, and at the time Hašek wrote to Jarmila expressing his surprise that the censorship had permitted it.

Some of these stories derive from Hašek's personal experiences. 'The Story of a Rogue' is about the perfectly respectable Mr Dolejška, who is innocently waiting for his girl friend, when he is caught up in a demonstration and arrested by the police. He ends up by getting a life sentence. Hašek himself was arrested in a similar incident and sent to prison for a month (his longest sentence) when attending an Anarchist demonstration in Prague on 1 May 1907. He said he was only there as an observer, but it is by no means certain that he was as innocent as Mr Dolejška was in the story.

It was not altogether true to suggest, as Hašek often did, that the police were necessarily clumsy in their methods of trying to recruit and train informers. They succeeded in suborning some quite influential Czechs, including Karel Sabina, the librettist of 'The Bartered Bride', a political radical who was in touch with all of the leading anti-Austrian elements, as well as Karel Šviha, president of the Club of the Deputies of the National Social Party. And there were no doubt countless others whose names have not come to light.

Hašek's dislike of the 'arm of the law' naturally inclined him to sympathise with criminals and underdogs, and he wrote many stories in which convicts outsmart the police or are portrayed as better men than those who have convicted them. He also likes to show officials in the Justice Department or in the law courts as particularly idiotic. One of his best stories is 'The Criminals' Strike', where he depicts with masterly irony the terrible consequences for all who make a living out of the law of a decision by criminals to 'down tools' and commit no further crimes. In the end even the highest members of the judiciary, now unemployed, are driven to parading the streets with banners, 'give us work!'[12]

Somewhat perversely Hašek was sometimes prepared to make

fun of those would-be do-gooders who try to reform the institutions in a liberal and humanitarian direction. In 'The Judicial Reform of State Counsellor Zákon' an enthusiastic civil servant proposes to his ministry in Vienna a reform by which criminals would be released, trained and eventually appointed judges, on the supposition that criminals do not lie to fellow criminals and would not perjure themselves, if they appeared in court before judges who were ex-criminals. But when this idiotic proposal is put into practice, the inevitable result is that crime increases. 'When he [Mr Zákon] took up his evening paper, he read that an excellently organised band of young thieves and burglars had been caught by the police. A remarkable phenomenon was that allegedly the whole of this group consisted of lawyers under articles or those who had just qualified [...] When the Judge asked the accused why they stole and committed burglary he heard one of them reply, "So that we could become Counsellors one day." '[13]

Another story, written in a Gilbertian vein, 'The Bold Attempt at Escape of Two Warders from Pankrác Prison' satirises attempts to liberalise the prison system. It tells of a prison where the inmates have been granted every privilege, while the warders are treated like convicts. In the end two of the warders try to escape but are caught by the convicts who are suitably rewarded.

In his vein of black humour Hašek tells in 'Saved' how criminals sentenced to death are given a feast before they are hanged, but one of them overeats himself and falls ill. The prison doctor does his best to save his life – so that he can be duly hanged.

It would be wearisome to try to explore the whole varied range of Hašek's satire. He laughed at schoolteachers, joked about animals and their owners, made fun of modern poets, ridiculed the complications of getting married and married life, the irritating habits of children, the idiocy of the censors and the stupidity of professors and experts in general. He laughed not only at German nationalists but at Czech patriots as well. But were all these stories – over a thousand of them – really funny? Certainly not all of them; but some were very amusing, especially those where he described entertaining situations which come as a surprise. In 'The Expedition of Šejba the Burglar' a burglar tries to get into the attic of a house but is attacked in the dark by two women, one on each landing. Each thinks it is her husband coming home drunk – in the one case the President of the Senate and the other an examining magistrate.

Hašek had a keen eye for the absurdities of administrative practice and its red tape, and was masterly in parodying its officialese. A man is caught committing a nuisance in the street just in front of Police Headquarters. The correspondence between the City of Prague and the offender which ensues is a delightful take-off of Bohemian municipal officialdom ('Justice and the Lesser Bodily Needs').[14] In the old days there used to be toll-booths on some of the Prague bridges. 'The Official Zeal of Mr. Štěpán Brych, Toll Collector on the Prague Bridge' relates how a conscientious toll-collector refuses to let a Town Councillor go past the toll-gate without paying, although he knows him well because he is his chief. Eventually, in a fit of anger, the Town Councillor forces his way past him, but the toll-collector pursues him all over Prague and threatens to shoot him until at last the Councillor jumps into the river followed by his pursuer. The last that is heard of them is the frantic cry of Mr Brych from the water, 'Give me the *Kreuzer*.' Both their bodies are washed up three days later. Mr Brych's hand is still clutching the *Kreuzer* which he has succeeded in wrenching from the Councillor's pocket.

The theme of 'Theirs but to do and die' – the thoughtless execution of orders without consideration of the fatal consequences dominated Hašek's mind. It is the key-note to much of the theme of *The Good Soldier Švejk* in its various stages. And 'The Story of the Good Swedish Soldier', which Hašek wrote in 1907, is probably its first appearance in his work. It relates how a Swedish sentry freezes to death in a temperature of 25° below zero because he refuses to desert his post. Just before he dies he realises that when he falls down dead, as he inevitably must, his rifle will fall too and may get damaged. God forbid that he should cause Sweden further expense! And so he carefully lays it down, although he knows his soldierly honour will suffer because it is against regulations to part with a rifle when on duty. With his last dying movement he writes in the snow the words 'For God, Country and King'.

There are plenty of stories showing Hašek's black humour. In

'Trade in Coffins' he tells of a businessman who has always been unlucky throughout his life. Finally as a last resort he decides that the best thing is to sell coffins, which he imagines to be a thriving business. Unfortunately the town he is unlucky enough to choose is renowned for its good health and no one dies. In the end he hangs himself, comforting himself with the observation, 'At least one coffin will be sold.' Or 'Peace to His Ashes', which describes how an interview between a young and personable undertaker and a tearful widow ends in her removing the urn in which she has kept her husband's ashes and promising to marry him.

Finally there is the proposal to restore the finances of the Monarchy by conferring on the government the monopoly of death. There will be a new tax on death and burials. The proposed law is set out in Hašek's best officialese and includes the following clause, 'whoever fails to report his own death or his own burial will be fined double the highest tax – 96 crowns – or, if need be, sentenced to 14 days imprisonment with four days on bread and water'. ('To His Excellency Herr von Biliňský, Minister of Finance, Vienna'.)[15]

In his numerous stories about children Hašek specialises in the mischievous and sly child who is against his parents or against grown-ups in general ('The Second and Third Main Prize'). Reminiscent of the characters in Wilhelm Busch's *Max and Moritz*, his children are not sweet and innocent angels, but cunning young devils. According to modern Czech critics, Hašek was attacking 'hypocrisy vis-á-vis children which was of course an essential ingredient of the bourgeois social system'. The moral of the story, 'A Children's Game' is – 'Don't tell children what they must not do, otherwise they will straight away go and do it.' Thus on their summer holiday children are to be allowed to do whatever they like. And so they get into bad company and steal sticks of dynamite with results to be foreseen! In 'A Conversation with Little Míla',[16] the writer gets so tired of the questions his little nephew keeps on asking on a walk that he takes him by train to the middle of the Hungarian *puszta* and dumps him there.

Hašek deals quite often with relations between master and pupil at school. The teachers are often shown to be sanctimonious

Jaroslav Hašek

hypocrites. They are full of *Schadenfreude* and take pleasure in asking questions which will stump the class, and fail them in their tests. They even dream up ways of taking vengeance on their pupils ('Alarm Signal') and the only escape for the intended victim is repeatedly to ask to 'leave the room' ('Classical Education'). In 'The Adventures of Government Counsellor and School Inspector Kalous' the staff try to scare the children into being good by depicting terrifying pictures of hell.

The size of the classes and the unruliness of the boys intimidate a new young teacher, who is horrified when he has to take them out for a day in the country. 'It was one of the most frightful schools in Bohemia. The teachers, the headmaster and the catechist were people who believed that schoolboys were a necessary evil, outcasts, young ne'er-do-wells, who must be kept firmly on the rein so as not to become criminals.' He cannot keep order, so he decides to tell them all the awful things they might get up to and what he will do to them if they do. 'If any one of you does anything of these things', he says, 'you don't have to come to school next day and can regard yourselves as excluded from all middle schools in Austria.' The story ends as follows: 'The next day after the school excursion only five of the forty-five pupils appeared. The rest considered themselves excluded from middle schools all over Austria...' ('The School Excursion').

Hašek's characteristic style in story-writing can perhaps best be gauged from an examination of one of his tales, 'The Cynological Institute' – the name he had coined for the kennels he set up. The first point to note here is that the background to the story is based on fact.

In the story the author advertises his 'Cynological Institute' in the paper and when he receives an order for dogs he sends his servant around Prague to steal dogs or catch stray ones; he then cleans, trims and dyes them so that they are unrecongnisable to their former owners and can be offered for sale as the very article the customer wants.

Here at once we come on two characteristics of Hašek's storytelling. First, many of his stories are based on true incidents in his life. Next, some of the themes he uses in them recur in *The Good Soldier Švejk* (see p. 173 for Švejk's account of his 'doctoring' of dogs).

90

Typical of Hašek too is his solemn justification for the name he has chosen for his kennels. A favourite theme of his is that in Bohemia names of animals are used as terms of abuse, which is unfair to animals. The word for dog in Czech is *pes* and for kennels *psinec*. Hašek says he did not want to use the word *psinec* because 'a distant relative of mine is in a ministry and he might have protested'. To Hašek the bureaucracy was always a 'dog-house' or 'a dog's breakfast'. The allusion has more point in Czech where the term has a more insulting meaning than in English. But he admits that his real reason for choosing the name was that it meant that at last he was 'the proud owner of an institute', which was probably the true one.

Hašek is in his element when he parodies advertisements. 'A dog is the most suitable gift for birthdays, first communion, engaged couples, married couples, wedding or jubilee presents. For children it's a toy which cannot be easily broken or torn. The dog is a faithful guide, who will not attack you in a wood. All varieties in stock. Direct connections with abroad. In the Institute there is a reformatory for unmannerly dogs. In a fortnight the savagest dog is taught to stop barking and biting. Where do you put your dog during your holidays? In the Cynological Institute. Where will a dog be taught to perform tricks in three days? In the Cynological Institute.' Puff or blurb of this kind – totally dishonest, because the 'Institute' had no dogs at all – was something Hašek parodied especially well.

As we continue reading the story we become conscious of some of Hašek's shortcomings – his tendency sometimes to miss a good opportunity for creating humorous situations. When the writer advertises for a servant, one of the applicants confuses 'cynological' with 'gynaecological' and says he was a servant in a maternity home and at women's clinics. This would have offered a splendid opportunity for a short amusing scene, if the applicant had been allowed to come to the Institute and had gradually revealed his misunderstanding in a dialogue full of such *doubles-entendres* as the censorship and the editor would have permitted. Instead Hašek rehearses in some detail all the applicants and their various qualifications, which is circumstantial detail but not particularly funny.

In the end Hašek chooses the applicant who says nothing about himself but asks boldly, 'When can I start?' It saves him the trouble of making a choice. Čížek, the successful candidate, is Švejk-like in his first greeting: 'The weather probably won't clear up until tomorrow. Did you hear that at 7 a.m. two trains collided again on the Pilsen highway?' When asked to go and get hold of a dog, he comes back drunk dragging behind him a lead and a collar, but nothing else. Then he collapses in a chair and starts to snore. Afterwards he explains that he had the dog but on his way back called in at a tavern.

A customer comes in and asks for a really savage dog as a house guard. He asks the price and Hašek says 100 crowns. Čížek is at once sent off to find a suitable animal but thinks only of the profit. So he decides to buy cheaply from a butcher a very old dog, which can no longer draw a cart and is growing savage. He thinks it will be a splendid guard dog but in any case a thief will probably poison it sooner or later and its master will then come and purchase another. Čížek paints it in an effort to make it look terrifying but it goes off quite happily with the purchaser. That very night his house is burgled.

In the end Čížek brings in so many puppies that Hašek decides to hire a stall in a busy Prague street just at Christmastime and to offer them for sale there. He leaves it to Čížek to arrange the matter.

In the afternoon he goes to see what his servant has done. From a distance he can see crowds of people and he rushes on, convinced that the stall is a great attraction. But when he comes near he hears voices raised in protest. 'Unspeakable brutality!... Where are the police...?' The cause of all this is that Čížek has decked out a Christmas tree and hung the puppies on it as if they were candles or sweets. 'Those poor wretches were suspended there with their tongues hanging out, like medieval robbers hanged on a tree. And underneath was the notice, "You will make the happiest Christmas for your children, if you buy them a lovely healthy puppy."'

The ending is not untypical. The madhouse, suicide, or some other form of death are often Hašek's final resort. But the exact form of the final dénouement does come as a surprise even to those who are quite inured to Hašek's quirks. And the way it is described is particularly tasteless, reminding one uncomfortably of the episode of the German soldier who in *The Good Soldier Švejk* was transfixed on the railway points-lever (p. 485). The story appeared in *Horizon* in April and May 1914. In a few months time many Austrians, including Czechs, would themselves be hanging on real trees.

The analysis of this particular story, where Hašek was not subjected to the usual limitations of space, since it was published in two parts and is twice the average length of his other stories, shows up his strengths and weaknesses as a story-teller more clearly than pages of discussion. To embroider a real-life incident, especially if it is autobiographical, is fraught with difficulty. There is always a temptation to stick too closely to what actually happened rather than let the imagination run loose. In this story Hašek was unable to avoid the expected, except at the very end. When Čížek is sent out to buy dogs, one knows what will happen, and the unhappy consequences of a visit to a tavern are a device which he draws on all too often. After its promising beginning one reads on with a certain disappointment. When Hašek ran out of inspiration or was too lazy to draw on it, he took refuge all too easily in banality, vulgarity (not so much in this story) or tastelessness.

4
THE ORIGINS.
THREE ŠVEJKS OR ONE?

'Humbly report, I was born and...' (Švejk in 'Švejk Stands against Italy')

The critics who wrote about Švejk before the war made no serious attempt to examine his character in depth. They contented themselves with one or two broad generalities, such as, whether he was an idiot or just shamming idiocy; whether he was a figure inseparable from his environment and historical period, or international and for all time; whether he was a credit to his country or his class, or a threat to the next generation; and finally to what extent he was a revolutionary and a freedom fighter or just a mere 'dodger'. Some thought that his character was not worth exploring further. Others could not figure him out at all. Certainly Hašek made it difficult for his readers to come to definite conclusions about him and it was probably his intention to do so, mystification being his second nature. Everything *might* have been made clear if he had only completed the book.

In the next chapters the various facets of Švejk's character, many of which are contradictory, will be examined, but first let us enquire into the origins of 'that heroic and valiant good old Soldier Švejk' and try to discover the intention Hašek had in creating him.

He wrote three versions of the Švejk 'mythos'. The first took the form of a set of five stories which saw the light of day in 1911 in *Caricatures*. The second version was written in 1917, while Hašek was serving as a war correspondent in the Czech Legion at Kiev in Russia. It was published by the Slav Publishing House in that town in the spring of the same year and was designed as propaganda for the Czechoslovak cause – to pillory Austria and attract volunteers to the Czech Legion, which had been formed to fight for Czech independence. It was a much shorter and cruder version of the final book.

The third version – the final novel as we all know it – was written after Hašek's return to Prague from Russia. It appeared in instalments from 1921 onwards, the first volume in 1921, the second and third in 1922. He left the fourth unfinished and it was published in 1923 after his death.

According to what Jarmila told her son Richard it was in May 1911 that Hašek first hit on the idea of creating the character which was afterwards to make him so famous. One evening he had returned home late and exhausted. Hardly had he woken up the following morning, when he was feverishly searching for a scrap of paper, which he had left about the night before. Before going to bed he had jotted down a 'brilliant idea' and now to his horror he had completely forgotten it.

In the meantime Jarmila, with her fetish for tidiness, had thrown it onto the rubbish heap. Hašek rushed out to search for it and was delighted when he found it. He carefully picked up the crumpled piece of paper, reread its contents, crumpled it up once more and threw it away. This time Jarmila rescued it and pre- served it. On it she saw, clearly written and underlined, the heading of a story, 'The Company Idiot'. Underneath was a sentence which was just legible: 'He had himself examined to prove that he was capable of serving as a regular soldier.' There followed some further words which were illegible.[1]

Here was the first embryo of the Good Soldier Švejk. When everyone else was trying to dodge service in the Austrian army, the 'idiot' insisted on having himself examined to prove that he was fit to serve. It will be recalled how in the final book Švejk appeared before a commission of medical experts, which had to examine his mental state, and made the case 'as clear as day- light when, observing a picture of the Monarch hanging on the wall, he cried out: "Long live our Emperor, Franz Joseph I, gentlemen"'. (p. 28.) No one but a complete lunatic could have said that!

But why did Hašek suddenly think of a *soldier* in the rôle of an idiot?

Hašek was never himself a soldier in peace time and, when he wrote his original stories about Švejk, he drew only on what he had heard other people tell him about army life. In the autumn of 1906 Ladislav Hájek, his writer friend, had been called up and sent to Lemberg (Lvov) in Galicia for a year and on his return was in contact with Hašek again. Another friend and contemporary writer, Josef Mach, served in the Austrian army in Trient (Trento). From these two and others Hašek probably learned all he needed to know about the army at this stage of his life. Otherwise his sources would have been his usual ones – magazine articles and reference books and in this case perhaps military manuals.

Hašek was an ardent anti-militarist and had no doubt learned to be such from his earlier association with the Anarchists, who used to spit on the Austrian uniform and openly refuse to do military service for 'the enemies of the Czech people'. Here Anarchist pacificism no doubt went hand in hand with nationalist sentiment, because, according to Hašek, Czech conscripts were often ordered about by German N.C.O.s, and the language of command – and of vituperation – was German. He claims in many parts of *The Good Soldier Švejk*, and no doubt with justification that the Slav personnel were often treated like dogs by their German superiors.

But the Austrian government was quick to clamp down on any signs of anti-militarism. In 1909 there had been a trial of young people in the National Social Party connected with the journal *Young Currents*, led by two of the editors who were Hašek's friends. Forty-four were convicted, the editors receiving two years' imprisonment each. There was also a trial of Anarchists. At the end of 1910 one of them, named Vlastimil Borek, was brought to Prague in handcuffs. According to the police records Hašek, who was in contact with these groups, was summoned to the police in that year for having once gone to the Albrecht Barracks in Prague and asked for Borek, a one-year volunteer from Galicia.

It was doubtless as a result of this that, according to the same source, Hašek's apartment in Prague was searched on 11 December 1911 without any incriminating material being found. Jarmila wrote an imaginative description of this experience in a story called 'The House Search' (although it may have been written by Hašek himself over her signature as sometimes happened).[2]

> Once in 1911, at the time of the trial of the anti-militarists, Mit'a [Hašek] came home in the early hours of the morning.

'Hasn't anyone been looking for me, darling?'

'No, no one.'

'Listen, they took me to the barracks and confronted me with soldiers. Tomorrow we'll probably get a house search.'

'Oh, my God!'

'My dear stupid angel, a house search – that's just fun. You'll soon see.'

The day was already beginning to break when we fell asleep. We were aroused by a loud ringing. . .

According to the rest of the story the police officials dragged husband and wife from their beds, but were helpless in the face of the ironical composure of Hašek.

' "I would go on looking," he advised the police. "The Devil never sleeps and Christ said: 'Seek, and ye shall find'."

'They looked in the various drawers in the bookcase and under the carpet, they stirred around in the stove; and finally when they could not find anything else they impounded some of Jarmila's old love letters.

"When shall I get them back?' asked Jarmila, when later she happened to meet one of the police in a tram. "They are all ready, but if you only knew what trouble we had with them! They had all to be translated into German and sent to Vienna."

"But you forgot one packet."

"Then, please, don't tell anyone, madam." ' '

Hašek's advice to the police, as supposedly recorded by Jarmila, sounds remarkably like the voice of Švejk, and it was indeed just about this time that he was inspired to write stories about the Good Soldier and his encounters with the Austrian military authorities.

(a) The First Švejk

The first of the five Švejk stories to be published in *Caricatures* in May 1911 was called 'Švejk Stands Against Italy'. It describes how Švejk was sent on manoeuvres near the Austro-Italian frontier.

A few years earlier Austrian relations with Italy had been tense. This would explain the otherwise curious fact that, as related in this particular story, two members of the Triple Alliance were both having manoeuvres along their common frontier, each preparing to attack the other or to parry such an attack. No wonder it was cynically said that Austria and Italy were 'allies but not friends'.

From 1903 onwards the Austrian Chief of the General Staff had begun to think seriously of transferring troops from Galicia to strengthen the garrison in the Tyrol. By the summer of 1904 relations with Italy had become so strained that the Austrian Foreign Minister felt it necessary to warn him not to make tours of inspection on the frontier. In 1907 the new Chief of the General Staff, Conrad von Hötzendorf, made no secret of his desire for a preventive war against Italy. Italian intrigues in Albania, Italian anti-Austrian irredentism and finally the end of the Austro-Russian *entente* in 1908, which had hitherto safeguarded Austria's Eastern frontier, had turned the Italo-Austrian frontier in the west into one of Austria's most vulnerable points. Fully aware of this, the Italians might easily be tempted to try something on. It was to this hot spot that Švejk was sent and one can only wonder that his presence there did not produce a major explosion.*

Hašek makes it clear in his first story that his hero is no mere idiot and that his innocence is only simulated. He tells us that Švejk went to join up *with a joyful heart*. 'For him it was a question of *getting some fun out of the army*.' Švejk is 'inwardly content that all the officers of the whole garrison are afraid of him, *not because of his rudeness but*, on the contrary, *because of his polite answers, polite behaviour and kindly and friendly smiles*'.

It is Švejk's cheerfulness, politeness and *apparent desire to do his best* that infuriate his superiors, who are not prepared for this and have no weapon against it at all, except to put him in gaol. But this is really no answer, because sooner or later he will have to be let out, and then the whole process will start all over again. 'With complete calm he went again to have himself gaoled.'

* In 1904 the Austrian Ambassador was asked by the Italian Finance Minister if 'as a man of honour' he could assure him that Italy would not be attacked by Austria. He gave that assurance. But he wrote in his memoirs later that he was justified in doing so because at that time Conrad's plan to make a sudden unprovoked attack on Italy at a time when relations were peaceful was 'still slumbering in his mind'.

In despair of how to handle him, the army authorities assign him the soft job of serving the one-year volunteers in their their club, where he is no doubt able to scrounge food and drink, enjoy cigarettes and puff smoke into the air. When the bells ring for the midnight mass Švejk may be sitting in gaol again, but he has at least escaped the long and boring experience of having to attend it.

Švejk of this early vintage already has many of the characteristics of the product of the maturer *cru* – his *amiable smile*, his *sweet and extremely pleasant manner*. And when he is asked by a new officer, 'Man, how on earth did you get here?' he starts a typically Švejkian rambling story:

'Humbly report, I was born and. . .'

In the course of this he reveals that he lit a cigarette in the ranks, lost his bayonet and nearly shot the Colonel at the rifle-butts. After admitting all this 'he fixed the officer with *the radiant look of a child* and the latter did not know whether to laugh or get angry'.

Švejk is punished again later for his over-zealousness. When he is told by a cadet that he is to imagine that Italy has declared war on Austria and they are marching against the Italians, he cannot control himself and immediately shouts, 'All right, then, forward march', for which he gets six days.

But the final irony is that Švejk actually succeeds in crossing the Italian frontier, which in itself might have provoked an international incident, and in bringing back with him a specimen of the latest Italian machine-gun, which up to then had been kept a secret from the Austrians – not a weapon of one of Austria's enemies, let it be noted, but of one of her allies.

The second of the five Švejk stories was published in *Caricatures* a month later. Its title, 'The Good Soldier Švejk Obtains Wine for the Mass' and the other character in it, the army chaplain Augustin Kleinschrodt, suggest immediately that we are dealing with an earlier version of the episode of the drunken chaplain Katz in the final novel. But in the event the story turns out to have more resemblance to Švejk's notorious 'anabasis' – his cheerful but hopeless attempt to get back to his regiment in České Budějovice by starting off in the opposite direction in his apparent pathetic faith that 'all roads lead to Rome'.

Jaroslav Hašek

In a manner somewhat reminiscent of Katz, Kleinschrodt's gaze falls on the good-natured face of the soldier Švejk. He pats him on the shoulder and says: 'You'll come with me!'

Beguiled by Švejk's *honest eyes* and *good-natured head* the chaplain does not trouble to look at his punishment record and soon Švejk is leading a life of bliss, secretly drinking the wine for the mass. Then he sets out from the camp in Hercegnovi in Dalmatia to get to Vöslau in Lower Austria, where he thinks he must go to buy the specially good wine of that region, which Kleinschrodt prefers to use at mass. When he finally gets there, he makes the mistake of asking where the nearest barracks are, and is sent off to Kornenburg, which is in the surroundings of Vienna. When the authorities learn that he has come all the way to Kornenburg from Dalmatia to obtain wine from Vöslau, they are convinced that it is the chaplain who sent him, not Švejk himself, who must be mad and, after he has gone to sleep in the happy knowledge that he was 'doing what he could for the State', they send him back to Hercegnovi via Vienna, Graz, Zábřeh in Moravia, Trieste and Trient. But the chaplain is not mad, neither is Švejk. The latter has, as could be expected, only interpreted his instructions too literally – overreached himself as usual. He was supposed to go into the town of Hercegnovi and buy Vöslau wine there, which as a famous brand was presumably readily available in the local shops. Instead he had gone half-way across the Monarchy to get it from its place of origin.

After waiting all this time for Švejk's return, the chaplain is convinced that he has deserted and as soon as he appears in the camp, he has him put in irons. When Švejk explains what he has done, the chaplain advises him to get 'superarbitrated' i.e. pensioned off, so that they can have peace from him. The story ends with Švejk making the historic affirmation that he will serve His Majesty the Emperor *to the last bone in his body* – an early example of the fun Hašek has with the conventional phrases from the patriotic literature of the time.

The third story which might be called 'The Good Soldier Švejk is Cashiered' (literally 'The Superarbitration Process with the Good Soldier Švejk') reveals for the first time the important fact about Švejk, which we learn later from the novel, that he had at some stage of his army career been *'finally certified by an army medical board as an imbecile'.* In this story the 'superarbitration process' is fully explained.

But in fact we seem to be reading an earlier version of the treatment handed out to malingerers in *The Adventures of the Good Soldier Švejk.* 'Whenever I examine a soldier who has reported sick', says staff doctor Jansa in the story, 'I do it out of the conviction...that in fact a man who has reported sick is beyond all doubt as fit as a fiddle. And it is on that principle that I proceed. I prescribe quinine and strict diet. In three days' time he begs me for God's sake to discharge him from the hospital. And if in the meantime a malingerer like that dies, then he does it on purpose just to annoy us and to get out of serving a sentence for that fraud of his...' 'Suspect everyone to his last breath!' Hašek comments.

When they decide to 'superarbitrate' the good soldier Švejk, the whole company regard him with envy. But Švejk will not accept it. 'When I am a soldier, then I must serve His Majesty the Emperor and no one can throw me out of the army, no, not even if the general comes, kicks me in the backside and tries to chuck me out of the barracks. I would simply turn round and tell him: "Humbly report, sir, I want to serve His Majesty the Emperor to the last bone in my body and I am returning to the company. And if they don't want me here, I'll go to the navy so that I can serve His Imperial Majesty at sea at least. And if they don't want me there either and the admiral gives me a kick in the backside, then I'll serve His Imperial Majesty in the air." '

After that he is given over to the staff doctor, who subjects him to the same sort of treatment which the later Švejk receives at the hands of Dr Grünstein in *The Adventures of the Good Soldier Švejk* (p. 62). Struggling with the effects of an enema, Švejk says 'with dignity in this delicate situation': 'Brother, don't spare me. If I was not afraid of the Italians I shan't fear your enema. *A soldier must fear nothing and serve, remember that!'*

'And so Švejk is transferred to the arsenal, so that he can fill torpedoes with gun-cotton', as is told in the next story, 'The Good Soldier Švejk Learns How to Handle Gun-Cotton'.

Out of the frying-pan into the fire! After having been sent to one of the most politically and military sensitive spots, he is now transferred to an explosive one. The hope is no doubt that he will blow himself up, but it does not work out like that. As Hašek says, 'Such service is no fun, because you have all the time one foot in the air and the other in the grave.' But Švejk is equal to all situations, even that one. 'Like the honest soldier he was, he lived quite contentedly in the middle of the dynamite, ecrasite and gun-cotton.'

One day the Colonel comes upon Švejk puffing at his pipe right in the midst of the gun-cotton. Seeing him like this, he says: 'Švejk, go on smoking!' which, as Hašek points out, were wise words, because 'it was definitely better to have a lighted pipe in one's mouth than in the gun-cotton'. After three days' excavation in the rubble left by the ensuing explosion, Švejk is identified when his voice is heard singing a patriotic Austrian army song from underneath a heap of ruins and fragments of human bodies. When he is pulled out, he takes his pipe out of his mouth, salutes and says, 'Humbly report, gentlemen, there's nothing to report and everything is in order.'

As the only survivor, Švejk is given a banquet in the officers' club and promoted corporal. On returning to his barracks in Trient he reads a notice asking for volunteers for the newly constituted flying corps and at once applies. 'Humbly report', he says, 'I've already been in the air, and I know it and would like to serve His Imperial Majesty there.'

The last of the stories follows on from the others and is called 'The Good Soldier Švejk Operates in Aeroplanes'. When trying out with Švejk a new mechanism, a Romanian major in a fit of despair says to Švejk, 'Švejk, you ass, fly to hell.' Švejk takes the expression literally in its Czech form ('Fly to all devils'). Dutiful as ever, he seizes the joystick and does exactly as he is told.

Here one of the principal traits of the later Švejk is worked out in considerable detail – his unflinching resolve to carry out to the letter the orders given him, no matter how idiotic they may be or how perversely he may interpret them. This determination is a source of continual perplexity to the authorities, who again do not know how to deal with it.

With his third story, 'The Good Soldier Švejk is Cashiered', Hašek played a low-down trick on the kindly editor Lada. Because he had to wait longer for his fee than he liked, he cheated him by publishing it not only in the National Social *Caricatures* but in the rival Social Democrat *Good Joker* as well. Lada, who had good reason to be furious with Hašek, at once resolved to pay him back in his own coin. He said to himself: 'Rather than share Švejk with another paper, I'll have him executed at once.' And so he commisioned another humorous writer to prepare a spurious fourth Švejk story, in which the Good Soldier would meet his death in a perilous adventure, and published it over the signature 'Jaroslav Hašek'. He relished the thought of how angry Hašek would be when he found that his hero had been killed. But his *Schadenfreude* did not last long. When the next edition of *Caricatures* returned from the censors, out of the whole story only the headline had survived: 'Jaroslav Hašek: End of the Good Soldier Švejk'.[3]

It looked as if this was Švejk's grand finale, but in 1912 Hašek had all five stories republished in book form in Prague under the title *The Good Soldier Švejk and Other Stories*.

It is important to bear in mind that these early Švejk stories were written during the period when Austrian censorship was strict. Consequently they present a harmless, bowdlerised version of the Good Soldier. He is a mild figure who lacks the depth or subtlety of the finished article. The satire in these stories is much less drastic than in the ensuing version, *The Good Soldier Švejk in Captivity*, which was not subject to Austrian censorship, but they do present some of the basic characteristics of Švejk as he appears in the final novel.

(b) The Second Švejk – 'The Good Soldier Švejk in Captivity'

The reappearance of Švejk in book form in Kiev in 1917 is something of a mystery. There are several curious things about *The Good Soldier Švejk in Captivity*, as the book it called. First, little seems to have been known about it, until is was published in Prague for the first time in 1947 and 1948 and then again 25 years later in 1972 and 1973. It is seldom mentioned in articles about Hašek in Czech literary encyclopaedias. Next, although it clearly derives from the first Švejk stories and foreshadows the final version of the book, its tone is very different from either. One may be excused for suspecting that it was not written by

Hašek at all but 'ghosted' by someone else on the basis of some of his ideas.

In *The Good Soldier Švejk and Other Strange Stories* Švejk is a joiner by profession. *In the Good Soldier Švejk in Captivity* he is a cobbler, discharged from the army, who has taken a small shop at Vinohrady. He is in fact a master cobbler and has an apprentice, which argues a certain seniority in age and profession.

In this wartime version, Švejk speaks all the time of serving, literally, *until his body is torn to pieces*, or, in English, 'to his last breath' or 'to the last bone in his body'. But by continually asserting this, he leads the forensic doctors to the conclusion that it is only his idiocy which has prompted his action, because any sane individual would do his best to get out of military service. According to this diagnosis Švejk's love for His Imperial Majesty is abnormal, arising exclusively from the low level of his intelligence. And on these grounds he is turned down. Shattered by this rejection, Švejk haunts the barracks at night screaming out his desire 'to serve His Imperial Majesty to the last bone in my body'. One winter's morning he is found lying on the pavement near the barracks beside an empty bottle labelled 'The Emperor's Devil's Own Liqueur'. It is from this time, we are told, that his rheumatism dates.

After this long flash-back, the main story opens with Švejk having himself rubbed with embrocation by his apprentice, Bohuslav. He is visited by a neighbour, the umbrella-maker, Bílek, who has just received his call-up papers. And while Bílek complains bitterly about having to leave his family and fight the Serbs, Švejk can hardly restrain himself from volunteering, but his rheumatic pains are so severe as to 'put His Imperial Majesty completely on one side and to blot out totally for the moment his consciousness of loyalty'.

But the next day, Švejk, with crutches in his hands and pushed by Bohuslav on a wheelchair, 'meant for victims of the drying up of the spinal marrow', cries out to the excited crowd, 'To Belgrade, to Belgrade!' A powerful squad of mounted and infantry police intervenes and, after some rough handling, Švejk is propelled to police headquarters. But the nearer he approaches his destination, the less his rheumatism troubles him. He even tries to jump out of the wheelchair, but is hustled upstairs to the investigation department.

As in the final version of the novel, there follows a description of the other arrestees, who all claim to be innocent, after which Švejk is taken off to be confronted with the Police Commissioners Klíma and Slavíček. Švejk repeats his wish to serve the Emperor to the last bone in his body, but in the police report his utterance is reproduced as follows: 'Rather than serve His Majesty he would break the monarch's bones'. After a period of detention, he appears before a military court and is sentenced to eight years' imprisonment. He is then sent off in a group to a military prison in Thalerhof-Zelling in Styria. When the prison director visits him on his round of inspection, Švejk repeats his wish to serve the Emperor to the last bone of his body and is promptly taken off to the hospital on a stretcher in a strait-jacket. As he is carried away 'frothing at the mouth', he can be heard singing the Austrian national anthem 'through the froth'.

Next day he is sent to a psychiatric clinic in Vienna for observation. In answer to the question, 'Who is the president of the Negro republic of San Domingo?' he replies, 'The only ruler I recognise is our most gracious Emperor Francis Joseph I', and goes on repeating these words in the prison at night at the top of his voice, until he is finally taken off to a lunatic asylum in Halle in Germany.

But Austria is in such dire straits that it is reduced even to calling up lunatics, and Švejk is summoned to appear before a recruiting commission. He is pronounced fit and, like Hašek himself and the later Švejk, sent to the 91st Infantry Division in České Budějovice.

When he reaches the military camp at Bruck an der Leitha, he finds himself under the command of Sergeant-Major Sondernummer and Corporal Althof, both German N.C.O.s, who abuse the Czechs and treat them as animals. He also comes to the notice of Ensign Dauerling who, when telling the Czech rank and file that they must not speak their Czech gibberish but learn German, notices that Švejk's attention appears to be wandering. When Dauerling roars at him, 'Why am I bothering to say all this?' Švejk replies in German, 'Humbly report, sir, the Czechs must anyhow peg out sooner or later' – a saying popularly ascribed to the Austrian Chief of the General Staff of the time. This infuriates Dauerling, who sends Švejk on Battalion Report, but, after talking it over with Cadet Biegler, he thinks better of it, because the battalion commander, 'the mad Major Wenzel', hates it when men come up before him for trivial offences. Both Dauerling and Biegler are deadly afraid of Wenzel and so Dauerling decides to let Švejk off. But when Althof comes to release him, Švejk is defiant. He insists on going on Report. 'It's an order and it must be obeyed!' he maintains. When this is reported to Dauerling, he sends for Švejk and abuses him roundly, but in vain. Švejk still insists. Then Dauerling tries to bribe him, but it is of no avail. Finally he hits on the idea of getting him off Battalion Report by appointing him his batman. In this way he somehow manages to exclude him from the battalion list and Švejk dutifully complies.

After describing the life of a batman, its advantages and disadvantages, Hašek tells how Švejk has to take a letter from his chief to the Hungarian lady, Mrs Kákonyi. In doing so he gets involved in a street brawl (as the later Švejk does in the final novel, when doing a similar errand for Lieutenant Lukáš). This is followed (as in the later book) by the appearance of anti-Czech reports of the affair in the Hungarian press, in which Dauerling is personally named. Dauerling gets into even more serious hot water when he asks Švejk to find a dog for him. He steals a dog, but, while he is taking it for a walk, meets Lieutenant-General von Arze, who recognises it as his own. As a result Dauerling is promptly transferred to a battalion which is to be drafted to the front and Švejk is sent with him. As they approach the front, Dauerling grows more and more jittery, especially when they find themselves surrounded by the Russians. In terror he begs Švejk to shoot him in the shoulder, so that he can be invalided out. Švejk carries out the order too well and, instead of shooting to wound, shoots him dead. After this he goes over to the Russians, and here the story ends (although it appears not to be complete, judging by the dots after the last word).

The company commander, Lukáš, is mentioned in passing and one of his orders is cited, but he does not appear in person. The same applies to Captain Ságner. In fact Dauerling has taken Lukáš' place and neither Lukáš nor Ságner are leading characters.

The main fault of this second Švejk version is that it is not
really funny, partly because the characters are not life-like. They
are grotesque pasteboard figures. But Švejk too acts out of character. The language of most of the persons in the book is bombastic
and violent, and the whole action of the story is strained and
unreal. There are none of the amusing episodes, with which the
final version of Švejk so happily abounds, and none of the anecdotes which in Švejk's telling provide such enjoyable digressions.
The book's recipe is simple. The Austrians and Germans are to be
presented as either feelingless monsters or pitiful cowards.

And, as for Austria, we are asked to believe that the whole
Monarchy is run by lunatics, who should be in an asylum and
many of whom are. It is typical of the crudest anti-German war
propaganda on the Allies' side during the First World War, which
is not to be wondered at, because Hašek had temporarily almost
ceased to be a humorous writer. After he had joined the Legion
the bulk of his writings had been war propaganda and followed
a stereotyped pattern. Later they became Bolshevik propaganda.
No doubt *The Good Soldier Švejk in Captivity* would be welcome
reading for those Czechs who were full of hatred for the Austrian
leadership – whether they were blind Czech nationalists or
equally blind Czech anarchist socialists. But as literature it could
only be ephemeral and quickly forgotten. Indeed it only interests
us today for the way Hašek presents Švejk, which shows that at
that time he had not quite made up his mind how the character
should develop. It is true that this second version of the Švejk saga
derives to some extent from the first one. But after having been
'superarbitrated', the carpenter has apparently become a cobbler
with a shop in Vinohrady. He has, as is stated by the author, and
as Švejk himself tells everybody, been cashiered from the army as
an idiot, because he keeps on saying he wants to go on serving the
Emperor. In this the authorities and the doctors see a proof that
his mind is disturbed. His persistence in wanting to serve is indeed
characteristic of the Švejk we know, but it is quite unlike him to
spend the night on the pavement near the barracks with a bottle
of liqueur at his side. Nor would the authentic Švejk, when put in
gaol, 'cover his face with his hands, burst out crying and complain that he was continually being unjustly suspected of evil
intentions'. It is equally hard to imagine him throwing himself on

his bunk in his cell and starting to shout: 'I am innocent. I am innocent.' Further, the real Švejk would never wander among the prisoners in Thalerhof-Zelling, hanging his head and continually saying to himself: 'But surely you are not mad? You remember everything quite well.' This particular Švejk is overcome by a deep melancholy: 'He took no notice of anyone about him, and sad days, spent between bare walls, passed hopelessly *ad infinitum.*' This Švejk not only dreams about the Emperor at night, he has a fixation about him and begins to see his image everywhere by day as well – even in the beans he eats. Indeed the reader has the impression that Švejk is being driven mad by the drastic treatment he is subjected to, whereas the Švejk we know would have remained imperturbable in the face of all the indignities imposed upon him. He drove others mad while remaining sane himself.

Thus throughout this second version of the *Švejk* mythos the Good Soldier behaves in a totally unexpected way until finally, as batman to Ensign Dauerling, he shoots his master dead. One could argue at this point Švejk was again simply carrying out his orders and carrying them out too conscientiously as usual. But it seems unlikely that the Švejk we know would ever have pointed a revolver at a superior officer under any circumstances, let alone have shot him.

(c) The Third and Final Švejk – 'The Fortunes of the Good Soldier Švejk during the World War'

Shura tells us how the thought of writing a long novel first crossed Hašek's mind. It seems that he and a dubious bohemian friend, František Sauer, had hatched the plan together in Prague towards the end of February 1921. 'Jaroslav [Hašek] and Sauer came home in a good mood', Shura recalled. 'They laughed and hugged each other, and Jaroslav said that he'd had an idea: he would write about the soldier Švejk again [...]. This time it would be something different; it would be real literature. "I shall laugh at all those idiots and at the same time show what our real character is and what we are capable of doing." '[4]

He certainly achieved the first part of his resolve, but did he manage the second? His remark is a trifle cryptic, but presumably he meant to end the satirical part of his book with a patriotic epilogue or peroration, designed to show that the Czechs were not 'those doves' which he had often proclaimed them to be. If we are to believe the suggestion made (without any authority) by the Marxist novelist Ivan Olbracht that Hašek's intention was to make Švejk cross over to the Russian side and join in a revolution in China, we can perhaps feel relieved that he was never able to finish it.

As usual with his writing, Hašek's immediate motive was financial – to make enough money to pay his debts and to provide for his and Shura's keep. He could not manage to do this out of the proceeds of the twenty or so articles he had contributed to the press in January and February 1921. He was even living on advances paid to him for articles he never wrote, with such titles as 'Švejk among the Bolsheviks' and 'Švejk in Holy Russia'. Possibly these last two commissions helped to inspire him to decide to write a full-length novel about Švejk. At the beginning of January he was not even able to pay his landlady her rent, and he and Shura would have been on the streets if they had not been taken care of by Sauer, who invited them to live with him. As it was, he left a bill of 100 crowns still unpaid.

And so he hoped to earn more by publishing books. The first and second consisted of selections of stories which he had written in Prague during the war and had not yet had an opportunity to publish. Now he thought of a third book, which would consist of new and original material. To return to the subject of Švejk for the third time was hardly original, but he clearly wanted to write a book which would encapsulate all his experiences in the Austrian army during the war and possibly as a prisoner of war in Russia. It would draw on, but improve on, *The Good Soldier Švejk in Captivity*, because he would feel free to write as he liked, instead of having to write under the restrictions of censorship – as happened when he wrote his pre-war Švejk stories – or possibly to order, when he was a war correspondent of the Legion at Kiev.

Hašek and Sauer decided to publish the book together in weekly parts and distribute it themselves. But Sauer had insufficient money to pay his share of the printer's bill and so he brought in his brother Arnošt and an estate agent V. Čermák, both from Žižkov, to form a company. It was decided that only the names of Arnošt Sauer and V. Čermák should appear in the book as the publishers.

Hašek and František Sauer sought out the artist Josef Lada, whom Hašek had worked for and lived with in the years immediately preceding the war. They asked him to make one sketch for the covers of the weekly instalments.

'I started to do so', Lada relates. 'I did not create the figure of Švejk after any definite person, but according to Hašek's concept, as described in the book. I drew the figure of Švejk filling his pipe in the midst of a rain of shells and bullets and exploding shrapnel. I tried to depict his good-humoured face and calm expression, which showed that he had all his wits about him, but could if necessary act stupidly. On the pre-arranged day I brought my sketch to the wine cellar, where we were to meet. Hašek and Sauer were very pleased with it, and after lengthy consideration Hašek promised me a fee of two hundred crowns.

'Sauer thought that this was too little and raised it to five hundred. Hašek, after a long silence, ended the discussion by banging his fist energetically on the table and deciding that I should get a thousand crowns. Instead of getting any money, however, I was left to pay the restaurant bill for both of them. The cover was printed, but I never got any money at all for it. I had never had great expectations of getting any, but after I had forgotten all about it, the accountant came from Sauer, who kept some kind of shop for underwear, and brought me some pairs of underpants and stockings with a message that his chief presented his compliments and this was the fee for the cover illustration. He had not been able to send it before, because he had gone bankrupt.'[5] This was the only illustration of Švejk which Hašek saw and approved. The rest were drawn some years after his death and portray Švejk rather differently.

Sauer found that Hašek was so slow in getting on with the writing of the novel that he was in despair. He contrived Hašek's move from Prague to the country town of Lipnice in July 1921 in the hope that in the peace and solitude of the beautiful Bohemian-Moravian Highlands and safe from the Prague bars, Hašek would be less distracted. He proved to be wrong. Hašek said, 'Now I live bang in the middle of a pub. Nothing better could have happened to me.' But he did not get on too badly with his writing. He had completed Volume I before he left Prague and it was published by the late autumn of that same year. Writing from Prague, Sauer begged him to send more copy, but he could squeeze very little out of him. At length he came to Lipnice himself for the second time and stayed a fortnight. During this time Hašek did no writing and Sauer returned empty-handed to Prague, exhausted by the round of pub-crawling and revelry to which he was nightly exposed. And so Sauer decided to revoke the contract, the partnership was dissolved and the publishing taken over by a professional publisher, Synek.

At about this time Hašek scalded his hand and could not write, and so he engaged the son of the local policeman as his secretary; but time after time the new employee had to return home, because the writer did not feel like working. Often he used to dictate in the bar during conversations with other guests. Under such conditions it was difficult for either author or secretary to concentrate. Considering that Hašek had intended the book to be in six volumes, progress may have appeared to be slow, but by the end of 1921 Hašek had completed the second volume of a book he had only started in February, and was ready to start on the third volume. This was no mean achievement, when one considers that by that time he was quite ill. Emil Longen, who had staged some scenes from *The Good Soldier Švejk* in Prague in November 1921 came to Lipnice to see Hašek that same month and wrote afterwards: 'He walked round the room choking with his cough and then rushed out of the door into the fresh air [...] He couldn't sleep on the bed in his room, but sat down in the inn near an open window, where he slept until dawn.'[6] He also said that Hašek suffered from great lassitude and every movement seemed to tire him. Despite this he managed to finish the third volume in time for it to appear in the course of 1922.

The Good Soldier Švejk was by this time selling like hot cakes. Already in 1922 Volume I had run into five editions, Volume II to four and Volume III to two. Volume IV, the last, appeared unfinished in 1923, the year of his death. By 1936 each volume had appeared in ten editions. Before he died Hašek negotiated the stage and film rights for the novel. It had proved an enormous success and for the first time in his life he had been well enough off to build himself a house. The erstwhile vagabond had become almost domesticated!

As with Schubert's 'Unfinished Symphony' attempts were made to complete Hašek's unfinished epic. His closest friends, including Lada himself, maintained that the author had no idea how to end it. In 1923 Karel Vaněk who, from a commercial traveller became an editor of *Red Right* and had known Hašek in the Legion, was bold enough to do it for him. He published two concluding volumes which he called *The Fortunes of the Good Soldier Švejk in Russian Captivity*. To read this work (which has been translated into German but not into English) is one way of learning to appreciate Hašek's genius.

Vaněk parrots Hašek's style, but his version betrays at once that he has no understanding at all of the spirit of the book or the likely intention of the author. As might be expected from an editor of *Red Right*, he turns Švejk into a political figure, who emerges as a conscious crusader against war and capitalism and consequently is bereft of all his original naïve charm and magic. What is less to be expected from a Communist in that position is that the version is heavily larded with vulgarities and obscenities – the very first pages recount Švejk's supposed views on venereal diseases and their cure. Unfortunately, since Vaněk's continuation was printed uncritically in the Czech edition of the novel from 1924 onwards and was included in the subsequent German translation, some readers were at first confused by it and failed to differentiate between the original and the false imitation. Even Piscator, when he planned to make a film of the novel, was prepared to include in it some of Vaněk's continuation. Fortunately, since the war it has been omitted from editions of the book.

5

THE CHARACTERS IN THE BOOK –
ŠVEJK HIMSELF

'He's a screaming half-wit and an interesting personality.' (Katz)

Presumably the authentic account of Švejk's physical appearance comes from Captain König, the Commander of the Gendarmerie at Písek, if he describes him accurately: 'A shortish stocky figure, a symmetrical face, and nose and blue eyes without special characteristics.' This is an extract from the report he sends to Regimental Command at České Budějovice (p. 283) and it squares pretty well with Lada's drawings, especially if we add Hašek's description of him (p. 308): 'Švejk's figure at this moment was characterised by his full smiling face, bordered with great ears. They stuck out under his military cap, which was rammed down over his head.' Unfortunately Hašek seldom provides us with detailed physical descriptions of his characters, even his chief one. In the only one of Lada's illustrations which Hašek saw and approved – the drawing for the cover of the first instalment – the figure of Švejk is anything but stocky (see illustration on p. 4). František Strašlipka, who was in real life the batman of Hašek's company commander and who is supposed to have been his model for Švejk (see photograph on p. 5) had a 'symmetrical face, but unfortunately the only photograph of him we have reveals no more than his head and shoulders. It seems unlikely that he had a stocky figure, but we cannot judge his height. However Jan Morávek,[1] a journalist, who served in Hašek's regiment, and who wrote in 1924 that 'Hašek's Švejk was to a large extent Strašlipka himself', went on to describe him as 'enormously tall' which, allowing for some exaggeration, would fit Švejk's figure in Lada's first drawing. In many of his illustrations Lada portrays Švejk as fat rather than stocky (p. 693 for instance). On the other hand if, as Hašek says, three more Švejks could have got into an old uniform which was given him and had belonged to 'some pot-bellied fellow', he could not have been all that fat (p. 99). Another particular where Lada's illustrations may mislead us is Švejk's age. Strašlipka was obviously quite young. Švejk is depicted in all Lada's later illustrations as an older man. Indeed he looks much older than Hašek was in 1915, when he was 32. The impression which the author himself leaves of Švejk's age is ambiguous. At the very beginning he appears quite mature but at the end (p. 726) the allegedly homosexual colonel says, 'What a nice lad!' and is obviously attracted by him. This is more like Strašlipka. Indeed Švejk's general attitude and deportment suggest a younger man. It is interesting to find that in most of the later Lada illustrations Švejk is shown as having a close-cropped or bald head, whereas in the earlier ones he is shown to have normal hair with a curly turned-up fringe (see illustration on p. 8). This makes him appear younger. But for better or for worse, Lada's portrait of Švejk – the short stocky figure of indefinable age – is now the accepted one, however differently Hašek himself may have visualised him.

As to Švejk's character we must first collect any evidence we can find in the book about his earlier life, always having in mind that we cannot obviously take as gospel anything he himself says. He may be speaking with his tongue in his cheek, or his creator may be 'manipulating' him to add to the irony of the situation. Thus, some of his remarks may not arise from his character at all but from the author's wider intentions.

Švejk tells the examining magistrate, 'My papa was Mr Švejk and my mama Mrs Švejk' (p. 24), because he did not wish him to entertain any doubts about his legitimacy. On another occasion he says to the judge advocate that he was a foundling (p. 94); but he presumably invented this story to arouse the sympathy of his interrogator. It is on a par with his remark to Dr Grünstein that Baroness von Botzenheim was his step-mother who abandoned him 'in tender years' and later found him again (p. 74). Švejk tells us himself that he once worked at Ostrava, is an old soldier and served in the Austrian army before the war (p. 336) at Budějovice, Mníšek and Velké Meziříčí among other places, and took part in manoeuvres at Písek in Southern Bohemia in 1910 (p. 263) and at Veszprem in Hungary (p. 587). In 1912, when there was tension because an Austrian consul in

Serbia was supposed to have been maltreated, Švejk was preparing for orders to march on Serbia. Later he was discharged from the army, after having been certified as an imbecile by an army medical board. We must take this as a fact, since it is what the author tells us too at the beginning of the book, and is repeatedly confirmed by Švejk himself throughout. ('When I was serving as a regular I got a complete discharge for idiocy and for patent idiocy into the bargain') (pp. 3, 20, 35, 66, 168). Hašek also tells us that at the time when the story begins Švejk is making a living by selling dogs whose pedigrees he forges. We also learn from the author at the beginning (p. 3) that Švejk suffered from rheumatism in his legs, although there is little sign of his being troubled by it in the further course of the book.

He claims that his brother, who was a schoolmaster (which Lukáš confirms), served in the army too and passed the officers' examination. Švejk himself had been anxious to educate himself, so as not to be left behind, but had difficulties, because they would not let him into the reading room of the Industrial Union in Prague. He was so shabbily dressed that they suspected him of coming there to steal the overcoats – a Chaplin-like incident ('The light shone through the holes in the seat of my trousers'). But by putting on his best suit he managed finally to obtain access to it (p. 459).

He appears never to have married (or at any rate we never hear of it) and indeed to have been singularly unlucky in love. During the whole time he was serving at Budějovice he received only one letter and that was from a girl called Božena, who reproached him for having gone dancing at 'The Green Frog' with 'a stupid tart' and having completely thrown her over. But when he returned to Prague, he found that Božena had been far from faithful herself, and so, as he tells Lukáš, he preferred country wenches to 'worn-out young misses in the towns who go to dancing classes'. They were more sincere, as exemplified by Karla at Mníšek, who told him exactly what she thought of him with a horrible laugh and with disgusting frankness (pp. 628–9).

At the same time he tells Lukáš that once, when he brought a 'young lady' home and was in bed with her, his charwoman, who was bringing in the coffee, was so startled that she spilled the coffee all over his back (p. 170). Since 'they were enjoying themselves immensely' at that moment, it seems that he was sexually normal, as his adventure with Mrs Katy was also to prove (p. 183), but the charwoman's shock suggests that this was certainly not a common event.

He confesses to Lukáš to having had bad luck all his life. ('I always want to put something right, to do good, but nothing ever comes out of it except trouble for me and all around' p.172.) He repeats this later (p. 350) in such a plaintive tone that Lukáš thinks he is crying. It is certainly true that he makes a mess of almost every assignment given him by Lukáš. He lets his cat bite off his canary's head (p. 172), allows it to eat up the boot polish and pass out (p. 208) and steals a dog for his lieutenant which turns out to belong to the Colonel (p. 209). On the journey to Budějovice he loses the Lieutenant's luggage (p. 219), infuriates a general, who is on a journey of inspection, by confusing him with a bank official and by making tactless remarks about his baldness. Then he pulls the communication cord, allegedly by mistake (p. 224), with the result that he is forced to get out of the train at Tábor and leave his Lieutenant to go on to Budějovice without him. On the station he gets involved in a drinking session with a Hungarian, whose language he cannot understand, and in the process succeeds in missing all the remaining trains to his proper destination. He is then forced to walk there, but consistently goes in the wrong direction, because he assumes that 'all roads lead to Rome' (Book 2 Chapter 2). At Királyhida he bungles his delicate mission to Mrs Kákonyi (pp. 366–70); later infuriates Lukáš and others by his incompetence on the telephone (pp. 423–4); and gets into further trouble in Hungary, when he goes in search of a bottle of cognac for the Lieutenant and a hen for his supper (which he injudiciously scrounges from some Hungarian peasants, when Hungarian–Czech relations are already strained enough by his failed mission to Mrs Kákonyi and the ensuing brawl.) (p. 544). In the end Lukáš is forced to tell him, 'You've already had so many peculiar incidents and accidents, so many little "mistakes" and "errors" as you call them, that the only release for you from all your misadventures would be a stout piece of rope round your neck and full military honours in square formation' (p. 550).

But these little failures on Švejk's part cannot obscure his

touching devotion to Lukáš, expressed in the personal sacrifices
he makes in his master's interest but concealed by him out of
modesty or loyalty to others (c.f. the episode of the double
portions of lunch which he brought for Lukáš and paid for
himself (p. 480), his claim that he, not Lukáš, wrote the incriminating letter to Mrs Kákonyi (p. 368) and his attempt to shield
Baloun by falsely claiming to Lukáš that it was he, not Baloun,
who ate up his pâte (p. 510)).

Apparently, when the book first appeared, most readers were
convinced of Švejk's idiocy. Hašek tells us in the Epilogue (p. 216)
how he heard one man swear at another and say, 'He is about
as big an idiot as Švejk.' He suggests that if that is the way the
character is being interpreted, he, the author, may have failed in
his purpose. But the public had at that stage only read Volume I.
The other volumes would have raised their doubts. Was his
idiocy genuine or was he only shamming? It is not surprising
that the reader is confused, when so many of the characters in
the book are equally bewildered. When Švejk loses his luggage,
Lukáš tells him, 'I still don't know whether you're just pretending to be a mule or whether you are a born one' (p. 219). And
earlier, when he learns that the dog Švejk has found for him has
been stolen from the Colonel, he says, 'Either you're a cunning
blackguard or else you're a camel and a fatheaded idiot' (p. 209).
These doubts are harboured by someone who is more sympathetic
to Švejk than any other character in the book. On the other hand
there are others who have no doubt at all that Švejk is a rogue
and nothing more. One of these is Lieutenant Dub. 'This man,
sir', he tells the Colonel, 'pretends to be a half-wit for the sole
purpose of concealing his rascality under the mask of imbecility'
(p. 722). The interrogator 'of bestial type', who is the first police
official to question Švejk, says that what he has already 'committed' proves that he has all his wits about him (p 20). But the
examining magistrate, on the other hand, seems to think he is
genuinely feeble-minded and sends him to be examined by
forensic doctors. They, for their part, have no doubts at all
about his idiocy and send him to a psychiatric clinic for observation: not to establish whether he is a lunatic – they are fully
satisfied about that – but whether he is a public danger. However, the panel of doctors, who examine him in the clinic, come

to the conclusion that he is 'a malingerer, whose mind is affected'. Finally the police inspector at police headquarters thinks differently: with his *absence of intelligence* Švejk must obviously have been led astray by others. Who was it who influenced him to commit such stupidities? (p. 44). With an expression of injured innocence Švejk denies that he has committed any stupidities at all, but the inspector, who does not accept his protestations at their face-value, suggests that the public regarded his patriotic shouts and gestures as ironical. And so Švejk is dismissed without being disciplined further. But, whatever Švejk's intentions may have been, whether his actions are genuine or merely play-acting, the authorities cannot prove his guilt. Thus he wins his first battle with them. He has succeeded in foxing them all. The best evidence that Švejk is only pretending comes from the advice he gives to Marek when the latter is accused of mutiny. 'The best thing you can do now is to pretend to be an idiot' (p 385).

Later, when he has had himself trundled 'to the war' in a bath-chair, this is somewhat perversely taken by the authorities as proof that he is a malingerer, and he is sent for treatment by the ruthless Dr Grünstein. But the latter, who is obviously perplexed by his case, has him examined by a commission. The commission visit him in the ward and are divided in their opinions: half of them insist that he is an idiot, and the other half that he is a scoundrel who is trying to make fun of the War (p. 76). Its chairman says, 'The swine thinks he'll be taken for a genuine idiot. You're not an idiot at all, Švejk, you're cunning, you're a fox, you're a hooligan etc.' The senior staff doctor then orders him to be sent to the garrison gaol, where 'they'll knock all this drivel out of his head.'... 'The fellow's as fit as a fiddle. He's only shamming and talking rot into the bargain in an attempt to make fun of his superiors. He thinks they're only here for his amusement and the whole war's a joke and a laughing matter. At the garrison, Švejk, they'll soon show you that war's no picnic' (p. 77).

But in fact there is no need for this demonstration, because Švejk knows it already, as his black humour has proved. 'I think that it's splendid to get oneself run through with a bayonet', he says, 'and also that it's not bad to get a bullet in the stomach.

It's even grander when you're torn to pieces by a shell and you
see that your legs are somehow remote from you. It's very funny
and you die before anyone can explain it to you' (p. 153). When
Vodička tells him, 'I've never had such a blasted silly war'
(chiefly because he can't hit back at the Hungarians) Švejk
counters with 'As for me I'm quite happy' (p. 387). Yes, Švejk
knows very well what war means, even though he hums aloud:

> I always thought
> That war was fun.
> A week or two
> And home I'd run... (p. 77)

It is sometimes rather hard to keep clear in one's mind that
whereas Hašek is writing his book in the Czechoslovak Republic
after censorship had been abolished, the events he describes are
happening under Austria during a period of severe censorship.
Hence Hašek can comment as he likes, but Švejk can seldom
speak out and must generally wrap up his meaning.

Švejk's 'gallows humour' is a feature of his utterances throughout the book. It is partly a take-off of the sentimental claptrap of
Austrian war propaganda – that it is glorious to be destroyed
or crippled for one's country – and partly a tragic and ironic
commentary on the frightfulness of war. By seeming to make
fun of its horrors he draws attention to the ghastly waste of
human life in a way that no one can fault. 'Are you happy?'
Lukáš asks him. 'Humbly report, sir, I am awfully happy. It'll
be really marvellous when we both fall dead together for His
Imperial Majesty and the Royal Family...' (p. 213).

Strangely enough, in the garrison gaol, where he comes into
the hands of the most sadistic instruments of 'the law', who have
a prophetic resemblance to those who were to run the concentration camps in the Third Reich, Švejk's attitude raises doubts
even in their minds. When he affirms that he has no complaints
and is completely satisfied with his treatment, he does so 'with
such a sweet expression on his face' that even the brutal staff
warder himself takes it 'for honest zeal and decency'. Consequently he talks to him 'without adding either 'shit', 'stinking
vermin' or 'lousy oaf' as he usually did (p. 82).

At the prison service Švejk bursts into tears on hearing the
chaplain's sermon. Afterwards the chaplain sends for him and

accuses him of 'having blubbed for fun'. Švejk freely admits it.
'I saw, Venerable Father, that you needed a reformed sinner.
[...]and so I really wanted to give you a pleasure[...]and at
the same time[...]to have a little fun on my own to get some
relief'. Is it possible that this 'confession' is wrung from him
because he recognises in the chaplain a kindred soul, to whom
he can speak from his heart as with Lukáš? In any case Švejk's
'honesty' and 'artless countenance' pay off once again. 'I'm
beginning to take a fancy to you', says the chaplain, and as a
result he gets his release from gaol and a soft berth as the
chaplain's batman (pp. 88–9).

Švejk's unorthodox and unexpected replies repeatedly con-
found his superiors, and his 'innocent and kindly' eyes exert their
irresistible spell. 'How can I look into his stupid kind eyes?'
says the chaplain, after bartering him away to the lieutenant at
a game of cards (p. 156). Lukáš too is immediately struck by the
innocent expression on Švejk's face at his first encounter with
him (p. 168).

Švejk annoys Lukáš by obviously allowing his attention to
wander towards his canary, just when he is getting his instructions on how to behave as a batman. Lukáš wants to say something sharp, but checks himself on observing the innocent
expression on Švejk's face. When Švejk later confesses to him
that he has sacrificed his canary in vain, his 'kindly innocent
eyes[...]glow with gentleness and tenderness', and so the lieutenant stays his avenging hand (p. 172). Sergeant Flanderka at
Putím, who sends Švejk under escort to Písek, is so touched by
the good-natured expression on his face that he disregards his
official regulations and lets him go to Písek unhandcuffed
(p. 273). Even in the presence of the formidable Colonel
Schröder, Švejk's eyes ask: 'Have I done something wrong,
please?' They speak: 'Don't you see I'm as innocent as a
lamb?' (p. 309). But the Colonel is not impressed. For him there
is at first no doubt at all that Švejk is an idiot and he gives
'this mentally deficient animal' three days' 'severe'. But later
even he is impressed by him and thinks he 'has character'
(p. 378).

After Švejk has caused Lukáš untold difficulties by stealing
the Colonel's dog, the Lieutenant can hardly bear to set eyes on

him again. 'First I'll give him a few across the jaw', he thinks, 'then I'll break his nose and tear off his ears. After that we shall see' (p. 208). But he melts before the 'honest and kindly gaze of the good and innocent eyes' of his batman. The latter's entry to the room is 'sweet and simple'. It is the same after the fiasco with Mrs Kákonyi. Švejk looks at Lukáš 'with moist tender eyes, as though wanting to say, "United, heart of mine! Now nothing will separate us, my pet."' When Lukáš preserves a menacing silence, Švejk's eyes speak 'with sorrowful tenderness'. 'Speak, my darling, say what you are thinking' (p. 404–5). It is the same with Colonel Schröder and the doddering old Polish inspecting General. Švejk looks at the latter 'somehow so trustingly' that he senses a wish on the part of the men that he, the General, should help them (p. 536). And Schröder tells Lukáš, 'One really feels sympathy for such a man' (p. 378).

Švejk employs various techniques to baffle the authorities: a favourite one is to resort to an anecdote in any situation which is likely to be troublesome. There are countless instances of this, but a good example is his eagerness to tell the story about the tailor and the ham, immediately after having infuriated the General by commenting on his baldness (p. 223). It is not merely an attempt to change the subject. To forestall the inevitable abuse which Lukáš will rain on his head, he launches into a long tale and hopes that his anger will have evaporated by the time he has finished.

Lukáš, however, takes Švejk's 'anecdotism' as further evidence of his idiocy. After listening to one such story, he says to himself, 'My God! I often talk drivel like this too, and the only difference is the form I serve it up in' (p. 170). His conclusion is that if Švejk were to go on talking until evening, the longer he went on the more rot he would talk (p. 661). Once, when Švejk threatens to tell another long story, he cuts him off by saying, 'Švejk, you're starting to talk frightful tripe again' (p. 653). But in the case of Lukáš at least, Švejk's technique is successful, because, we are told, the Lieutenant was 'obviously beginning to enjoy' his conversations with Švejk (p. 570).

When the chaplain Martinec comes to see Švejk to offer him 'spiritual consolation', Švejk defeats him by subjecting him to an uninterrupted rain of stories (p. 699) so that 'the whole of his spiritual consolation seemed to him now rather difficult' (p. 701). The main features of Švejk's stories are their length and their detail – 'He told his story with all possible detail, not even forgetting to mention that forget-me-nots were blooming on the dam of the lake' (p. 734) – and when he mentions the names of the Tartar prisoners he adds just for the fun of the thing a whole string of pseudo–Tartar names he has invented. This confirms an observation of the *Prager Tageblatt* that Hašek 'told the most improbable things with a professional thoroughness[...]with many quotations and supporting examples, given in such detail that the listener could be made to feel ashamed of himself if he did not believe him'. But these interminable stories sometimes irritate Švejk's comrades, because they want to get something off their own chests and cannot get a word in (Marek, p. 749).

Švejk's utterances are often a mixture of exaggerated loyalty and plain treason. His 'loyalty' is often ironical and is to be judged as treason too. But not always. We can look on the episode where he feverishly sings war songs in bed and later insists on having himself pushed in a bath-chair to the recruiting office as a grand joke, but in one of his moments of apparent sincerity, he confesses to Lukáš that he always wanted to do good. So is there perhaps a genuine intention behind what seems to be his simulated patriotism? Is he not perhaps doing his best to get to the front in his rather idiotic way? The author presents it as a grand satire – the genuine patriot coming to the aid of the threatened Monarchy, when it is clear that a crazy cripple can be of little help to it, and Švejk in particular can only bring it misfortune.

In spite of his protestations of devotion to the Monarchy, at the very beginning, when discussing the Sarajevo murder with his charwoman, he speaks disrespectfully of monarchs in general (pp. 4 and 6) and comes very near to making treasonable utterances in the presence of Bretschneider (pp. 9, 12) or elsewhere (pp. 18 and 30). Probably his true feelings are revealed in his conversation with an orderly (p. 207), where he speaks most disparagingly of the Monarchy ('so idiotic that it ought not to exist at all') and of the Emperor ('He wets himself and they have to feed him like a little baby'). He gives vent to the views of the average Czech about the war, 'which would certainly have been defined in the court as treasonable and for which both of them would be hanged'. Some of his more general utterances are in the same vein. 'Two-handed *mariáš* is more important than the whole war', he says (p. 456).

Apart from speaking treasonably against Austria and the monarch himself, when he is out of Lukáš' hearing, Švejk is later rebuked by him for the disrespectful way he speaks to him about all officers (which contrasts with his respectful and obedient attitude to them in their presence). 'As I've already told you many times, you have a habit of speaking in a specially disparaging way about the officers' ranks.' Of course Švejk characteristically denies this (p. 657).

On the other hand, when Baloun complains about the difficulties of the war and the attitude of the officers, Švejk considers it 'proper to stand up for army life in the present war' (p. 470). On a later occasion, when talking to Vaněk, he says, 'We need another Radetsky' (p. 341). Several times in the book he protests that he wants to do his bit and get back to his regiment (p. 679). He complains that he has not even got the small silver medal for valour yet (p. 175). At the beginning of the book he makes abundant protestations of his loyalty to the Emperor (pp. 12, 43 and 45), rejects with injured innocence the idea that he might have committed treason against him (pp. 688, 716), and confesses to Lukáš that 'what His Imperial Majesty ordains, he ordains well...' (p. 655). On another occasion he tells himself that 'all his patience in aid of His Imperial Majesty would one day no doubt bear fruit' (p. 675). He frequently shows an awareness of his responsibilities. He tells Lukáš in Ságner's presence, 'When a man is in the army he has to be conscious and aware of...', but never completes the sentence because Ságner tells him to clear off (p. 736).

He tells the magistrate 'There must be law and order' (p. 18), and justifies the police arrests after the assassination of the Archduke (p. 25). In fact he uses the law in his own defence. When he is under escort and forbidden to go to a urinal, he says: 'Very well, you'll have to give me that in writing so that when my bladder bursts it is established who is responsible for it. There is a law about that, corporal' (p. 717). He claims to want to do what the authorities require of him (p. 22). With fine irony he is even ready to accept the rigours of an enema, if only it will help Austria. 'Don't spare me[...]Try hard to think that Austria rests on these enemas and victory is ours' (p. 69).

Among Švejk's many indisputedly positive qualities is his ingenuity. It is not always happily exercised, as when he cites alimony as one of the grounds for the Chaplain's urgent need to borrow money, but justifiable perhaps when he goes on to give the address of an old deaf lady in the street where he lived as that of the imaginary pretty girl, not yet fifteen, whom the chaplain had to pay alimony to. Even Lukáš respects Švejk for his good ideas. When he is perplexed about how to get rid of Katy Wendler, he asks Švejk's advice and follows it successfully (p. 184). It is true that he has reason bitterly to regret that ingenuity when it works out badly, as in the case of the copies of '*The Sins of the Fathers*', about which Švejk says he had 'ideas of his own' (p. 473). (Actually these ideas were quite logical.) On the other hand one must admire the masterly way Švejk deals with Sergeant-Major Nasáklo, who was ordered to give him an hour's rifle drill (p. 556).

The question whether Švejk is totally honest is, in spite of his many protestations to that effect, open to doubt. He protests to Lukáš, 'I've always been honest' (p. 173) and refuses to accept a bribe from Mrs Katy (p. 172), but he is able to lie and trick when he thinks it is in a good cause, as is proved by the deceit he adopts to wheedle a dog for Lukáš out of the Colonel's maid (p. 191). But the tricks he uses when trying to sell a miserable mongrel as a thoroughbred (p. 174), show that he can do the same to benefit himself (although he maintains to Lukáš that he 'was too honest to make a profit'). He also tells Vodička that during an investigation by an examining magistrate it is his duty to lie, because at a court martial one must never confess anything (p. 392). When the Pole who cannot pronounce the Czech words correctly, shouts out 'coffee' instead of the password 'copy', Dub is probably right in suspecting that Švejk immediately shouts the order, 'All outside with mess tins' and thus mischievously succeeds in creating chaos (p. 572). And, of course, Švejk is always capable of inventing a good lie to save the situation, as when he claims to be the 'stepson' of Baroness von Botzenheim – in other words, her bastard (p. 74), or when he tells

Lukáš that the lunch he is bringing is for him when in reality it was intended for Father Lacina (p. 349).

One of the Švejk's greatest qualities is his imperturbability. After he has made a colossal gaffe in the train with the inspecting general, he is found standing by the window 'with such a blissful and contented expression as could only grace a month-old baby which had drunk and sucked its fill and was now enjoying its bye-byes' (p. 223). He also faces with remarkable equanimity the fuss about his allegedly unintentional pulling of the communication cord (p. 227). Sergeant Flanderka, who is under the impression that Švejk is a Russian spy, is deeply impressed by his calm when he puts him in the guardroom. 'He acts as though it did not concern him. We must respect a man like that' (p. 256). The sergeant does not realise that Švejk has nothing to fear, because he is not a Russian at all; but, this *sang-froid* is an essential part of Švejk's make-up. When he is about to be brought before the judge advocate, Švejk comforts Vodička with the words, 'Don't worry, Vodička. Take it calmly. Don't get nervy. What does it matter being brought before Divisional Court like this?' (p 387). It is this coolness which riles his superiors more than anything else. Švejk shows it especially when Dub is on the warpath (p. 587), when he is arrested by Bretschneider (p. 14), when he is being examined by the man 'of criminal type' (p. 20), or indeed in the presence of any authority cross-examining him.

Švejk is something of a philosopher. He likes to improve the hour by drawing a moral. Looking at the dog he has stolen from the Colonel, he says, 'After all, by and large, every soldier's stolen from his home too' (p. 199). When warned that it would be best for him not to stay too long at the front, he says stoically and ironically, 'You needn't worry about that. It's always interesting to see foreign parts free' (p. 230). Under this category come his various rules for getting on in life. 'At a court martial no one must ever confess anything,' and 'It's your duty to lie' (p. 392). (But he does not quite practice what he preaches because one of the complaints the authorities hear about him is that 'he admits everything' (p. 237).) Although this contrasts with what he says to Lukáš, 'There's nothing worse than when someone tells a lie', Švejk means here not that lying is wrong, but that it brings you into difficulties (p. 169).

Some of his theories are exceedingly worldly-wise and very shrewd in the context of the Austro-Hungarian Monarchy. 'There are lots of things in the world which are not allowed to be done and can be done. The main thing is that everyone should try to do what he's not allowed to do, so that it can be done' (p. 611). 'Every hasty action only does harm' (p. 682). Some are rather involved:

> Anyone who speaks ambiguously, has got to think carefully before he opens his mouth. A straight-forward chap who calls a spade a spade seldom gets a swipe across the jaw. But if he happens to get one several times, then he's careful and prefers to keep quiet when he's in company. It's true that people think that a fellow like that [i.e. someone who stays mum] must be up to some trick or other, and that he often gets beaten up too, but that's what his deliberation and self-control bring him [...] A chap like that has got to be modest and patient (p. 732).

This is after all one of Švejk's principal rules of life.

Some of his principles he has learned from his officers. 'In the army you must have discipline, otherwise why would anyone bother at all? Our Lieutenant Makovec always used to say, "There's got to be discipline, you bloody fools, otherwise you'd be climbing about on the trees like monkeys..." And isn't that true? Just imagine a park, let's say at Charles Square, and on every tree an undisciplined soldier! It's enough to give you a nightmare!' (p. 8).

Švejk has a strong feeling for justice and is quite capable of standing up for a comrade who is unfairly atacked or indeed for himself. He reports the 'old sweat' Sergeant Major Schreiter for calling the men 'a pack of lousy watchmen' (p. 336). But yet his advice to others is to the contrary – not to worry about injustice. 'Jesus Christ was innocent, but all the same they crucified him. No one anywhere has ever worried about a man being innocent. *Maul halten und weiter dienen*, as they used to tell us in the army. That's the best and finest thing of all' (p. 19). He is a human and forgiving man. 'I think we should be fair about everything. After all, anybody can and must make a mistake, the more he thinks about a thing. Medical experts are human beings and human beings have their faults[...]Even ministers make mistakes' (p. 27). He is a great optimist, a well-wisher to humanity, who thinks that all can and should be settled for the best. 'And so, sir, you see that everything can be settled peacefully. . .' 'It's always best if everything passes off without a scene and a lot of fuss' (p. 546).

But although he preaches moderation and restraint and shows goodwill to all, he can use strong-arm tactics if the situation demands it, particularly if it is in the interest of his superior. Witness his uncompromising attitude to Kolařík over the field-altar (pp. 128, 130). Or, 'I'll break this saint on your head', he says to the tram conductor who won't allow them to get into the tram with the field altar (p. 135). He kicks 'the stern gentleman' out of the door (pp. 147–50). There are many occasions when Švejk shows initiative and takes charge, as with the drunken lance-corporal on the way to Písek (p. 278). He is especially severe with the corporal in the train (p. 321). He bullies Mikulášek, the weak batman of Major Wenzel (p. 352) but stands up for Kunert, the equally weak batman of Lieutenant Dub. On the latter occasion Lukáš notices that Švejk's face 'lacked its accustomed good-humoured expression and instead boded some new un-pleasant development' (p. 606). He uses his full authority as company orderly when sending Platoon Sergeant Fuchs about his business (p. 414). He even tries the same tactic on Quarter-master Sergeant Vaněk with success at his first meeting with him (p. 407). His treatment of Baloun, who keeps on filching Lukáš's supplies, prompts Ságner to punish Švejk by giving him some unauthorised tough rifle drill (p. 554). But he can also deal effectively with a superior who asks stupid questions or mis-behaves himself. He is cheeky to Major Blüher (p. 429) and puts the drunken Chaplain Katz in his place. 'Look, I'm fed up', he says to him. 'Now you'll climb into bed and snooze, do you under-stand?' (p. 121). He also exerts his authority when he goes in search of Lieutenant Dub in the brothel (p. 623). He is indeed quite remorseless when dealing with someone whom he believes is cheating; witness his treatment of the mayor of Liskowiec (p. 644) or of the Austrian spy who speaks Czech with the Polish accent (pp. 685–7).

He is totally uncompromising when he returns home to his flat from prison and finds a night porter and a woman together in his bed. 'If you don't dress, I'll try to fling you out just as you are on the street. It'll be a great advantage, if you're properly dressed when you fly out' (p. 51). He knocks the Polish brothel-keeper at Sanok down the staircase (p. 621). He is quite inflexible too when carrying out orders. 'Until I receive orders from the lieutenant I don't even know my own brother[...]In the army there's got to be order', he says to Mrs Katy (p. 177), from whom he refuses to accept a bribe. This is one of his qualities which is valued by Lukáš. He has determined views about war. 'When there's a war on, let it be a war. I certainly won't hear of peace until we are in Moscow or Petrograd. After all, when there's a world war on, it's not really worth it just to sit about on our arses near the frontiers' (p. 739).

One of Švejk's main characteristics is his inflexible resolution 'But I'm going to Budějovice all the same', he tells Sergeant Flanderka; and Hašek characterises his words as 'more effective even than Galileo's famous statement'. ('But it turns round all the same.') (p. 253). It is also to be noted that on the march to the front, when all the men are tired and have thrown their packs on Dub's cart, Švejk alone goes 'bravely ahead, carrying his pack and singing as he marches' (p. 631).

Švejk is of course a master of speaking with his tongue in his cheek and many of the remarks I have quoted are double talk, but to those who do not know him, he appears to be arguing seriously. An example of this is that when suspected of stopping the train he 'spoke continually of his honesty and how he had no interest in making the train late, *because he was going to the front*' (p. 225).

Apart from telling stories, one of Švejk's favourite occupations is to sing songs. He does this when he has war fever so that his charwoman is seriously anxious about his state of mind (p. 56). He carols cheerfully as he walks along on his 'anabasis' to Budějovice (pp. 239–41). He sings together with Marek in prison, doing 'three days' severe' (p. 310). He sings while taking his early morning walk after waking from his pleasant sleep at his post as telephonist (p. 427), when he is jauntily marching to the front (p. 631), again when he is in gaol at Przemyśl (pp. 697 and 704), and when he is finally marching to the headquarters of his company at the very end of the book (p. 734).

Many of his remarks are witty. When Sergeant Flanderka asks him, 'Is it difficult to photograph a station?' he replies, 'Easier than anything else, because it doesn't move but always stands in the same place, and you don't have to tell it to smile' (p. 273). 'How long do you think the war will go on?' Vaněk asks him. 'Fifteen years', he replies. 'That's obvious, because once there was a thirty years war and now we're twice as clever as they were before, so it follows that thirty divided by two is fifteen' (p. 739). Another example of his wit is his sudden change of tone when Lukáš accuses him of not respecting his superior officers. He composes a mock speech about Colonel Fliedler in which he only sings his praises (p. 570). Or there is the occasion when he punctuates the last words of Lieutenant Dub's speeches with ribald remarks in rhyme (p. 632).

Does Švejk's character develop as the action of the book proceeds, or is it just that Hašek changed his mind in the course of writing it? Hašek, like Dickens with *The Pickwick Papers*, was writing a book for publication in instalments and had not necessarily thought out the full implications of his leading character when he recreated him. There is a notable difference between the style of Part I of the book and the remainder. It seems that Hašek's original intention was to create as many comic scenes as he could, so as to secure a rapid sale for the first instalments. In the first volume Švejk is mainly a figure of fun and a lot of the episodes are sheer farce. It is not possible seriously to assess his character in those scenes of buffoonery where he is singing army songs in bed, being pushed to the front as a cripple in the bath-chair and making astonishing replies to his questioners, whether police or doctors. Here he is a clown figure. It is only when his character is put to the test that he emerges as a strong and sane force in a weak and apparently demented world. At the same time it is noticeable that Švejk moves from the centre of the stage at the end of Volume II. His name disappears from the chapter-headings and the epic story of the 11th March Company and its fortunes takes over. Švejk is no longer the only pebble on the beach. He is joined by Vaněk, Baloun, Chodounský, Jurajda and others. As the battalion draws nearer to the front the perspective broadens out.

So much for Švejk's character. It will be debated further when its appraisal by Czech and German critics during the last fifty-seven years is discussed.

6

THE OTHER CHARACTERS:
THE ARMY

'Long live Imperial and Royal cretinism!...Cadet, ensign, second
lieutenant! I'll shit on them...You see, old man, what kinds of
bastards are born under the sun.' (Marek)

Several of the other leading characters in the novel were modelled
on members of the 91st Regiment – the regiment Hašek served
in. Their names are to be found in the army records of the time,
and after the war some of them personally confirmed in press
interviews that they were the prototypes.

Hašek's portraits of the officers are, with the exception of
Lukáš, unfavourable. Most of them are plain idiots (*blbci*) like
Colonel Friedrich Kraus von Zillergut who 'stopped officers in
the street and engaged them in unendingly long conversations
about omelettes, the sun, thermometers, doughnuts, windows and
postage stamps', and who was so 'colossally stupid that officers
avoided him from afar...' Fit companions for him are the
speechifying brigadier (p. 626), the Polish 'latrine general'
(p. 535) or the 'old deathwatch' (p. 521), who is crazy about
army 'bull' and has two lads at home whom he makes line up
before him and 'number'. Or they are shown as having no
principles or sense of dignity, like Colonel Schröder and the
sordid and licentious 'entertainments' he and his fellow officers
organise in the officers' club (p. 305). Some thirst for the men's
blood like the 'hanging' General Fink von Finkenstein or Major-
General von Schwarzburg, whose inspections are so drastic that
officers shoot themselves afterwards, which he of course welcomes.
Some officers filch what they can from army supplies, keep
prostitutes who are entered on the books as nurses and participate
in orgies like Captain Tayrle (p. 618). They treat the men and
sometimes even the N.C.O.s like slaves or dogs (Captain Tayrle
again). In this way they manifest their low opinion of the army
by divesting it of its dignity.

Oberleutnant Rudolf Lukas, the commander of Hašek's company was different. He is said to have been exactly like his namesake in the book, Heinrich Lukáš – honest and fearless, a man to whom any kind of bootlicking or flattery was totally alien, qualities which stood in the way of his promotion. He was not particularly popular among his fellow-officers, but the men thought highly of him in spite of his strict discipline, thanks to which he brought order into the chaotic affairs of the Company. A Czech by birth, he concealed, his true origin in public and spelled his name in a foreign way – *Lukas*.

Lieutenant *Lukáš* of the book is similarly strict but fair. He has no compunction in swearing at his subordinates (though they accept this) and punishing them; but he is human too and shows he has feeling for them. He orders Baloun to be tied up as a punishment and afterwards feels remorse for having done so. Hating inefficiency, service in the Austrian army must be particularly difficult for him. He obviously feels like a fish out of water in the company of his fellow officers and is reluctant to patronise the officers' club (p. 304), although he could have contributed to their entertainment by singing couplets. Probably his frequent love affairs and his fetishism (p. 171) were expressions of his escapism. But what did the real Lukas think, when he read about the totally fictitious love affairs which the batman to whom he had been kind had wished on him? It is a testimony to his good sense and moderation that when interviewed after the war he never complained but spoke very favourably of Hašek. He said: 'He surprised me. He was a really good soldier. He did not drink [sic], although he had enough opportunities to do so, and by his humour he kept his comrades in a good mood[. . .]He was not a coward. A most strange person! But suddenly he would play some idiotic trick[. . .]'[1]

It is noteworthy that the most attractive character in the book, Lukáš, and the most repulsive, Dub, are both Czechs. Dub is a caricature of a type of Czech who was by no means rare at that time and was an object of popular scorn, a *Rakušak* – a pejorative word for a Czech who flaunts his Austrianism. (An alternative name was *Čehona*, invented by the satirical writer Dyk who made it up out of some syllables of the servile words of the Czech version of the Austrian national anthem.) He is totally subservient to the Habsburgs. According to Jan Morávek, Dub was modelled on a lieutenant in the reserve called Mechálek, who was always saying: 'You don't know me yet, but, when you do know me, you'll be crying your eyes out.'[2] But Chaplain Eybl, the original of Field Chaplain Ibl, apparently maintained that Dub was a portrait of the Jewish regimental doctor. According to yet another account, one of Hašek's Lipnice friends gave him the idea for the character.[3] Finally, it has long been whispered that the model for Dub was in fact the famous linguistician and member of the Academy, František Travníček, but no one dared to state it because he held a place of honour in the Communist republic until his death in 1961.

In the book Dub is described as a schoolmaster and teacher of Czech in civil life who 'manifested an unusual alacrity for expressing his loyalty to the crown on all possible occasions'. In society he was shunned, because everyone knew him to be an informer. 'In the town where he taught he was one of the members of a triumvirate of the biggest idiots and mules, consisting of the district *hejtman* (the government's representative) the headmaster of the grammar school and himself.' (p. 519.) He bores his fellow officers by constantly repeating what he once said to the *hejtman*, to prove what foresight he had shown. When he exclaims in German, 'Blood and life for the Habsburgs! For an Austria inviolate, united and great...' even Captain Ságner, not a specially loyal Czech, but contemptuous of reserve officers, ignores the remark and abruptly changes the subject. In fact all the officers find Dub unbearable (pp. 518–20).

It seems that Hašek had not originally intended him to be the foil to Švejk and the main target of his satire. On his first appearance Dub is shown as reacting quite sensibly to the nonsense going on around him. He whispers to Lukáš that Cadet Biegler 'had put it across Ságner and no mistake' (p. 468). But when Biegler disappears from the scene because of his suspected cholera, Dub takes over from him the rôle of principal butt of the comedy. He is gradually unmasked as a fool, hypocrite and habitué of brothels.

Captain Sagner, the battalion commander – also a Czech – had the reputation of being in real life a very slippery customer

1 Portrait sketch of Hašek by Josef Lada

2 Hašek soon after his call-up in 1915 (right, marked with a cross)

3 Hašek back in Prague in 1921, on an excursion

4 Cover-illustration by Lada to the first instalment of *The Good Soldier Švejk* – the only portrayal of Švejk Hašek saw and approved

5 František Strašlipka, reputedly Hašek's model for Švejk

6 Principal characters according to Lada: Vaněk, Lukáš, Biegler and Ságner

7 Contemporary photographs of the 'originals' of Vaněk, Lukáš, Biegler and Ságner

8 Švejk and his landlady Mrs Müller: two successive versions of Lada's
illustration to the opening scene

indeed and Hašek initially describes him as such. But according to Morávek's more favourable recollection of him, he was in reality 'elegant, tall, strict and good, protecting Czechs, providing it did him no harm'.[4] In the book he is shown as stupid, even in comparison with a young ass like Biegler, who makes a fool of him. Ságner's revenge on the officious young cadet may be cruel, but he has his good sides: he treats Dub with the contempt he deserves and at one moment even protects Švejk. His attitude to Marek is indulgent and human. When Vaněk tells him that the one-year volunteer is 'politically suspect', his comment is: 'My goodness, there's nothing very remarkable in that today. Who is there who doesn't have that reputation?' (p. 560). By and large, the picture Hašek draws of him is of a man who is not very clever – indeed a disaster in the field – but otherwise neither good nor bad, and trying to do his duty. Although in the book Vaněk does not give a good report of him to Lukáš and describes him as ruthless (p. 401), he was probably no worse in real life than many officers in the Austrian army. War was war. Lada's portrait of him is pure caricature (see p. 6).

The one-year volunteer, Marek, studied classical philosophy in civilian life and is brought in as an intellectual to be a mouth-piece for the author, where Švejk cannot fill that role. This device enables Hašek to let off some steam, which he was no doubt dying to do, since the narrative method he had chosen for the book did not encourage comment by the author. Many of his experiences were Hašek's own – including his expulsion from the Volunteer School, his trick with the hospital book (p. 288) and his adventures as editor of *Animal World* (p. 323). He is also a convenient medium for telling the reader more about the conditions in the Austrian army and giving the author the oppor-tunity of satirising them as shown in his accounts of Lance-Corporal Müller, Corporal Althof, Ensign Dauerling, Captain Adamička and Colonel Schröder.

If Švejk is one facet of Hašek, Marek is another and much harsher one – a sort of Hyde to Švejk's Dr Jekyll. Appropriately enough, some of the stories he tells come from *The Good Soldier Švejk in Captivity*. He has something of Hašek's anarchism in him, and indeed arrives at the regiment with a personal file in which there is a secret report on him marked, 'Politically suspect!

Caution'. When he is called up he is up to all the tricks of the proverbial 'dodger'. He does everything he can to catch a disease which will invalid him out, but soon lands himself in trouble. According to Ságner he behaved like 'a thorough devil' and, instead of trying to do well and get promoted as his intelligence deserved, he 'drifted about from arrest to arrest'. When held in arrest he makes as much noise as he can, bawls satirical songs at the top of his voice, infuriates the gaoler and later baits the corporal in charge of his escort. But Captain Ságner recognises his intelligence and appoints him as battalion historian, where he turns history into a witty charade.

There was a cadet Biegler in the battalion, but we know little about him except that, according to Eybl, Lukas became engaged to his sister. In the book he is a second Dub, but a more intelligent one. He is ambitious, officious and a 'Jimmy Know-all', who is only too keen to show off his knowledge and consequently draws on himself general unpopularity, as well as the scorn of his superiors, who would have valued his zeal if it had not shown up their own slovenliness and ignorance. In the sordid saga which follows he pays the price for wanting to be the one keen officer in Austria.

Jan Vaněk, the prototype of the Czech Quartermaster Sergeant-Major in the book, was like that character a chemist in real life. Moravek's reminiscences of him, which are based on the Quartermaster Sergeant-Major's own diary, show that he was a good friend to Hašek and tried to protect him from the justified wrath of the lieutenant. He scarcely deserved the portrait Hašek drew of him – a lazy man, too fond of the bottle, taking life easy ('Only no flap!') and making sure that he got a good rake-off on the stores and cornered the pick of the rations for himself and his friends. Such a portrait may well have fitted many quartermaster sergeant-majors in the Austrian army. Hašek, who was attached to the company staff and helped him in the office, was able to observe him from close quarters. More important, he was able to see quite a number of military documents which he could parody. The true state of their relationship is shown by the fact that Vaněk flouted orders and revealed to him that his papers were marked 'a swindler and deceiver'. So in the book Vaněk tells Marek confidentially that his papers are similarly marked.

Vaněk's reminiscences give a rather different account of the Czech attitude to the war than some Czech critics would have us believe. He describes, for example, the dangerous expedition he and Hašek undertook, for which no one else would volunteer and which earned him a bronze medal and Hašek a silver one.[4]

Although there is no mention in the regimental records of the orderly Baloun, the telephonist Chodounský or the cook Jurajda, they might easily have been real people. Their conversations are so natural and plausible that they come alive as we read the scenes in which they appear. It takes all sorts to make a world, and a gluttonous orderly, a psychic cook and a calculating telephonist are all credible components of it. In a book in which more than usual attention is devoted to food and eating, a glutton is perhaps most of all in place. Hašek had already portrayed a less sympathetic one in his short story 'Director Behalt' in 'Stories from a Water-Bailiff's Watch-tower.'

So much for the officers and men from the regiment, whom Hašek drew from life. We can add Chaplain Otto Katz who, as Hašek tells us in his epilogue to Part I, was still alive in the time of the First Czechoslovak Republic. If Hašek is stating a fact and not just spoofing, Katz was by that time manager of a bronze and dye factory in Northern Bohemia and wrote him a long letter threatening to pay him out for what he had written about him. However, everything was allegedly put right when Hašek called to see him – hardly surprising since, when he left him at 2 a.m., Katz 'could no longer stand on his feet'. But all this is presumably only a joke.

Katz is depicted as having been educated at the Commercial Academy, where Hašek himself studied, and having joined up as a one-year volunteer, like Hašek himself. He is probably the most debauched character Hašek ever depicted. He gambles illegally, has obscene pictures in his room, frequents brothels, swears and blasphemes, takes part in drinking orgies with the officers, and tries to seduce another chaplain who is one of his colleagues to deny his faith – in fact there is no sin he would not commit.

There is no trace of a living model for him, nor need this surprise us. It is highly unlikely that in Catholic Austria the Cardinal Archbishop of Prague would have permitted a man of such low morals to be ordained. Nor could one seriously imagine that such a desecration of the sacraments could be tolerated in a country where there was an alliance between the Altar and the Crown.

On top of everything else Katz is presented as a Jew. Hašek comments: 'By the way there's nothing odd about that. Archbishop Kohn was a Jew too. . .', but he is being disingenuous. He knew very well that in the prevailing climate of the time the Chaplain's jewishness would endear him even less to many of his readers.

Like many of the army officers the military chaplains are shown as rotten to the core. If they make the slightest effort to resist vice, it is not long before they succumb to it. Hašek tells of a 'high military clerical dignitary' who passed through ravaged Galicia 'in a car with some tarts' (p. 637). A fitting companion to Chaplain Katz is Father Lacina (p. 315), whose only interest in life is finding opportunities to scrounge food and drink. Representatives of the weaker brethren who struggle against temptation are 'the pious chaplain' (p. 136) and Chaplain Martinec (p. 694) whom General Fink has already debauched. The Archbishop of Budapest deserves passing mention as one of those prelates who pray to the merciful Lord to 'make a paprika goulash out of the enemy' (p. 523).

Of Bretschneider Hašek only tells us that 'there are lots of people of the type of the late Bretschneider, who [. . .] are still knocking about today in the Republic. They are extremely interested in what people are talking about' (p. 216). Hašek was probably thinking of secret police sent to interview him on his return to Prague. He affected to see little difference between police surveillance under the Monarchy and under President Masaryk. But as he had been sent to Prague to start a revolution, he could scarcely expect to escape police attention. It was not only because of his Communist background, but also in preparation for the possible charge of bigamy, which might be brought against him. In depicting Bretschneider Hašek appears not to have anyone special in mind, which is not surprising since he had friends and protectors among the police who were quite tolerant to him.

According to Hašek, Palivec spent the whole war in gaol. He came to see Hašek when he read that he appeared in *The Good*

Soldier Švejk, and bought more than twenty copies of the first instalment, which he distributed to his friends. He seems to have been proud of the way Hašek portrayed him – particularly his foul mouth.

There are of course a vast number of people who make brief appearances in the novel such as Mrs Müller, Baroness von Botzenheim, Dr Grünstein, Sergeant-Major Řepa, Judge Advocate Bernis, the 'obstinate man' whom Švejk threw out and who remains anonymous, Katy Wendler and her hop-merchant husband, Blahník, the dog-stealer, Colonel Kraus von Zillergut's maid, the corporal who escorts Švejk and Marek to Királyhida, Major Wenzel's batman, Mikulášek, Mr and Mrs Kákonyi, the violently anti-Hungarian Sapper Vodička, Dr Welfer, the orderly Matušić, Sergeant-Major Nasáklo, Dub's bat-man, Kunert, Captain Tayrle, the Major of the Ukrainian village, the Jew and his wife, Major Wolf, and Colonel Gubich. Then there are the various characters Švejk meets on his 'anabasis' – the shepherd, the tramp, Sergeant Flanderka, Pepek Vyskoč, old Pejzlerka and the lance-corporal who led Švejk to Písek (or, rather, was led by him). I have mentioned only a few of them, there are even more if one includes the characters in the various anecdotes, which are often colourful and original. No doubt many of them were drawn from life and were people Hašek had en-countered in Bohemia in peace time on his travels throughout the Monarchy or in the army during the War, not just figments of his imagination.

All these lesser beings – tailors, carpenters, millers, inn-keepers, foresters, gamekeepers are of the essence of Bohemia albeit in somewhat distorted shapes, and it was from their milieu that the men of the Czech National Revival sprang. The Czech political leader, Rieger, was the son of a miller, the poet Čelakovský of a poor carpenter, Dvořák of a butcher, Smetana of a brewer. Hašek certainly understood his people. He knew the petty problems which worried them and the troubles they got themselves involved in. If he depicted them only from the comic side, it was this aspect of them which formed a popular subject of conversation in taverns and sheepfolds, in railway carriages, over card-games or in gaol.

A by-product of satire is the insight it offers into the society it is exposing. The light which Hašek's works throw on the Austro-Hungarian Monarchy enables us to see it through the eyes of the common man, albeit one of the nationalities and a dissident. It is a useful corrective to the angle of vision to which we are used – the view of the statesmen of the period and some historians. It is of course the army we learn most about. What sort of an army was it?

By tradition it had been a picked force of long-term professional soldiers, but Austria's humiliating defeat by the Prussians in 1866 brought a change in its structure. Compulsory 3-year service was introduced for all male citizens between the ages of 19 and 42 (reduced to two years in 1912) and what had once been a comparatively small élite force, on whose loyalty the dynasty could rely, was turned into a much larger levy of short-service men, 72 per cent of whom were drawn from the nationalities (44 per cent Slav), and many of whom were lukewarm in their allegiance to the Monarchy.

The variety of regiments which the Monarchy had at its disposal in these later years can be seen if we refer to the list which the drunken Captain Spíra was rehearsing in *The Good Soldier Švejk* (p. 304).

> Consider it carefully, please. We have fully mobilised the Austrian Landwehr Uhlans, the Austrian Landwehr, the Bosnian Rifles, the Austrian Rifles, the Austrian Infantry, the Hungarian Infantry, the Tyrolean Imperial Sharpshooters, the Bosnian Infantry, the Hungarian Honvéd Infantry, the Hungarian Hussars, the Landwehr Hussars, the Mounted Rifles, the Dragoons, the Uhlans, the artillery, the train, the sappers, the medical corps, the marines. Do you understand?

It will be noticed that in the list there are Austrian, Hungarian and Bosnian formations, but neither Czech nor Polish and no specifically Serb or Croat either. The reason for this is that as a part of the *Ausgleich* of 1867 the Hungarians were allowed to have their own forces (*The Honvéd*). To equalise the situation in Cisleithania an Austrian *Landwehr* had then to be created. The provinces of Bosnia and Hercegovina were not parts of Cisleithania or Transleithania – they formed a special entity governed jointly by Austrians and Hungarians.

When the First World War broke out a military establishment of five hundred thousand had to be brought up to a strength of over three and a quarter million. The age of conscription was reduced to 18 and the maximum raised first to 50 and later to 55. The army was now flooded with elements 'who were still civilian at heart and who brought politics, nationalism and even pacifism into the barrack room'.[5] According to Hašek the regular officers felt hatred and contempt for their reservist colleagues, whom Ságner is said in the book to have called 'civilian stink'.

Only the German, Hungarian and Bosnian troops were considered 100 per cent reliable. Regiments from other nationalities had to be stiffened by the inclusion of 'loyal' elements. Experience proved too that not all nationalities could be used on all fronts. As the war proceeded Bohemia tended to be garrisoned by Hungarian troops and Hungary by Czechs. The hostility between the two nationalities was an effective *cordon sanitaire* against the spread of disaffection.

The results of this interchange are amusingly described by Marek in the novel:

> It was known a long time ago that we'd be transferred to Hungary [...] The Hungarians'll come here to Budějovice to do garrison duty and the races'll get mixed [...] it won't be rape with gross violence [...] Fair exchange is no robbery. A Czech soldier will sleep with a Hungarian girl, an unfortunate Czech girl will take a Hungarian Honvéd into her bed and centuries later there will be an interesting surprise for the anthropologists: why did people with protruding cheekbones appear on the banks of the Malše? (pp. 309–10)

The officers were normally professional soldiers who had graduated from one of the Cadet Schools or Military Academies. The N.C.O.s were regulars too. After the officers and the N.C.O.s came the one-year volunteers. These were usually intellectuals who in peace time undertook to feed, clothe and equip themselves for a year of voluntary enlistment. (This did not apply in wartime.) By this undertaking they avoided having to serve the full term. They had various privileges including that of obtaining a commission after their year of service. They usually went into the technical, administrative, or medical branches of the army.

Ensigns were non-commisioned cadets who were gazetted as junior lieutenants after two years' service with the regiment.

Of the officers and N.C.O.s 75 per cent were German. In the top ranks the proportion was considerably higher. In the novel the most senior Czech officer we hear of is an unnamed Colonel whom Švejk chances to meet when he asks the way to his regiment. Major Wenzel may have been a Czech – one cannot be sure – but otherwise the highest Czech officer we meet or hear of is a captain.

In the book we do not merely read about the animosity between the various nationalities, we feel it. The Hungarians seem to be the most hated of them. They are presented as cruel, quarrelsome and inhuman in their treatment of Russian prisoners, the civil population, Ruthenians and Jews. After the Kákonyi episode (where it is the rascally Czech Magyarophobe Vodička who starts the brawl) the Austrian German Colonel Schröder makes it plain to the Czech Lieutenant Lukáš that Austrians and Czechs stand together in their dislike of Hungarian arrogance (p. 375). And the Hungarians in their turn have no hesitation in showing their contempt for the defecting Czechs by making the 'hands up' sign at them in a gesture of surrender (pp. 232, 589).

The Poles are not shown in too good a light. It is typical that the spy who is infiltrated into Švejk's cell in order to incriminate him, the doddering 'latrine general' and the sentry, who mispronounces the pass-word, all have Polish accents. The Bohemian Germans are full of blind war-lust and jingoism. The Germans from the Reich, Austria's allies, who are far better treated than their Austrian counterparts, with higher pay and better rations, look down with scorn at their less fortunate and, in their eyes, less capable brethren. ('Like an élite army among them all, Reich Germans were strolling about and aristocratically offering the Austrians cigarettes from their lavish supplies' (p. 724).)

In spite of the modernisation of the Austrian army, which was intended to place it on the same level as the armies of the other great powers, something of the old feudal spirit lived on. The Emperor, who was supposed to be supranational but was not, was made into a symbol of unity: the men took a solemn oath to him that they would 'faithfully and obediently serve him' wherever 'the will of His Royal and Imperial Majesty demanded it'; as late as 1914 the elderly Archduke Friedrich was appointed titular Supreme Commander (although the effective head was Conrad von Hötzendorf); and the men when addressing their officers still had to preface their remarks with the German feudal sound-

ing phrase 'humbly report' (literally; 'obediently report'), translated into the various languages (although stereotyped phrases
of this kind, for all their feudal sound, have very little meaning:
British Ambassadors felt no humiliation when they had to end
their despatches to the Foreign Secretary 'I have the honour to be
Your Lordship's Obedient Servant').

The language of command throughout the army was German.
The language of instruction in the Hungarian regiments was
Magyar, and this privilege of the use of their native tongue was
extended to some other non-Germans if the proportion of them
was high enough, but in general all the troops learnt a kind of
German patois which in the case of the Czechs was a broken
German.

In the story 'Švejk Stands Against Italy' the German Major
Teller addresses Švejk in pidgin Czech and asks him if he knows
what a *kver* (*Gewehr* for rifle) is and Švejk says (literally) 'I
obediently beg, I don't know.'

Feudalism had another and more positive facet: in the Austrian
army there was a more humane and paternal relationship between
the officers and men than in the Prussian, even though the
Austrian 'parent' did not spare the rod if he felt it was needed,
but Hašek appears not to have accepted this view.

If we are to believe the book, some of the higher officers,
irrespective of nationality, would have liked to see Prussian iron
discipline applied in their army, but the less harsh Austrian
character and the multi-racial composition of the *K. und K.*
made this impracticable. The bald-headed major-general in the
train thinks that Lukáš is far too familiar with the lower ranks
and believes that soldiers must be kept in a state of terror (p. 222)
and Ensign Dauerling, who is of course a caricature, reads in the
Ministry of War's book, *Drill or Education*, that 'Terror is
essential for the soldiers' (p. 296).

The N.C.O.s are shown to be the worst. Hašek gives many
instances of the inhuman way they treat the men (mainly German
N.C.O.s handling Czechs). They take a pleasure in ordering
recruits to prostrate themselves 'flat on the ground!' an exhausting number of times and are only too glad to make them wallow
in puddles – particularly if they are intellectuals who have been
called up in war time (p. 297). Here we have the lower ranks

taking it out on the 'civilian stink'. But the bullying sergeant humiliating the hapless educated conscript was not a preserve of the Austrian army – as we can see from *Punch* cartoons in the First World War.

The forms of punishment used in the Austrian army are shown to be medieval and indeed were so. For the most trifling peccadillo the men are handcuffed, tied up with their feet above the ground or trussed. In fact up to 1917 the field punishment was to imprison a man in hand- and ankle-cuffs so that he could neither sit nor lie. 'One over the jaw' can be the immediate response of an N.C.O. to a soldier who dares even to question an order. It is horrifying to read Hašek's claim that, as they draw nearer to the front, the authority to order an execution is devolved lower and lower, so that, allegedly, in the end a corporal can order a 12-year-old boy to be hanged for 'suspiciously cooking potato peel'. But the number of photos from the Eastern Front of bodies hanging on gallows show only too clearly that in wartime this may have been no exaggeration.

And there appears to be scant justice. When the rank and file are sent 'on report' or ask to go on it, they have no chance. A soldier of the 11th Company presents himself on battalion report with the complaint that one evening in the streets Ensign Dauerling called him a Czech pig. Captain Adamička's comment is: 'Now we shall have to see whether you had permission to go out of the barracks.' Later he summons him and says, 'It has been ascertained that you had permission [...] And so you will not be punished. Dismiss!' (p. 297). The only resort is an approach to a deputy or a letter to the press. But a volunteer risks losing his stripes if he dares to do so (p. 339).

Marek, who is of course not merely a misfit but a wholehearted dissident, sees ruthlessness everywhere: 'In the military business your mentality gets completely brutalised [...] In the cadet school they never worried about previous education because it was generally unsuitable for Austrian regular officers [...] Their one military ideal was the Prussian drill sergeant. Education ennobles the soul and this is useless in the army. The coarser the officers the better' (p. 295).

Some of the officers in the novel show human feelings and a sense of humour, although not very many. Their brutality can be gauged from their talk. 'Consumptives should be sent to the front. It does them good and after all it's better for the sick to be killed than the fit', says an admittedly tipsy young officer. 'If the enemy breaks a soldier's leg [. . .],' says the latrine general, 'that's something praiseworthy, but crippling yourself by uselessly jumping out of a van when the train is in full motion is a penal offence' (p. 535). Marek comments ironically, 'A battalion without dead is no battalion at all', as he writes his 'history' of the battalion (p. 582). Earlier on he quotes Ensign Dauerling's remark, 'What a lot of fuss about a bastard that'll peg out anyhow' and adds, 'Field Marshal Conrad von Hötzendorf [the Chief of the Austrian General Staff] used to say the same' (p. 296). (There is no confirmation he ever did.)

Of course this is the product of Hašek's usual hyperbole, but few would deny that such ideas were held in some quarters of the army. Feelings were aggravated by the fact that the Reich German officers showed contempt for Austrian laxity and that some Austrian Germans shared their view. Not just shortage of food, but a certain bureaucratic inhumanity combined with hopeless disorganisation, of which there is repeated evidence throughout the book, result in the troops spending hours in the train on empty stomachs. This is almost certainly what Hašek underwent himself, because at this point of the book Hašek's experiences and Švejk's must have been almost identical. In protest Švejk scratches on a wall a three-column list of all the soups, sauces and main dishes he has eaten in civil life (p. 717). Incidentally it is notable how many pages of *The Good Soldier Švejk* are concerned with food. Conversation continually returns to this subject – more evidence of the men's hunger and neglect. ('The neglected Austrian soldiers with their bellies distended by filthy concoctions [. .] hung around [the Prussians] like greedy cats' p. 724). On the other hand the officers are depicted as feeding pretty well. Lukáš's lunch at Királyhida consists of soup with liver dumplings, beef with gherkins, two slices of roast with Frankfurter stuffing and two portions of *apfelstrudel* (p. 397).

Corruption among the officers and quartermaster sergeant-majors appears to be a staple ingredient of army life. But so it is in most armies today. Quartermaster Sergeant Bautanzel makes no bones about all the fiddles that go on (p. 529). The men say

that those convicted of theft are soon reinstated (p. 346). Maltreatment and poor feeding inevitably lead to disaffection and
bad will, which in turn produce slovenliness and inefficiency. No
one cares; no one can be bothered. At Putím the Gendarmerie
lance-corporal allows two tramps to escape 'because he had not
wanted to trudge with them through the snow all the way to
Písek' (p. 266) and he is just as careless about Švejk. Indeed the
gendarmerie are as bad as the regular troops, if not worse. They
too find it simpler to give an offender 'one across the jaw' and
do not scruple to blackmail the population into shutting their
eyes to their own horrendous breaches of duty. The Captain of
the Gendarmerie at Písek is firmly convinced that all his gendarmes are 'a bunch of do-nothing egoists, bastards and crooks
for whom nothing else but brandy, beer and wine had any
meaning. Because they had low wages they accepted bribes so
as to be able to booze and they were slowly but surely breaking
Austria up' (p. 280).

Little wonder that with all this corruption and *Schlamperei*
there was a great temptation for the men to desert, especially
when the gendarmes could be squared to turn a blind eye. The
number of Czech 'dissenters', as the people called them, appears
to have been considerable. On his 'anabasis' Švejk is immediately
taken for one, because 'the country around Písek is infested with
them' (p. 244). Even when they have been conscripted, enrolled
in a unit and packed off to the front, they do what they can to
get left behind on the journey.

It has been said that throughout the greater part of the novel
the action takes place in a train or around it. This is very relevant
to the actual happenings, because transport was the Achilles heel
of the Austrian war effort, due mainly to shortage of rolling
stock. Four trains were needed to take each regiment. The men
were put into cattle trucks, the officers and the regimental colours
into carriages and the Colonel with his staff and the regimental
cash box had a carriage to himself. But with all this, progress was
so slow over the railway lines that it has been claimed that the
so-called 'March Battalions' would have reached the front quicker
if they had marched the whole way on foot.

7

STRUCTURE AND FORM

'There exists the non-being of all phenomena, forms and things. . .
Form is non-being and non-being is form.' (Jurajda)

Structure

Hašek himself would almost certainly have been incapable of
enlightening us on the question of the structure and form of his
novel, because he did not bother his head about literary theories,
and there is no trace anywhere in his biography or works of his
having taken any particular author or literary form as his model.
Jarmila describes how he wrote with incredible ease and alacrity
and was capable of working at any time or place and on any
subject.[1]

> 'What are you going to write?' I asked, while he was getting
> ready to dictate to me.
> 'Something eight pages long!'
> That was his whole programme of work. A subject obediently
> presented itself, whenever he called for it.
> He kept strictly to his programme and on page eight I had to put
> the full stop.
> 'Write another page,' I begged sometimes.
> 'No, let's kill the hero at the third line from the end.'

We know from Hašek's secretary, to whom he dictated his
manuscript of *The Good Soldier Švejk* after he had scalded his
hand, that he did not give much thought to a plan for the book
but just dictated whatever came into his head, referring from
time to time to the map and marking the route followed by the
company to the front. He undoubtedly drew on his pre-war tales
about Švejk, of which the opening chapters of the novel are
strongly reminiscent; certainly too, on his countless other stories,
some of which contain episodes similar to those in the novel or the
tales told by its characters; and finally on the second version of

'Švejk', *The Good Soldier Švejk in Captivity*, which was published only four years before he started writing the final novel. The most original parts of *The Good Soldier Švejk* – those concerning the First World War itself – are, as we have seen, based closely on Hašek's own experiences, with many of the characters drawn from real life. With so much live material, and bound together by Švejk's itinerary, which was the same as his own, the novel needed no structure. The rough mould was already there and all Hašek had to do was to empty into it the fruits of his memory and imagination. This has prompted the Soviet critic, S. V. Nikolsky, to suggest that the novel is in fact a 'string of novellas'.[2]

There are, however, some critics, mainly in Eastern Europe, who believe that on the contrary the novel has a carefully thought-out structure. The Soviet critic, Bernshtein, for instance, believes that 'a careful analysis reveals behind the supposed carelessness of composition a very original and carefully thought-out artistic structure', which the first critics of the book mistook for the author's carelessness or incompetence.[3]

This is no doubt what the Bulgarian critic, N. Georgiev, had in mind too when he found elements of parody both in the contents of the book and in its structure. Hašek, he believes, made fun not only of state and society in Austria but traditional forms of narrative fiction as well.

He mentions three examples of this structural parody. First, although the battalion moves slowly towards the front 'in orderly progress', Švejk's 'own war' remains stationary. In other words the action recurrently goes round in a circle and returns to its starting point. ('Švejk Home Again After Having Broken Through the Vicious Circle', Švejk's repeated returns to Lukáš after separation, Švejk's gravitating more than once towards Marek.) Georgiev sees the incident with Baroness von Botzenheim (or as Švejk interprets it to Dr Grünstein) as a parody of the 'recognition scene' common in epics and tragedies. The Bulgarian critic also believes that an element in this structural parody is the high 'coefficient of frustrated expectations'. Švejk's adventures (literally 'fortunes') in the First World War belie their title. He is not engaged in war at all, and the reader, who expects many breathless adventures, is deceived.[4]

There is no doubt that in the novel the 'War' is only the base and its 'glories' are reduced to Baloun stuck in the barrel and Švejk's heroics in the latrines; but I would see this as part of its divine irony rather than as a structural parody.

Is Švejk a real hero or is he too only a parody of one? In one of his poems about the war Hašek says, 'There are no heroes', and in the novel Marek, who is Hašek's mouthpiece, echoes this remark when he exclaims, 'Heroes don't exist, only cattle for the slaughter and butchers in the general staff.' But one of these 'cattle' might be a hero in his bovine way.

Indeed, there are passages in the book where the author leaves us in no doubt that he sees Švejk as a hero. In the preface he describes him as 'heroic and valiant' and refers to him as 'this modest anonymous hero'. But he sometimes depicts him as a martyr too. Near the beginning of the book he writes: 'And so, mounting the staircase to the Third Department for questioning, Švejk carried his cross up on to the hill of Golgotha, sublimely unconscious of his martyrdom' (p. 19). And after he steals the hen from the Hungarian peasant, 'at the head of the strange procession marched Švejk, grave and sublime, like one of the early christian martyrs being dragged into the arena' (p. 544). Should one perhaps classify him as an unconscious hero? Or an unconscious martyr? Or perhaps a martyr-hero, because he starts by being a martyr and ends by being a hero?

There is a class of fiction which is epic in form but in which the heroes are not 'dignified', as Aristotle believed epic heroes should be, and this is the picaresque novel. Does *The Good Soldier Švejk* fall into this category, or should it be regarded as a parody of it? The picaresque novel is the classic type of epic romance, in which a rogue is the central character and the whole story is built around his exploits and misadventures. From the point in the narrative when Švejk sets out on his so-called 'anabasis' to walk to his base, *The Good Soldier Švejk* seems to show some of the characteristics of this type of fiction. It is typical of a picaresque novel, for instance, that the hero survives by his wits. He has numerous adventures and misadventures as he travels on his way, but generally succeeds in the end in getting the better of his enemies. But if Švejk is a hero of this type, he is no active one, like Don Quixote, Tom Jones, Gil Blas or Roderick Random.

He does not seek adventures; they come his way. In the 'anabasis' he is like a clockwork mouse, which is wound up and goes straight on until it is halted by an obstacle or runs down. In many picaresque novels the action and continuity are interrupted from time to time by stories told by characters whom the hero meets, which have little or no relevance to the main plot – a feature of some eighteenth-century novels and of the nineteenth-century *Pickwick Papers*. Hašek does not resort to this delaying device or 'filler', although Biegler's dream and Marek's endless monologues, which have some narrative features and which hold up the action of the novel, could be said to fulfil an analogous function. But Švejk is no Jonathan Wilde. He is certainly no rogue in that sense. Moreover in *Tom Jones*, *Roderick Random* or *Humphrey Clinker* the reader's attention is concentrated on the central character, whereas in Hašek's novel we are told little about Švejk's character and background, and our attention is consequently divided between Švejk himself and his world. We are almost as much intrigued by the various types Švejk encounters, as we are by the Good Soldier himself, and we learn a great deal about the state of the Monarchy from the wide panorama of Austrian life which the author sketches in. In a similar way Gay's 'Beggar's Opera' tells us more about London's underworld in the eighteenth century than about Macheath. The highwayman is an engaging personality, but we do not know him well enough to be sentimentally committed to him.

Satire

The Good Soldier Švejk is of course a highly satirical novel. One of the perennial functions of satire has been to deflate the great – especially where the satirist believes them to be unworthy of the respect in which they are held. Hašek's main target is the Austro-Hungarian Monarchy, those who run it and life within it.

The assassination of the Archduke, with which the book opens, provides a masterly example of continuous satire. By the time discussion of it has ended, Hašek has not merely debunked the Austrian ruling house, he has annihilated it.

Švejk himself appears not even to have heard of the assassination. When his charwoman, Mrs Müller, tells him, 'Now they've killed our Ferdinand', it gives Švejk the opportunity of asking innocently which Ferdinand she means, the messenger at the chemist's who drank a bottle of hair oil by mistake or the fellow who sweeps up dog manure in the streets? If the scene had been laid in England, and the Prince of Wales had been assassinated, a charwoman would not have said: 'Now they've killed our Edward', but 'Now they've killed the Prince of Wales.' In Czech Mrs Müller uses an untranslatable ethical or possessive dative in the following sense: 'They have killed Ferdinand for us', 'Do you know what they have done to us? They have killed Ferdinand', or 'They have killed *our* Ferdinand.' The choice of this possessive form (totally unjustified by the real relationship) enhances the irony. Whoever did the deed, certainly did not do it *against* the Czechs, who would have been indifferent about it or glad that it happened. But it can of course be read either way – that it has been done *in* or *against* Czech interests.

In any case the familiar use of the name 'Ferdinand' combined with the possessive dative prompts Švejk to think at once, not of the heir apparent, but of two quite insignificant and incongruous characters who would be close enough to him to deserve the possessive dative. This shows what little importance he attaches to the Archduke himself.

From that point on, the rest of the conversation tends to belittle not only the Archduke but the whole imperial family. Švejk's immediate unrehearsed reaction to the crime is: 'What a grand job!' Then he utters various confused reflections, apparently grudging the Archduke his expensive car, suggesting that he had been rash in not taking into account the risk of an assassination, and that Sarajevo was a danger spot, because the Austrians had taken Bosnia and Hercegovina from the Turks. (Švejk knows perfectly well that if anyone was responsible it was almost certainly the Serbs, but he is not going to incriminate fellow Slavs.)

As the conversation proceeds, it centres on the type of revolver used in the murder and its mechanism, and branches out into a trivial story about 'a gentleman in Nusle' (a suburb of Prague) who also 'fooled about with a revolver'. Although Švejk says that shooting an Archduke is 'not like a poacher shooting a gamekeeper', he goes on to talk of the murder of royal personages as an almost everyday and inevitable happening, bringing in the

Empress and the Tsar and Tsarina of Russia and then hinting that the same fate awaits the Austrian Emperor; and he ends by relating two ridiculous episodes. One is about a man who made a similar prophecy in a pub and was arrested afterwards and taken away in a drunks'-cart, because he had no money to pay his bill and had struck the landlord in the face; the other concerns an infantryman who shot his captain. This episode is a masterpiece of irrelevant triviality; the bullet smashes a bottle of ink; the ink messes up the official documents; the infantryman hangs himself on his braces; the braces are not his, because he had borrowed them from the warder on the excuse that his trousers were falling down; should he not have waited to borrow the braces until after they had shot him? As a result of having lent the braces the warder is reduced to the ranks and gaoled for six months, but he then escapes to Switzerland and becomes a preacher.

By the time Švejk has finished with the subject, such emotion as the assassination might reasonably have been expected to arouse has been effectively defused and Švejk emphasises the point by jauntily going off to the pub, as if nothing had happened, and leaving a message with his charwoman for the man who has bought a toy dog from him.

Meanwhile at 'The Chalice' the police agent Bretschneider is eagerly listening to conversations in the hope of being able to catch one of the customers out and make an arrest. In his presence Švejk talks easily, even flippantly of the murder, the dark beer reminding him irreverently of the mourning flags in Vienna. He relates a string of trivial anecdotes which are supposed to have some relevance to the Archduke's death. At a review a general falls off his horse during an inspection 'without any fuss' just as he was about to be promoted Field Marshal; which reminds Švejk of how at a similar parade he had twenty buttons missing from his uniform and was trussed up and sent into solitary confinement for a fortnight. Later on, Švejk makes a strange comparison between the supposedly widowed Archduchess and a gamekeeper's widow, who was married five times, the last time to a pig-gelder. Then he brings in the Emperor's son and two of his brothers to finalise the ridicule.

The innkeeper, Palivec, who prides himself on his caution, lets fall some tactless remarks, which reveal his own indifference to the crime. 'Sarajevo, politics or the late lamented Archduke are nothing for people like us', he says. Later he throws discretion to the winds and says, 'It's all the same to me whether our Ferdinand was done in by a Serb or Turk, Catholic or Moslem, Anarchist or Young Czech*...'

Švejk's remarks to Bretschneider are even more incautious. The Archduke ought to have been fatter. If he had been, he would have had a stroke long ago 'when he was chasing those old women at Konopiště who were collecting firewood and picking mushrooms on his estate'. (Although the Archduke Francis Ferdinand was married to a Czech and had his main estate at Konopiště not far from Prague, he was not popular in Bohemia. His marriage had not been approved by the Emperor and so his wife had not been accorded royal status. To the court at Vienna she was not legitimate and to the old Czech nobility in Bohemia she was not noble enough. The Archduke, who was a morose man, bitterly resented these slights.)

Continuing in much the same vein, Švejk mentions in the same breath with the Archduke a 'first class bastard' of a cattle-dealer. Even more risky is his observation that when people get drunk in Bohemia, they at once begin to make insulting remarks about the Emperor. ('Get drunk, have the Austrian National Anthem played and you'll see what you start saying'.) Probably even these remarks would have been accepted by Bretschneider as inevitable and routine in Bohemia, if Švejk had not stumbled onto the subject of foreign politics. While Bretschneider blames the assassination on the Serbs, Švejk firmly asserts that it is the Turks who are responsible and that a war will follow, in which 'the Germans'll attack us, because the Germans and the Turks stick together. You can't find bigger bastards anywhere.' However, Austria can ally herself with the French.

It is probably this last remark, which is totally contrary to Austrian policy and fully in line with the pro-Entente sympathies of the Czechs, which prompts Bretschneider to arrest Švejk on the charges of 'high treason, insulting the royal family and incitement' (the latter because the offences had taken place in a public

* The Young Czech Party was one of the leading political parties in Bohemia (see Chapter 2).

place). The police are particularly interested in Švejk's certainty that war will break out. How well informed is he? War is just what the Austrians themselves are planning, and it would be convenient for them to have evidence that someone else is doing so too.

In the ensuing chapters the satire is largely directed against the police or the other instruments of the law, prisons and prison warders, doctors, malingerers and the lunatic asylum which (like enemas and latrines) is for Hašek a symbol of Austria itself. Then it finally settles on the Catholic Church with Hašek's stinging portrait of Chaplain Katz.

The Grotesque

Hašek's satire often assumes grotesque forms, as in his exaggerated accounts of Švejk's treatment in the garrison gaol, the antics of the Chaplain during the mass and his outrageous behaviour when drunk at the altar.

Some people are ready to accept insulting portraits of royalty or even Church dignitaries, but would draw the line at a parody of the mass. Hašek has no such compunction. Not only was the Church of Rome the age-old target for satire – in Bohemia itself at the time of Hus the Pope was carried through the streets in abusive effigy – but in Austria it was the pillar of the Monarchy. The 'Altar and Crown' ruled Austria jointly. Hence it was fair game to debunk royalty, court ceremonial, the senior officers and the aristocracy, the courtiers, the higher prelates and Church ritual. In the eyes of this former Anarchist, they were all branches of the same evil root.

The grotesque is one of the many forms of satire. A casual reader, turning the pages of *The Good Soldier Švejk*, might suppose that the book was grotesque from start to finish. It is true that like Cruikshank and 'Phiz', Lada turns many of the figures into caricatures, sometimes in the spirit of the book, sometimes not. There are several types in the novel which are too grotesque to have been real – like General Fink, who loves hanging people and writes a letter to his wife describing the fun of it, or indeed Chaplain Katz himself. (The Austrian general Haynau, known as 'The Hyena of Brescia', who just escaped a ducking at the hands of Watneys' brewery workers, when he came to England, seems to have enjoyed hanging rebels, but that was over sixty years earlier.) The scene depicting Dr Grünstein's ogrish method of treating the malingerers is a grotesque travesty of a military hospital in war time, and various events portrayed in the book or described in the stories its characters tell are grossly exaggerated. Generally speaking, satire is more telling, and often funnier, when it is closer to real life. We are much more ready to believe, for instance, that the senior officers in the Austrian army are inept dodderers (as shown in the episode of the muddle of the cyphers) than brutal hangmen. The humour of the book lies in its brilliant portrayal of stupidity rather than its more heavy-handed exposure of depravity.

It is not the task of a satirist to suggest a remedy for the evils he exposes. His object is to paint them in as lurid colours as he can, and, like Dickens and Gogol, he often deliberately chooses, or lapses into, the grotesque in the process. Indeed, Gogol said, 'If your face appears crooked in a mirror, don't blame the mirror.' As Alfred Polgar wrote: 'The book [*The Good Soldier Švejk*] makes unsparing but masterly use of the liberties which caricature offers: it has the right to be unjust and its legitimate artistic methods are distortion, exaggeration...'[5] But the mirror can be a distorting mirror, and if it over-distorts, the image it reflects lacks credibility and we are then justified in blaming it. The effectiveness of Hašek's satire undoubtedly suffers from exaggeration and distortion.

Irony

Irony is a staple element of satire, and Hašek is masterly in his use of it throughout the book, whose essence lies in its absurd ironic antitheses. It is a novel about war, which is a terrible calamity and a desperately serious matter, and yet the book is to all appearances wildly funny. In this war the régime expects the population to share its patriotic fervour, but patriotism for Austria is treason to the Czechs, just as to the Austrian Germans Czech patriotism is treason to Austria. Hence every patriotic formula, appeal or rallying cry is viewed by the Czechs through a distorting mirror.

The irony of the novel is centred in the character of Švejk himself, who protests at all stages that he wants to serve his Emperor and country. It brings out the contradictions between the way people talk and the way they think; the way they are expected to think and the way they act. There is hardly a page from which some example of irony cannot be cited. Jurajda, the occultist cook, writes a letter to his wife, which is sheer double talk. It is composed in a particularly servile tone in the hope that if it is read by his superiors, it may 'keep him a bit further away from the battlefield' and so preserve his skin. There is additional irony in the fact that in civil life he had written a long essay on how no one ought to fear death (pp. 456–7).

One of the few realistic descriptions of a battle, showing what war means while it is being fought and not after it is finished, comes from the telephonist Chodounský. And what is the reaction to it of his listeners (or non-listeners)? They do not attend, because they are wrapped up in their game of cards. 'Two-handed *mariáš* is more important than the whole war and that blasted adventure of yours on the Serbian frontier', says Švejk. 'Oh my God, what a bloody fool I am [...] why didn't I wait a bit longer with that King?' (pp. 452–6).

From reading the book one is left with the impression that senselessness guides the destinies of millions, and that those who are directed see things much more clearly than those who direct them. The world is portrayed as a madhouse and the lunatic asylum praised as a paradise – the only place in Austria where the individual can enjoy complete freedom and be happy.

Parody

Hašek was a natural parodist, not only in literature, but in everyday life and he revels in its use in *The Good Soldier Švejk*. When he observes that Senior Chaplain Ibl had taken the material for his address from army almanacs (p. 447), Hašek was no doubt thinking how much material for his novel he had taken from that same source. Švejk, speaking to Vaněk of the Senior Chaplain's 'oration', says. 'Won't it be marvellous when, like the chaplain said, the day draws to its close, the sun with its golden beams sets behind the mountains, and on the battlefields are heard, as he told us, the last breath of the dying, the death-rattle of the fallen horses, the groans of the wounded and the wailing of the population, as their cottages burn over their heads. I love it when people drivel utter bunkum' (p. 448). The story which follows, about Marshal Radetsky and the dying soldier, is lifted almost word for word from an article in 'The Grand Entertainment Calendar for 1915'. In one place Hašek has of course given the text a farcical twist, when he makes the standard bearer say to Radetsky, who dismounts and is about to shake his hand, 'It's no good, sir. Both my arms are shot away', which naturally cannot be found in the original (p. 449). A similar parody occurs in the account of the ambulance driver, Josef Bong (p. 234), which Švejk reads in a propaganda poster on the wall.

Hašek liked to parody regimental orders, bureaucratic laws and regulations and newspaper articles, so much so that one Czech critic has questioned whether on these grounds the book is a true novel at all, but rather a *collage* or a *montage*.[6] Hašek found it easier to demonstrate that the law was an ass by quoting or parodying legal passages of its own contriving, than by introducing lawyers themselves to speak incomprehensible jargon, as Dickens or Smollett might have done. In *The Good Soldier Švejk* Hašek was perhaps more addicted to '*collage*' and '*montage*' than most novelists, but it would be absurd to contend that on these grounds the book is not a novel.

Hašek also employs humorous contrasts in the course of the narrative, linking up important world events with events in the novel which are trivial in comparison, such as the following: 'At the time when the forests of the river Rabe in Galicia saw Austrian armies fleeing across the river and when down in Serbia [...] the Austrian divisions [...] got the walloping they had long deserved, the Ministry of War remembered Švejk' (p. 55). Or 'While masses of armies pinned to the forests by the Dunajec and the Rabe stood under a rain of shells and artillery of heavy calibre was tearing to pieces whole companies and burying them in the Carpathians, Lieutenant Lukáš and Švejk went through a far from pleasant idyll with the lady who had run away from her husband' (p. 183).

Jaroslav Hašek

Anecdotism

A feature of the book, which definitely marks it out from any other book we know of, is the abundance of anecdotal tales. Most of these are told by Švejk himself, but some are told by other characters. The real orderly of the real Lukas is, as we know, supposed to have been Strašlipka, who never stopped telling stories; and one of the reasons for all those stories in the novel is the author's attempt to make Švejk true to his prototype. In one of the poems Hašek wrote during the war he included the following lines:

> The most frightful of all war's hazards
> Are – Strašlipka's old chestnuts.
>> ('In the Reserve')

But Švejk's stories are often motivated by his own need to cause a diversion, perhaps to save his own position, when it is threatened. Sometimes they have no ostensible motive other than to make the book more amusing and colourful. But they are one of its more realistic features. In the world of 'Upstairs and Downstairs' this is just the way 'Downstairs' people talk all over the world. It offers them a chance to get something off their chests and to take the stage for a brief moment when they otherwise spend most of their time serving or genuflecting to those 'Upstairs'. The anecdotes Hašek introduces are nearly always documented with the names of the characters and the place and sometimes even the date. The author himself was a great retailer of anecdotes, which he made up to amuse his bohemian friends in the Prague tavern (who were not strictly speaking the 'folk' but the bourgeoisie, except that in the Bohemia of that time the *petite bourgeoisie* had not moved very far away from their original peasant stock). At the same time he listened to the conversations of others, who undoubtedly were the 'folk', and reproduced them in his novel. The trick is occasionally overdone, but on the whole it is remarkable how greatly these anecdotes brighten up the book and how little they hold up the action. Hašek had carefully observed how people tell stories, and he took from life not only the subjects they fancied, but their way of telling them. Long rambling sentences, which a writer would normally break up, are preserved by Hašek just as they are spoken, even if they

156

are repetitious, disjointed and often defy the rules of syntax. These frequent naturalistic touches are brilliant, but they are the translator's nightmare.

Pacifism

The Good Soldier Švejk is by its very nature an *anti-war* novel. Nonetheless, the war itself – the thick of it as opposed to its horrifying aftermath – figures very little in it. This is partly because Švejk never reaches the firing line and Hašek himself remained there for only a short time. Perhaps if Hašek had finished the novel, it would have included some scenes of action. As it is, his characters only *talk* about the war.

Volume III ('The Glorious Licking') begins as follows:

> At last the moment came when they were stuffed into vans in the ratio of 42 men to 8 horses. The horses travelled more comfortably than the men of course because they could sleep standing, but what did it matter? A military train was again carrying off to Galicia another herd of men driven to the slaughter house.
>
> But it brought these creatures some relief none the less; when the train moved off it was at last something definite, whereas before there had only been uncomfortable uncertainty and panic as to whether the train would go that day, the next, or the following one. Some felt as though a death sentence had been passed on them and waited in fear and trembling for the moment when the executioner would come. And then calm resignation followed: soon everything would be over. (p. 447)

In the second paragraph above Hašek captures admirably the mood of all soldiers in war as they approach the firing line. In the first paragraph we meet for the first time with that bitter note which intensifies as the book proceeds and turns the light-hearted humour of the beginning blacker and blacker. There is the incident of the German corporal from the *Deutschmeister* who falls out of the train and is impaled on the points lever. 'He's had his war', says Švejk [...] 'Everybody at least knows where he is buried [...] It's just on the railway line and you don't have to hunt for his grave all over the battlefields' (p. 485).

A part of Biegler's dream describes the various disabled soldiers pressing to get through the gates of heaven. 'They had lost some parts of their bodies in the war and carried them with them in their rucksacks – heads, arms and legs.' Curiously enough, this passage is reminiscent of an episode in Comenius' *The Labyrinth of the World*, which Hašek would certainly have read. It is from Chapter XX – 'The Estate of Soldiery' – and describes 'those who remain after the Battle'.

> Meanwhile I see that they lead and carry from the battlefield many whose hands, arms, head, nose had been cut off, whose bodies had been transpierced, whose skin was in tatters, and who were everywhere dabbled with blood. While I could, from pity, scarce look at these men, the interpreter said: 'All this will be healed; a soldier must be hardy.' 'What then', quoth I, 'of those who lost their lives here?' He answered: 'Their hides had already been paid for.' 'How this?' said I. 'Hast thou, then, not seen how many pleasant things were previously granted to them?' 'And what unpleasant things also had they to endure?' quoth I, 'and even if only delight had previously been their lot, it is a wretched thing to give food to a man only that he may be forced to go to the shambles directly afterwards. It is an ugly estate in any case. I like it not!'

In the second half of the long Chapter 3, 'From Hatvan towards the Galician Frontier', Hašek concentrates more and more on the terrible traces left after the fighting – the burnt-out villages, the torn shreds of Austrian uniforms lying on the edge of the shell craters, the boot of an Austrian infantryman with a piece of shin bone hanging in the branches of an old burnt-out pine, the freshly built cemeteries, the white crosses gleaming on the plains and a mud-bespattered Austrian cap fluttering on a white cross. But it is again the results of war rather than fighting itself.

Further on Hašek writes: 'Everywhere little heaps of human excrement of international extraction, belonging to all people of Austria, Germany and Russia. The excrement of soldiers of all nationalities and confessions lay side by side or heaped on top of one another without quarrelling among themselves' (p. 598).

Up to now the frightful reality of war has only been referred to in Švejk's black humour. Now Hašek brings the reader face to face with it in direct description; but even so the mood quickly changes and the horror is defused, as Švejk concentrates his attention on an old chamber pot, lying in a ditch – a splendid example of bathos – and makes a fool of Dub, when he comes up to rebuke him for hanging about and staring at it. Meanwhile Marek is writing his imaginary history of the regiment and devising harrowing deaths for most of the N.C.O.s and men in it.

Then comes the Brigadier's speech to his men, which gives the impression that 'all those people in grey uniforms should let themselves be killed with the greatest joy, just because field posts were installed at the front and, if anyone had both legs torn off by a shell, it would be a beautiful thing for him to die with the thought that his field post number was 72 [. . .] Then, after his speech. . .these various groups of human cattle which were destined for slaughter somewhere beyond the Bug, set out successfully on the march' (p. 627).

Vulgarity

An English critic wrote about Swift that 'he was often coarse, but never lewd'. This leaves unanswered whether it is less ignoble to be coarse than lewd, but the same remark might have been made about Hašek, who seems to have shared Swift's preoccupation with excrement. Swift is pardoned for his scatological excesses, which, we are told, were provoked by his moral indignation. Those who knew Hašek, including his wife, maintain that his conversation was 'clean' and that he did not enjoy 'dirty' jokes.[7] Indeed his wife objected to the tone of some of his stories, but he defended himself by saying that he had to cater for the public taste. This does not appear to be quite true, because many of the newspapers and journals he wrote for were meant for family readers and did not favour vulgarity. The frequency of 'lavatory humour' in *The Good Soldier Švejk* is probably due to Hašek's fixation that Austria was 'the dregs'. In his view it was so rotten that the only fit comparison for it was the latrine. 'Austria's victory crawled out of her latrines', he observes (p. 538). Consequently he thinks or affects to think that everything about it 'stinks'.

Hašek's anecdotes were the anecdotes of the tap-room, and as conversations there were by their very nature ribald, it is surprising that those recorded in *The Good Soldier Švejk* are so very seldom lewd. Censorship in the Czechoslovak Republic was naturally a great deal more lax than it had been under the Monarchy. Masaryk wished to preserve a high moral standard, but his anti-clericalism meant that he did not regard the Church's idea of what was sinful and impure as the supreme touchstone.

159

Songs

A striking feature of the novel is the large number of songs and verses quoted. Hašek himself could not sing in tune and resembled in that respect another humorist, W. S. Gilbert, who said of himself that he only knew two tunes: 'One was "God Save the Queen" and the other wasn't.' But Hašek belonged to a particularly musical nation, one to whom song and dance were part of their everyday life. He would certainly have heard many songs in the course of his bohemian life and in the army, when the troops sang on the march. Many of the army songs, as in all armies, had their obscene verses, but Hašek never reproduces these. Švejk sings very often, and possibly Hašek liked to do so too, however ill-equipped he was for it. Lada tells us that they once composed a comic opera together simply by singing what came into their heads.[8] The songs have helped to turn Švejk into a 'folk hero'. As the gaoler says in Smetana's opera *Dalibor*, 'Where is the Czech who does not like music?' A man who did not like to sing could hardly pass muster as a Czech folk hero. Hašek quotes the German line *Schlechte Leute haben keine Lieder* in his short story 'Before the Revolutionary Tribunal of the Eastern Front'.

Comedy

But we must never allow ourselves to forget that Hašek was first and foremost a humorist. (It is not uncommon for literary critics when judging great works of comedy to lose their own sense of humour, and critics of *The Good Soldier Švejk* are no exception.) Much of the book is comedy pure and simple, a patchwork made up of the various joking tales the author loved to tell at the pub in the company of his boon companions. The mood of Rabelaisian laughter and intoxication in which the book was conceived and born indicates that the author looked upon it as a rollicking comedy, and many of Švejk's satrical remarks were originally thought of as good jokes which Hašek was dying to pass on and which, he hoped, would attract purchasers and earn the author money; they were not moral exhortations.

The book abounds in purely *comic* episodes – the muddle over the cyphers (pp. 463–76), Švejk's encounter with Dub, when he has illicitly bought a bottle of cognac for his lieutenant (pp. 575–80), the scurrilous story of Švejk's about the rivalry between the private detectives and how one of them, Mr Stendler, got a 'cock-eyed nut' (pp. 459–62), the incident at the latrines with the Inspecting General (pp. 539–42) – to mention only a few.

Wit

There is no doubt that Hašek had a great gift for satire, irony, parody and humour, but did he have *wit*? They do not necessarily go together, but examples of it can be found sparingly in the novel. It is occasionally even displayed by Švejk himself, as quoted in chapter 5. It appears less often in the utterances of other characters, certainly not in the long tiresome tirades by Marek. It is found most of all in some of the comments which the author makes from the side-lines. After the muddle over the cypher books we are told that 'Švejk got solemnly into his van. He felt respect for himself. It did not happen every day, that he committed something so frightful that he must never be allowed to learn what it was' (p. 476).

And so the conclusion must be that the structure of the book owes less to Hašek's conscious intention than to his inexperience in the novelist's craft. He was used to writing humorous short stories, and the book is in fact a string of such 'humoresques', as they were called in Czech. Some of them are inherent parts of the novel, adventures which Švejk has with various characters in the book. Others are narrated comparatively briefly by him and his associates. The final structure of the novel was thus determined by Hašek's experience of writing short stories and *feuilletons* rather than by any grand design and it was crowned by his immortal experiences in the army itself.

8
THE CONTROVERSY

'He looks so stupid and idiotic, but it's just with people of his kind that you need to have all your wits about you.' (Sergeant Flanderka on Švejk)

To most readers it will seem strange that the book by a Czech writer which is today best known abroad and perhaps still most read in Czechoslovakia itself should have been all but ignored at its first appearance.

One reason for its tardy recognition is that it appeared too early. Most novels about the First World War did not come on to the market until some ten years after it had ended. The memorable English war books like Edmund Blunden's *Undertones of War*, Robert Graves' *Goodbye to All That* and Siegfried Sassoon's *Memoirs of an Infantry Officer* were published between 1928 and 1930, and the Germans had to wait until 1929 for *All Quiet on the Western Front*. Hašek made his contribution to this class of literature before a critical spirit about the war had become general. When Remarque's book first appeared, readers in Germany were outraged by its naturalistic details and anti-heroic tone, and not only the Nazis but the not-quite-so-lunatic Right protested and demonstrated violently against it. Published earlier in 1923, Hašek's book could hardly expect a favourable hearing even in Czechoslovakia, where literary opinion inclined to the Left.

People remained under the spell of the emotions the war had unleashed for years after it had ended. It had been grand and heroic from whichever side you saw it, and, after the terrible sacrifices borne by all who took part in it, it would have been treasonable to present it in any other light. Only after the lapse of some years were people able to free themselves from conventional romantic obsessions and view it critically and dispassionately. And for the Czechs it presented a particularly difficult problem. The bulk of the nation had been obliged to fight on 'the wrong side', and those who had served on until the bitter end felt that they had done their bit in their calling and were not unproud of it. After all, at the time they were Austrian subjects, and none of them could be sure that Austria would not survive the war. Why, up to the early years of the century even Masaryk had stood for the preservation of Austria. Opinion in Bohemia could not be expected to switch so rapidly in favour of its over-throw. Moreover, many Czechs had won promotion and decorations in Austrian service – among them, surprisingly enough, Hašek himself.

It is true that countless Czechs were taken prisoner by the Russians, but not so very many of these crossed to the other side of their own accord. The Czech Legion in Russia was raised first from volunteers among Czechoslovak settlers in Russia, many of whom were Russian subjects. Later it was increased by the addition of Czech and Slovak prisoners-of-war who were glad to get out of the appalling Russian internment camps. In a short time it grew to be the most formidable military force in Russia, inflicting defeats on the Red Army itself. Its exploits were famous all over the new Czechoslovag Republic; and when the Legionaries returned home, they felt themselves part of the national legend and were popularly accepted as such. Most of them were strongly nationalist and anti-Soviet, and could not be expected to condone those who like Hašek, had deserted from their ranks and fought and worked on the other side. And there were count-less Czechs who thought then and still think now that Švejk himself is a bad advertisement for the Czech character. At a time when the new Republic was trying to establish its identity and reputation abroad, patriots had no wish to be associated in the minds of foreign readers with the unheroic qualities of the Good Soldier or the unwholesome tone of the book, for Hašek had not minced words in it. He printed for the first time in Bohemia the language which soldiers use and the salty anecdotes they told.

Moreover, to most Czechs Hašek himself was an extremely dubious character. Very shortly after having been awarded the silver medal for valour and received promotion, he had let himself be taken prisoner by the Russians, when he still had a chance of avoiding it. After volunteering for the Czech Legion and becoming one of its recruiting officers, propagandists and war correspondents, he had deserted to the Red Army only to perform similar services for the Bolsheviks. After the Legion had issued a warrant for his arrest, he had escaped its vengeance by ignominious flight. Subsequently he stayed on in Siberia in Soviet service until he was sent to Prague with the express mission of helping to overthrow the liberal and democratic republic of Thomas Masaryk and replacing it by a Soviet totalitarian one.

Finally Hašek's personal reputation before the war as an anarchist, bohemian, vagabond and drunkard had not been forgotten and was certainly not enhanced when it became known that he had brought back with him from Russia a second 'wife', a Bolshevik, while his legal and eminently respectable Czech one, Jarmila, was still alive and faithful to him in Prague.

On his return to Prague, where the Czechoslovak government had just suppressed an attempt to start a Bolshevik revolution, Hašek found himself boycotted not only by the Right, but by many of his former friends on the Left as well. One of them refused even to shake his hand. To the Right he was 'the Red Commissar with blood on his hands', while the Left were sceptical about the sincerity of his commitment to Communism and refused to take him seriously.

The grounds for boycotting Hašek's novel were thus largely political and moral, but there were genuine literary grounds as well. The author's style was considered to be illiterate, uncouth and inartistic, and his writings were consigned to 'the borderland between literature and trash'. As we shall read later, a leading Czech critic, albeit a very conservative one, writing soon after the appearance of the book, described the author as 'an altogether unliterary writer'.

Two events at last broke the wall of silence which had surrounded the book. The first was the very great interest aroused in Germany and among the German-speaking public abroad by the appearance of a German translation in 1926. This pricked the conscience of the Czech literary world, and Czech critics felt obliged at least to notice it and counter the high praise the author was earning abroad. The next event was the sharp controversy which developed at home, between those who condemned or extolled the author and his book. Once *The Good Soldier Švejk* had become the subject of public polemics, its sales began to increase considerably, and some critics in Czechoslovakia started to pay it more serious attention. But prejudice persisted for a very long time, lasting, surprisingly enough, until some years after the Communist take-over in Prague in 1948.

During the Second World War the book was burned by the Nazi authorities, and this was a high recommendation for it after the 'liberation'. One might have supposed that one result of the Communist seizure of power in Prague would have been Hašek's complete rehabilitation: he had after all been a Bolshevik Commissar. But owing to certain 'contradictions' in his character, actions and even writings, there still remained doubts in high quarters in Prague whether he should be reinstated at all. As a result the period from February 1948 until the beginning of 1953 saw the publication of even fewer articles about him and his works than during the pre-war years. But once the Soviet Union had decided that 'Comrade Gashek', as they called him, was 'progressive' and respectable, he was not merely rehabilitated but his memory honoured 'this side idolatry' at home and throughout the Communist world – a circumstance which would have surprised and tickled no one more than the author himself.

Let us now examine in more detail the stormy controversy which raged round the head of the Good Soldier and his birth (or rather renaissance) in 1923 and especially from 1928 onwards.[1] We must first give due credit to those who from the outset had perceived that the book was no ordinary one and had recorded this opinion during the author's lifetime.

While he was writing the third volume of his book, Hašek must have had some faint premonition of the success it would have. He expressed delight when he was told that Max Brod, the Prague German writer, who was to write so perceptively about Kafka and Janáček, had published a favourable review of the first volume, and he at once sent him a message of thanks on a postcard. Off the record, he told his friends, 'Now I really start to believe that *Švejk* will have a great career. Trust me, my friends, anything a Jew touches succeeds.' And Max Brod was no ordinary Jew.

In the very year of the publication of the unfinished novel and of its author's death, Brod published his book *Prager Sternehimmel*, in which he wrote that Hašek's achievement in creating a figure which was both an individual human being and a human type was of the highest order. Brod felt that, on leaving the theatre in Prague where a play about Švejk was being performed, one was filled with the glorious certainty that 'Man is indestructibe'. Eight years later he wrote, 'I regard Hašek as a truly great satirist. From the outset I put him in the same class as Cervantes and Rabelais. My evaluation provoked opposition, not only among Germans, but also among Czechs, who were not willing to go further than to label Hašek a humorist of average quality. I had the same experience with Janáček. I was inured to such battles.'[2]

Praise for Hašek had come a little earlier from the Czech Communist novelist, Ivan Olbracht, who had written in superlative terms about *The Good Soldier Švejk*, after having read only the first volume – in fact on 15 November 1921. 'I regard it as a work of sheer genius', he declared.

> Hašek shows us the world war from a totally new viewpoint. The writings of the Viennese, Karl Kraus, had already thrown a little light on this aspect of it, but, strictly speaking, only a little, because [...] his horizon did not extend beyond Vienna's streets, cafés and ministerial offices. Hašek, on the other hand, experienced the war itself and saw half Europe and Asia [...]
>
> I have read several war novels and even written one myself. But none of them shows up the world war in all its infamy, idiocy and inhumanity so vividly [...] Hašek had no need to fight the war within himself and conquer it. He stood above it from the very beginning. He just laughed at it.[3]

There was some exaggeration in this otherwise very perceptive judgement. Hašek's experience of the World War was not quite as wide as Olbracht claimed. It was true to say that he laughed at the war, but did he stand above it from the very beginning? A study of his life does not necessarily support that claim.

It would have been difficult to find a more ardent Marxist than Olbracht. He had translated the *Communist Manifesto* into Czech, and his best known novel, *Anna, the Woman from the Proletariat*, was hailed by one Communist critic as 'the mother of Socialist Realism in Czechoslovakia' – a double-edged compliment indeed. As one of those who were chiefly responsible for bringing a somewhat unwilling Hašek belatedly back to Prague to start a revolution, which, by the time he arrived had already been suppressed, he must have felt some guilt towards him. He was sorry for him too in his difficult position and wanted to give him consolation and encouragement.

It was Olbracht who coined for Hašek the phrase 'idiot of genius', adding that there was no shame in the appelation, because all genius had within it a grain of idiocy.[4] When Hašek was told this, his dry comment was, 'Olbracht has got it wrong. I'm not an idiot of genius. I'm just an ordinary idiot.'

A contrary point of view, perhaps more representative of average Czech literary opinion, was put forward by Arne Novák, a leading Czech critic and literary historian and son of the well-known Czech woman novelist, Teréza Nováková. In an essay which appeared in German in 1923 in *The Handbook of Literary Studies*, he described Hašek as an 'altogether unliterary writer, who attained world fame through his pan-European defeatism and inexhaustible triviality, when he created that irresistible war-type, the Good Soldier Švejk – a cowardly and tasteless buffoon, who behaves like an idiot and with the triumphant smile of cynical superiority preserves his stinking hide from the Imperial and Royal Army.' It is of course as ridiculous to suggest that Švejk tried to 'preserve his hide from the army', as to say that his hide was stinking. On the contrary, throughout the first part of the book Švejk continually asserts his desire to serve his Emperor until his last breath, and, had Hašek finished the book, Švejk would certainly have got to the front in the end, even if he walks in the wrong direction at the beginning.

These reviews were written while Hašek was still alive. On his death the important Prague German daily *Das Prager Tagblatt* (on which Max Brod himself worked) was already describing him in an obituary as 'the best humorous writer in Bohemia'.[5] It went on to make a very good point: 'In its simplicity Hašek's humour was very close to genius [...] He told the most improbable things with a professional thoroughness [...] with many quotations and supporting examples, given in such detail that the listener would be made to feel ashamed of himself if he did not believe them.'

So, in the first year after his death, there were a few writers at least, and some important ones, who tried to give Hašek his due, although their judgement may not always have been founded on purely literary considerations.

One of the earliest favourable Czech criticisms of the book, after those by Max Brod and Ivan Olbracht, came from the young critic Julius Fučík, who compared Švejk to both Sancho Panza and Sam Weller. At the same time he suggested that the novel was dadaistic (probably because the magazine to which he contributed the article was itself dadaistic, and Olbracht had used the word 'idiocy' (blbost) in his review of the book).[6] Fučík was a passionate young Communist who was to become during the German occupation a member of the Second Illegal Central Committee of the Communist Party and to work underground, until he was arrested in 1942 and executed in Berlin 18 months later. During his imprisonment in Prague he wrote, and succeeded in smuggling out of prison, the manuscript of a book, *Report Written on the Gallows*. After 1948 a posthumous 'cult of personality' settled on his head which was out of all proportion to his merits. He was made National Hero and awarded the Communist 'International Peace Prize'. In the fifties and afterwards it was not easy to get any book on any literary subject published which did not include a quotation of his opinions, whether they had relevance or not, just as in Russia all books – even on bee-keeping – had to have somewhere a quotation from Stalin on the subject. But the fact that in Fučík's writings there were three enthusiastic references to *The Good Soldier Švejk* was a help to those who were working for the rehabilitation of Hašek.

In 1926 Greta Reiner translated *The Good Soldier Švejk* into German. It proved to be a landmark, which brought the book for the first time within the reach of the German-speaking world and especially of the brilliant Berlin theatre director Erwin Piscator and his friend Bertolt Brecht, who were later to present it to the public in a dramatised version and bring its author world fame. Hašek had already considered the possibility of having his novel translated into German. At Lipnice, a month before he died, he had written to his artist friend, Panuška, 'I should be happy if I could live to see at least one edition of *Švejk* in a foreign language. The Chief Forester here, my friend Böhm, wants to try to make a translation of it into German, but I don't know what will come of it.'

But in the event it proved difficult to find a German translator. By this time there were not many writers left in Prague who were still bi-lingual, and most of them were distrustful of the author and the book. According to Greta Reiner the novel was considered indigestible and worthless. 'The publishers insisted on radical cuts', she recalled. 'They wanted to telescope the four volumes into one, because they could not understand that a certain diffuseness was one of the most essential factors of the book's comic effect.' When she approached an eminent Czech to write a foreword to her translation, he implored her as a good friend of the Czech nation not to dishonour it by translating such a book.[7] Indeed the news that it would appear in a foreign language at all unloosed an avalanche of protest. This was due not only to ideological or moral objections or animosity towards the author, but just as much to the free, unconventional and 'unliterary' style of his writing. In Bohemia, where there had traditionally been one form of the Czech language for literature and another for conversation in the home or on the streets, it was at that time inviting criticism to try to break down the barrier between the two. Hašek's postscript to the first volume of *The Adventures of the Good Soldier Švejk*, where he defiantly defended his intention to go on letting his characters 'speak as they do in real life', was intentionally provocative (p. 214). But, once the fashion had been set by Remarque's *All Quiet on the Western Front* and other writers, his naturalistic language and descriptions were accepted as the inevitable idiom for literature about the war.

But it was not only the colloquial language in the book which upset the Czech critics; it was the fact that Hašek could no longer write good Czech. He made spelling mistakes and used russicisms. He had always been notoriously careless over the texts of his stories, leaving them to the sub-editors or even to the printers to correct. When the post-war editors in Czechoslovakia came to prepare carefully revised texts of his works, they found that the author had left them with many problems. He could not even spell correctly the names of the taverns he haunted! This was not because he was illiterate himself (he read a lot, even if it was often not 'literature') but rather that what he wrote was illiterate.

Greta Reiner's translation came just at the right time, when some sections of German opinion were already beginning to reappraise the war and to do so fearlessly. Unlike some other subsequent translations, hers was at least complete. Since a translator should have a better opportunity than most people to judge the author he is transposing (for no one is a hero to his valet) it is interesting to learn what she thought of the book, even though her enthusiasm for it was undoubtedly influenced by her left-wing sympathies. In her introduction to the first volume, like Brod before her, she characterises Hašek as the 'Czech Cervantes', who had created in Švejk a new type in Czech literature, the type of 'artful idiot', who in spite of his limitations, was fully equal to any situation.[8] The fallacy here is that there is no 'artful idiot' in *Don Quixote*.

Since Hašek was looked down upon and ignored by the 'bourgeoisie', because he not only debunked patriotism and lampooned the Church, but wrote 'unliterary Czech' as well, it was only natural that the first writers to praise him were Communists or people with leftist sympathies, who were prepared to excuse or even make a virtue of his solecisms. The Prague Germans too had less reason to be irritated by the faults in Hašek's style than the Czechs. Two of them, Karl Kreibich and F. C. Weiskopf, were the first to react to the book in Prague after its appearance in German. Kreibich, who was later to become the leader of the German section of the Communist Party of Czechoslovakia (for as long as it was permitted to exist) endorsed the translator's view that Hašek was an outstanding humorist and satirist of genius, but did not agree that he was a second Cervantes. Don Quixote, he argued, was international and eternal, whereas Švejk was a specifically Czech type and the product of a distinct period of Czech history. With the fall of the Austria-Hungary he had outlived his time and significance, and in Czech national life of the time there was nothing more senseless than 'Švejkism'. As a German, he regarded Švejk as the product of a certain passivity in the Slav character, which made him incapable of fitting into 'the system' or of fighting against it.[9] Weiskopf, a journalist and translator, took a similar view: Švejk was no Don Quixote; he was not universal and could only have existed in the conditions of *Schlamperei* (muddle and inefficiency) which existed in the old monarchy.[10]

On the other hand there were Prague Germans who appreciated Hašek and who were not Communists. Willy Haas in an article published in 1926 maintained that Švejk's personality 'radiates the glow of a popular fairy tale or Czech folk song [. . .] It is not a question of class, proletarians, peasants, petit bourgeois or *Lumpenproletariat*; in this book it is purely and simply the people who speak.' Švejk was a 'Sancho Panza without Don Quixote': an active Sancho Panza, who fought his way through the world in his good, cautious and anxious way. He was well and truly devoted to his master and his regiment, but he was perpetually their misfortune.[11]

In the face of the high praise the novel was receiving in the German-speaking world, official Czech critics, who up to that time had deliberately ignored the book, could no longer keep silent. In 1927, J. O. Novotný, a minor Czech literary critic, published an article in which he attempted a reappraisal of Hašek, quoting the favourable judgements of some German and Swedish reviewers. He was, however, the first to initiate the misconception, which dies hard in the West, that Švejk was 'the most perfect expression and type of Czech passive resistance to the war and personified the organised "dodging" of his nation'. He saw Švejk as the 'universal Czech' – a brother of the million nameless soldiers on all fronts, who cursed the war which had dragged them away from their homes. He added prophetically, 'In Jaroslav Hašek a great artist has passed away and his rehabilitation, which has come so belatedly, had to come from abroad, if it was to come at all.'[12]

This first favourable judgement by a Czech non-Communist critic aroused the anger of the leading Czech Catholic novelist, Jaroslav Durych, and evoked from him a bitterly ironical reply. With heavy sarcasm he described *The Good Soldier Švejk* as 'a work which not only faithfully mirrors the typical Czech before and after the War, but also is a wonderful memorial to the whole Czech people and all their aspirations'. Quoting the words of the Senior Staff Doctor in the book about malingerers (which presumably apply mainly to Czechs) Durych wrote, 'They are a gang of crooks' (p. 78). (The original Czech is terser and more expressive: 'Je to banda.' Perhaps 'riff-raff' or 'dregs' is nearer.) Durych went on: 'This is the only book from which foreigners can and must learn the true nature of the Czech nation. Its educational value is incalculable. It is a monument to the intellectual and moral qualities and the specific attributes of our people.'[13]

But the event which had by far the greatest effect on the fortunes of the book was its dramatisation by Piscator, in a version which was performed at his *Theatre am Nollendorfplatz* in Berlin on 23 January 1928. The rights for the stage production had been acquired by Max Brod and Hans Reimann, who had already made their own dramatic version of the book, although they had not yet been able to stage it. Unfortunately Brod, who had shown such discernment in his review of the book, was less perceptive when he came to dramatise it. When he had read his stage version, Piscator commented, 'It realised our worst fears. What was handed to us was not Hašek, but a pseudo-comic farce about a batman. To achieve "comic" effects and in an endeavour to knock together a real "theatre piece", Hašek's satire had been thrown to the winds.'[14] Indeed a serious love element was even introduced between Lukáš and Etelka (the wife of the Hungarian Kákonyi) and Švejk was asked to be godfather to their children!

Since he was not free to make his own independent version, Piscator tried to do the next best thing – to rework Brod and Reiner's version, which was the only one he was permitted to use, and at the same time to stick as closely as possible to the original novel. He hoped that when the copyright holders saw the finished product, they might accept his version, which in the event they did. The task of rewriting the script was entrusted to Brecht, aided by Felix Gasbarra, Georg Gross and Piscator himself. It is not clear who had the major part in the rewriting. Brecht claimed that it was entirely his work, but it appears that his memory of the event was not accurate. From this moment dates Brecht's great admiration for Hašek as a writer. The book was a revelation to him. 'If anyone asks me to pick three literary works of this century which in my opinion will become part of world literature, then I would say that one of them is Hašek's *The Good Soldier Švejk*.'[15]

The production was one of the most successful of Piscator's creations, but by no means faithful to the spirit of the book, as could well be imagined, coming from two ardent Communists who believed passionately in the political rôle of the theatre. But the greatest act of heresy perpetrated by Piscator himself was to kill off Švejk and tag onto the story a macabre 'Apostrophe' (approved, surprisingly enough, by Max Brod) in which Švejk and his fellow soldiers arise from the dead, 'bleeding, ragged, limbless or crippled', to the accompaniment of the Radetsky March. They confront God in the figure of 'The Supreme Commander-in-Chief' and berate him, while he visibly shrinks before them. The addition was only given one performance. Not only was it out of keeping with the spirit of the book; it proved too strong meat for the German authorities of the time, who prosecuted Gross on the charge of blasphemy, as a result of which he was sentenced to two months' imprisonment and a fine of 2,000 marks.

Piscator, like many other admirers of Hašek's works, was dedicated to the October Revolution and the young Bolshevik state. Max Brod's comment on his production was that he had made a conscious revolutionary out of an unconscious one,[16] but Willy Haas, when he saw it, expressed the opinion that Švejk – 'a most conservative being' – far from being an unconscious revolutionary was not a revolutionary at all. He wrote, 'Of course Piscator turned the action into a political one [. . .] Most of the public were enchanted, including many Czechs in Berlin – but then practically all of them were Communists and gave full support to the radical and ruthless way Švejk was turned into a political figure!'[17]

By this time *The Good Soldier Švejk* was on everyone's lips and it was now the turn of the Czech nationalist poet and writer, Viktor Dyk, a deputy and later senator for the National Democratic Party, the most conservative of the five main political governing parties in the Republic, to deliver his thunderbolt against it. Dyk knew what he was talking about. He had himself written satires about Austria in wartime. He was one of those Czechs who after the war had claimed that the Czech Home Front should have primacy over Masaryk's liberation movement abroad and had opposed the President's more conciliatory attitude to the Germans in Czechoslovakia. He had strongly condemned the October Revolution and attacked Bolshevism as a betrayal of Russia's national interest. Now, in an article in his party's paper *The National Newspaper* of 15 April 1928, he asked how it was

Jaroslav Hašek

possible that of all those who had fought and died in the war,
only one living hero seemed to have survived and he was a
'dodger'. It was totally untrue, he argued, to claim that Švejk
had been made a dodger by conditions in Austria. He was a
dodger on principle, and his elevation to the status of 'hero'
involved the risk that future dodgers would come to be regarded
not as a joke but as models and leaders for the new generation
to follow.

This attack on his highly prized 'folk hero' was swiftly
answered by Julius Fučík, in a rousing defence published in the
May number of the Communist cultural journal, *Creation*.
Under the headline 'War with Švejk', he argued that Švejk was
not merely a soldier of the Austro-Hungarian army, but an international type, representative of all soldiers in all imperialist
armies, which explained the ready acclaim the book had received
everywhere. 'Švejk is the type of the unrevolutionary little man,
the half-proletarian petty bourgeois, who, on joining the army,
comes into direct contact with the machinery of the capitalist
state.' He could well understand why Dyk objected to Švejk
being portrayed as a hero, because he made a mockery of all the
concepts which were especially dear to the hearts of the bourgeoisie, for whom Dyk was a mouthpiece. So Fučík had at last
come to realise that Švejk was no revolutionary at all but a petty
bourgeois, and was also now trying to establish that he was not
merely a Czech, but an international type. Švejk was indeed
rapidly becoming a football for the opposing political factions.
One of the reasons why the Left praised him so highly was that
they thought they could use him as a weapon in the ideological
struggle.

The acknowledged doyen of Czech literary critics at that time
was F. X. Šalda, and he now raised his authoritative voice in an
article called 'On the So-called Immortality of Poetical Works'.[18]
He made the point that Hašek's book showed the unavoidable
motions which everyone had been obliged to make, if he wanted
to come out of the War alive. 'The most important of these
motions was to duck as low as possible. For Švejk that is easy,
because he is small. That is what is really immortal about this
book [. . .] The little man is indestructible [. . .] Švejk's [. . .]
idiotic cunning protects him more and is of more use to him

than the greatest imaginable acumen and ingenuity. This is the new note which Hašek has found.' But was not Švejk's 'idiotic cunning' a combination of acumen and ingenuity?

Later in the same year, Šalda returned to the subject. 'The battle which Švejk wages', he wrote, 'is a deadly serious and tense one: it is a struggle for bare existence. The fact that Švejk wages it with the help of comedy, humour and parody [...] does not detract from its seriousness [...] he [Švejk] almost falls over backwards in his attempts to execute every order literally, but through his blind enthusiasm he stultifies its whole purpose [...]' Šalda called *The Good Soldier Švejk* 'for all its comedy a desperately sad book, because in it the individual fights against [...] a giant power, against the War. It is a struggle for his very existence (because the poor man has nothing else he can call his own). If he uses weapons which are mean and underhand, they are not of his own choosing but are forced upon him. He fights as slaves are prone to do.' In a riposte to Durych, he conceded that the book was certainly a monument of shame, but not of Czech shame, but rather of the shame of their oppressors.[19]

By now Hašek had been sufficiently rehabilitated in his own country to be included in the *Masaryk Encyclopaedia* in 1927. In the next year he could be found in the German *Grosse Brockhaus* (albeit recorded inaccurately). By 1933 he had even received a flattering entry in the excellent supplement to Czechoslovakia's main work of reference, the large *Otto Encyclopaedia*, where it was said of him that, of all Czechoslovak writers, he had won the greatest popularity abroad and that *The Good Soldier Švejk* had appeared in all European languages. 'In his life's work he [Hašek] shows not only wider ranges of vision and the ability to delineate character, but also lively narrative inventiveness, deep knowledge of psychology [...] bold social judgement coupled sometimes with class consciousness.' But even by 1929 he had still not made the pages of the *Encyclopaedia Britannica*. Indeed, as the Soviet critic Bernshtein correctly observes, Hašek was not even mentioned in the article on Czech literature in its 1960 edition.

After Piscator's great success in Berlin, it was now high time that the book should be dramatised and staged in Prague itself. During the 1935–6 session, the Communist avant-garde director

E. F. Burian staged it at his small experimental theatre D.35, presenting Švejk as a simple but artful man, who had managed to preserve his sound common-sense in a war-mad world which was doomed to destruction. Švejk was a Praguer, who even during the war remained closely linked to the Prague people and their whole environment. Burian's production was one more attempt to make Švejk topical, and followed logically upon Fučik's conception of him.

Another Prague German Communist writer, Kurt Konrad, after seeing the performance, wrote, 'The most important thing about the *Švejk* at D.35 is that he is not alone. He is inseparably linked with all voices from above and below. He has his double everywhere [...]' He cited Švejk's last words in Burian's version as evidence of the change which had taken place in him from passivity to 'revolutionary activity': 'To hell with you, you idiot, stop shooting! There are human beings here.' (A remark, incidentally, which is quite out of character with the original book.) The play was no longer a satire on the Austrian military, Konrad said, but an attack on war in general.[20] So the Left were trying to turn Švejk into what Dyk most feared he might become – a consciously subversive element.

There were however some important Communists who flatly refused to allow Hašek a place in the literary pantheon. The doyen of Communist poets, S. K. Neumann, who had influenced Hašek for a time in his Anarchist days, had described him in 1921 as a 'clown and anti-Bolshevik' when he appeared at 'The Red Seven' cabaret immediately after his return to Prague. He sneered at him as a 'lost son' who had only left Russia because there was no more alcohol to be had there. Although Neumann modified his view later, he was never an admirer of *The Good Soldier Švejk*. Strongly opposed to individual sabotage and regarding activities such as 'dodging' and malingering as pointless, as long as conditions for a general revolution were not present, he went so far as to suggest that the book and its central figure were detrimental to the coming revolution. For him Švejk was no active fighter but only a contemptible 'dodger', who 'dodged' purely out of self-interest.[21]

By 1939 Hašek's great champion, Fučik, had come to new conclusions: 'Švejk is not a static character', he maintained.

'In the course of the book his character gradually evolves into an active, if not always conscious, destroyer of the "system". When the situation becomes serious, he will fight very seriously and most thoroughly', he wrote under a pseudonym in January 1939.[22] This heralded renewed attempts by the Left to mobilise Švejk in the ideological war, particularly at the time of the imminent Nazi threat.

Thus criticism in Czechoslovakia continued to polarise along ideological lines, with Marxists harping on Švejk's 'revolutionary potential' and the non-Marxists condemning the moral cowardice which, in their view, his unheroic attitude and actions implied. However, there were various shades of opinion among critics of the same ideological convictions: the Communist Neumann's view, for instance, that 'Švejkism' was a danger to the revolution seemed to run parallel with extreme conservative opinion, who saw in it a threat to the survival of capitalist society.

In Germany, where trends tended to be more radical and extreme, especially at election times, this politicisation of Švejk was pursued even more intensely. At the beginning of 1929, Greta Reiner, who had by now adopted an all-out Communist approach, had written: 'On all sides Švejk was used as a weapon in the election contest. For the Left he was the embodiment of the struggle against divine right, faith in false authoritarianism and the scourge of militarism. The Right described him to their listening flock as the incarnation of "dodging" and defeatism.' She too had by this time convinced herself that Švejk was no symbol of passivity, but 'an active hero'. Her interpretation was in step with Burian's production and Fučík's article – the Party line.[23]

Piscator's production of *The Good Soldier Švejk* seems to have achieved in Germany what Burian's fail to do in Czechoslovakia. It alerted the non-Socialist writers to the importance of the book. After Švejk had appeared on the stage in the beguiling interpretation of the great German comedian Max Pallenberg, Hašek's book became widely popular in Germany, not only with Communists and revolutionaries but with non-political readers as well. Indeed, if Piscator's production had had the effect of making a political figure of Švejk, Pallenberg, who continued to play the rôle in the German provinces independently of Piscator, tried to depoliticise him for fear that Piscator's original presentation would be unacceptable to the wider German public. Thus the actor to some extent countered the growing tendency to regard Švejk as an ideological figure. Eventually he brought his company to Prague, where Max Brod saw his performance. Brod recalled that Pallenberg's acting was a *tour de force*, but that his Švejk was no longer the genuine Švejk, but merely 'a sly batman and, in some scenes, an idiot'. (Earlier Brod had said that Švejk *was* an idiot!)[24] Pallenberg certainly played about with the text. When Švejk was asked why he was in Budějovice he answered in Schiller's famous words: 'To free the town from tyranny'! Švejk *might* have known that tag, but it is doubtful.

After the Nazi takeover in Germany in 1933, German Communists in exile began discussing whether Švejk was relevant to the new conditions of Nazi domination and particularly whether he would have a place in the new Communist society which would come after its fall. Kurt Konrad believed that Švejk was the inevitable product of the abuses inherent in the old capitalistic order. In the new society which was to take its place, he maintained, an entirely different type of hero would be required, and the people would have to be mobilised in the fight against reaction by revolutionary songs instead.[25]

In 1936 Piscator, who was living in exile in France, sent Brecht, then in exile in Copenhagen, a draft scenario for a film about Švejk, which was to make propaganda for the anti-Fascist front, but was never produced because of the international tension. In it Piscator abandoned all attempts to give political colour to the character of Švejk; the good soldier is shifted from his rightful position in the centre of the story to a siding, and the main interest is focussed on a love affair between Lukáš and a totally new character called Dora, a dedicated anti-Fascist militant. Švejk helps to bring the couple together and Dora achieves the political re-education of Lukáš (according to the stock recipe of Socialist Realism).

Brecht himself was so fascinated by the story of Švejk that he was quite unable to leave it, in spite of having worked on two dramatic versions of it already. In fact jealousy between him and Piscator about who should be the first to bring Švejk back to the stage or screen is said eventually to have led to their estrangement. On May 27 1943 Brecht wrote in his diary 'Under no circumstances may Švejk be allowed to become a cunning, slimy saboteur. He is purely and simply the opportunist of those tiny opportunities which have remained to him.'[26]

Although Brecht's *Švejk in the Second World War* (first performed in Warsaw in 1957, a year after Brecht's death) took many of its comic ideas and situations from Hašek's original novel and harked back to the historic Piscator version, it cannot be classed as a dramatisation of the original book. By transposing the action to the Second World War and bringing in Hitler, Goebbels and Goering – even introducing a scene where Hitler and Švejk are on the stage together – Brecht consciously distorted the original. Part of the plot of the play consists of Švejk's attempt to scrounge food for Baloun to prevent him from joining the German army in order to get regular rations. When Brecht showed these passages to his son, the latter told him that Švejk would never have worried about Baloun's difficulties and it was more likely that he would have advised Baloun to join the German army. The actor Peter Lorre, whom both Brecht and Piscator had had in mind to cast as Švejk, told Brecht that Švejk, the dog-lover, would never have killed the Colonel's dog merely to quell Baloun's appetite; but Brecht argued – unconvincingly – that Švejk was a dog-dealer, not a dog-lover, which was a very different thing.

A German provincial paper wrote after the first performance of Brecht's play, 'No Švejk figure with its golden humour, full of Austrian, Imperial and Royal warmheartedness, can fit into that [the Nazi] system of terror and total warfare.'[27] And Brod commented, 'I do not know the play, but I cannot believe that it is a success, because the good Švejk belongs absolutely to the milieu of old Austria.'[28]

After 1945 no more articles appeared in Czechoslovakia disparaging Hašek's novel or suggesting that it was harmful to national morale. In the final revised edition of Arne Novák's *Handbook of the History of Czech Literature*, published in 1946, it was given a little more attention, although the critic's superficial knowledge is shown when he confuses the embryo and primitive Švejk in the pre-war stories with the finished article in the novel.[29] All attempts to turn Švejk into a contemporary figure were similarly abandoned. He was now set in his historical perspective, even if, under Leftist influence, that perspective was often distorted.

After the Communist takeover in 1948, there was a gap of a few years during which Hašek's works were not considered calculated to contribute to the advance towards Socialism, and he nearly became an 'un-person'. Writing in 1954, the Czech critic Jiří Opelík drew attention to the promise made in 1950 but not fulfilled, to publish all Hašek's works by 1953.[30] Then suddenly a new period of intense study of Hašek and Švejk was ushered in, due partly to the attention given to him in the Soviet press and literature. Several new editions of *The Good Soldier Švejk*, at least one of which was annotated, were published (although the number of copies printed seems to have been quite inadequate, judging by their scarcity in Prague during the years 1960–66 at least), and an intensive effort was made to track down all the works of Hašek, however insignificant, which had not been published in his lifetime. In doing this no expense was spared; but the quality of many of the stories unearthed was so unequal and the attention and praise lavished on them so disproportionate that one wonders whether the exercise as a whole has enhanced the author's reputation. More constructive was the immense work of scrutinising the texts and re-editing them, which was performed for the first time by Zdena Ančík, a Communist journalist who worked in Britain during the war, and who must be regarded as the doyen of 'Hašekologists'. On his death the work was taken over by his younger colleague, Radko Pytlík, who has done more than anyone else to popularise the author and make him intelligible to this generation. His biography, *The Roving Gosling*, is as readable as a novel, and at the same time presents all the latest discoveries about Hašek's life, which makes it invaluable for those who wish to study him.[31] Researchers into the life and works of Hašek are much indebted to these two scholars.

Naturally the feverish re-issue of Hašek's stories in Czechoslovakia was partly prompted by the lack of entertaining books being written there in the grim fifties. The justification for the subventions lavishly supplied was not so much that Švejk was a revolutionary figure (although attempts were still made to take him further in this direction than was justifiable), but rather that he was a 'folk hero' and, more important, that his creator had been (for a short time) a member of the Communist Party, a Soviet 'commissar', and, *ipso facto* had a keen social consciousness.

In Germany after the war there was no doubt about the acclaim paid to Hašek in the German Democratic Republic, where his book was almost as popular as in Czechoslovakia. In the German Federal Republic, Austria and Switzerland, *The Good Soldier Švejk* appeared in numerous new editions, but several of the versions were truncated and, paradoxically enough, even censored. One incomplete edition published in the German Federal Republic in 1952 had a preface by the well-known Viennese writer Alfred Polgar,[32] who wrote with some truth, 'The book makes unsparing but masterly use of the liberties which caricature offers: it has the right to be unjust, and its legitimate artistic methods are distortion, exaggeration [...]' In the German Democratic Republic and Czechoslovakia, however, critics could not be expected to write as frankly about Hašek's limitations, although they may privately have shared Polgar's view.

Criticism after the Communist takeover in Czechoslovakia followed the monotonous and often uninspired lines which Marxism-Leninism laid down. Hašek and Švejk were presented not as they actually were, but as the Communist authorities wished them to be seen. This resulted in several rigidly dogmatic and often forced or distorted studies of both. An example of the latter was the sycophantic remark of the Communist critic, Jiří Opelík in 1954, when Malenkov was President of the Council of Ministers in the U.S.S.R.: 'Fučík shows Švejk as an example of "typisation" in line with Comrade Malenkov's definition of typicality'![33] (After Comrade Malenkov's disappearance copies of the critic's article were no doubt hard to find!)

In the mid-sixties, as a more liberal atmosphere became noticeable in Prague, writers could be found who were bold enough to record a dissentient opinion, which in the fifties would have been regarded as ideologically unsound. Professor Václav Černý, a respected non-Communist literary critic, published in 1965 an article in the literary review *Honour the Guest*, which

Jaroslav Hašek

revealed the same sort of critical attitude which 'establishment' criticism might have taken if Communist rule in Czechoslovakia had never been installed. It is worth quoting an extract from a translation of its rather tortuous Czech, if only for this reason.

> And so it is a fantastic error to attribute [to Švejk] any kind of revolutionary, programmatically ideological or ethical meaning. In his character there is not the least trace of any intent to regenerate or construct. Only the naïvest literary misinterpretation of the book would enable anyone to believe that the fictional character created by a certain author can be credited with views held by that author in his capacity as a citizen at any given moment of a revolutionary situation. And this was *The Good Soldier Švejk* which was even recommended for school reading! For the time being only the gods know in whose tiny brain was born this plan of a direct assault on the standards of our young people's feelings for the serious things of life, but the picture of a schoolboy devouring *The Good Soldier Švejk* on official orders, with the object of strengthening his 'progressive and positive attitude', definitely merits a place in the history of our educational science and cultural wisdom.[34]

England had to wait for Švejk until 1930, when Paul Selver made the first English translation of the book for Penguin. He cut it so that it was reduced to about two thirds of the whole. This was either due to the translator's own prudishness and fear of offending opinion in England and America, or to a pardonable belief that the book was too long. He was in the service of the Czechoslovak Embassy in London and no doubt shared the view of those who thought that Švejk was not the best advertisement for the Republic. He has the doubtful merit of having imposed on the British and American public a spelling and pronunciation of the name 'Švejk' which exists nowhere else in the world, not even in Germany. Selver's 'Schweik' (Shvike) is a complete misnomer. The Germans call him 'Schwejk' and the French 'Chvéik', in their efforts to be faithful to the correct pronunciation (Shvake). Even Brecht spells his 'Schweyk' with a 'y' to come nearer to the Czech. In his *Schweyk in the Second World War* he makes Švejk say: 'I have luck with my name, because I am Schweyk with a "y". If I had written it with an "i", I should be of German descent and could be called up.'

In 1973 the first complete translation of *The Good Soldier Švejk* by the present author was published by Penguin and Heinemann throughout the world and by Crowell in the U.S.A. It is

182

important for readers who do not know Czech or German to make sure they have this new translation, since otherwise they will be getting a bowdlerised version with many of its piquant passages arbitrarily cut out.

9
WERE THE CRITICS RIGHT?

'I think we should be fair about everything. After all, anybody can and must make a mistake...Even ministers make mistakes.' (Švejk)

How far were the critics of *The Good Soldier Švejk* justified in the judgements they passed on it? Some of them made the mistake of reading into the book far more than the author intended. They failed to appreciate that humorists are often concerned more with creating comic scenes and comic characters than conveying a political or moral message. Of course Hašek was a satirist and was not short of arrows to shoot or targets for his shafts. But his humour, both as a writer and in his personal life, had always contained strong elements of parody and burlesque – spoof – and it is sometimes difficult to know whether it is not the sheer fun of 'guying' someone or something – the exuberance of the comic actor and impersonator – rather than the righteous indignation of the satirist and moralist, which is winning the day.

Can the book be regarded as a political one, as some of its critics on the left believed? Did the author intend it to be interpreted as such? It seems that Hašek took some pains to ensure that it was *not* politically motivated and that its leading character should not be identified with any political philosophy. Švejk is just a 'little man' who, with very few exceptions, recognises that political considerations are beyond him and leaves them to others to sort out.

Hašek had joined the Bolshevik Party in Russia in 1918. This was only five years before his death. It might have been thought that from then on he would have remained a Communist to the very end. In the First Republic one was free to nail one's colours to the mast, even if those colours were flaming red. Indeed Communists enjoyed remarkable liberty of expression and action and took part freely in political and administrative life. It is possible that the need to live down his recent controversial past may have enjoined on Hašek a certain measure of caution, but a firm believer in Communism as the great panacea for all social ills would surely not have been so easily discouraged.

But there is no evidence to suggest that after his return to Prague Hašek's allegiance to Communism remained as fervent as it had once been. He showed that he was quite prepared to satirise the way Bolshevik power had been exercised in Russia and the sort of people who were exercising it, when he published the delightful *Bugulma Tales* in the Prague press. The satire was gentle, but telling enough to arouse protests from the Red Army. It is true that Hašek was unwilling to go further and write pronouncedly anti-Soviet stories – to present the Soviet scene as it actually was or at any rate as public opinion wished to see it. And it can always be argued that if Hašek had not left his book unfinished but had written two further volumes showing Švejk in Russia, he might have given it a pro-Soviet and pro-Communist slant in its concluding parts. But, up to the point where he stopped writing it, there is no indication in it that Švejk plans to desert, and an analysis of Švejk's character suggests that if he had been captured by the Russians his attitude to them would have been much the same as to any other authority. In this respect Hašek seems to have avoided the temptation to draw Švejk exactly in his own image.

At all events Hašek's preface to the book, written in 1921, shows quite clearly that Švejk is already back in Prague. He has not stayed in Russia to become a Bolshevik, nor has he been in China, otherwise he would certainly have been 'bothered by journalists asking for interviews'. Nor is there the remotest suggestion that he is a member of the Communist Party.

The novel can be classed as 'political' only in the sense that it describes the attitude of many Czechs to the Austro-Hungarian Monarchy, to an army that they had no wish to serve in and to a cause which they did not believe in and did not regard as their own. But this attitude, which was shared by many of the other nationalities in the Monarchy as well, can hardly be described as 'political'. It was a well-known fact of life, and in an independent Czechoslovakia it was scarcely necessary to reassert it. The principal message which the writer seems to be trying to convey is that war is a ghastly and pointless thing and that the Austrians who were running this particular sector of this particular war made a great muddle of it and in the course of their mismanagement took little account of human suffering. Of course, as a Czech, Hašek does not conceal his hatred and contempt for the Germans (Austrians), especially the N.C.O.s who, as he alleges, treat the men in general and the Czechs in particular like dogs. And he also seems deliberately to have remained silent about the Russians (except for the Central Asian prisoners for whom Švejk has to interpret). If the novel had been intended to have a Communist tendency, Hašek would surely have seized the opportunity to show up the incompetence of the Russian Imperial General Staff and bureaucracy as well as the Austrians. But it should not be forgotten that while in Kiev Hašek was for some time pro-Tsarist; and during most of his service in the Austrian army he was no doubt thinking in terms of a national or pro-Slav revolution rather than a social one. As for the novel's anti-war tendency, everyone hates war and countless books have been written about wars which show up their futility and reflect on the ethics of those who wage them without necessarily being classed as political.

What is more surprising is that the book contains so little direct social satire – much less than Hašek's short stories. Although the officers in the novel are shown as stupid, unprincipled and sometimes corrupt, the N.C.O.s and the men are not much better. Nor is there much class distinction. Human beings in all strata behave grotesquely, and one cannot really claim that in the book the author was paying even lip-service to the aims of the October Revolution, which he had been assiduously propagating in his journalistic writings from the moment he deserted the Legion and joined the Red Army. It is certainly surprising that none of his preachings from that time survived to reappear in the novel he began to write only some three years later.

Still less can Švejk himself be described as a revolutionary. Throughout most of the book he claims to believe in law and order, discipline and loyalty to the Monarchy. This is, as we have often shown, partly ironical, but not always so. Perhaps it is part of his 'idiocy', but it is certainly not the attitude of a convinced revolutionary. And as soon as he finds himself in a position where he can wield authority, he ceases to have any qualities which might have been described as subversive. The leading non-Communist critic, Václav Černý, was quite right when he wrote that it was a fantastic error to attribute to *Švejk* any revolutionary meaning at all. By 1936 even Piscator, who had tried to make 'a conscious revolutionary out of an unconscious one' (to quote Willy Haas), had given up all attempts to present him as such, and even Julius Fučík, the young Communist critic, who had earlier labelled Švejk as a 'half-proletarian petty bourgeois', was forced to admit that he was 'the type of the *un*revolutionary little man'.

Hašek's apolitical approach separates him from Bertolt Brecht, with whose writings his own have been compared. It is difficult to draw parallels between a single novel and a series of dramatic works, because the theatre makes its own specific demands which are not necessarily applicable to fiction. The theatre has been *par excellence* the medium for revolutionary experiment, while the novel neither requires it nor necessarily lends itself to it, especially in the hands of a writer so inexperienced in that literary *genre* as Hašek. He was so conventional and unrevolutionary in his literary style and thought, that Brecht's and his treatment of the same theme would be bound to produce totally different results, as indeed did happen when Brecht took over the Švejk theme himself. With Hašek's Švejk it is Švejk's innocence which triumphs. He appears not to be consciously undermining authority, whereas Brecht's *Švejk in the Second World War* presents a Švejk who is boastfully conscious of his demoralising influence. This does not of course exclude certain similarities which were inevitable given that Brecht was such a great admirer of Hašek's *Švejk* and even fell into Hašek's style in some of his plays (*The Caucasian Chalk Circle, Man is Man* and *Mother*). Brecht was much struck by Hašek's use of the vernacular in *Švejk* and imported it into his plays, but he did not realise that the Prague germanisms of Greta Reiner's translation were not a true reflection of the natural Prague Czech of Švejk himself. If the two writers were alike in their use of distortion and grotesque caricature, Hašek, as a Czech, lacked that German aggressiveness and biting invective which characterises Brecht's work. Hašek could never have written *Die Dreigroschenoper*. The world of vice – of highwaymen, cutthroats and prostitutes – was not his. He was drawn to the society of drunkards, idiots, sinners, tricksters, scroungers and layabouts: but violence and real depravity were absent from it. It was a gentler world and one which came within his own experience. '*Erst kommt das Fressen und dann kommt die Moral*' they sing in *Die Dreigroschenoper*. But although the Czechs, like the Germans and unlike ourselves, have a double form of the verb 'to eat' – one to eat like a human being and another to eat like an animal – Hašek seldom uses the Czech equivalent of *fressen* (žrát) – even in the case of Baloun. In his novel the German N.C.O.s treat the Czechs as animals and call them such, but Hašek concentrates on the human qualities even of outcasts of society.

A question which was debated by Communist critics was whether Švejk was a 'universal type', who can still be found today, or whether he could have existed only in the peculiar conditions of the old Austro-Hungarian Monarchy. Is he essentially Czech or could he equally well have been of another nationality – and 'universal'? And finally is he, as Kurt Konrad believed, essentially the product of the abuses of the capitalist system, or could he, as no Communist dares mention, exist even under a Communist system? The answer is of course that some of the conditions which Hašek holds up to ridicule continue to exist today, especially in countries under Communist rule. Indeed in some respects the conditions of idiocy, mindlessness and hypocrisy which he describes as existing under the Monarchy are more prevalent in the world at large today than they were in Hašek's own time. In some sector in all societies in all countries of the globe Švejks can still be found struggling with the system in which they are involuntarily involved. In that sense Švejk is not exclusively a Czech phenomenon and still less a typically capitalist one. Certainly, under the harsh repressive rule of Nazis or Stalinists, Švejk would not have been able to survive as easily as he did under the far milder and less oppressive régime of the Austrian monarchy. In that sense – but in that sense alone – he belongs to a past epoch.

Most people who have read Švejk or have heard of him, assume that he is specifically Czech, and that he embodies the virtues, vices and characteristics of that nation. A special kind of passive resistance under Fascism or Communism is referred to as 'Švejkian tactics'. But in times of war, occupation, oppression or even only unpopular rule, there will always be Švejks and Švejk-like tactics without regard to the nationality of those who perform them. They were to be found, for example, among the Norwegians under German occupation during the war and occur today among the Poles under Soviet domination. They have occured in many countries where conditions gave rise to them. It may be that Švejk's passivity and caution are to be associated with certain identifiable facets of the Czech character. He is no Captain from Köpenick, prepared to run the risk of *actively* making fun of the whole Prussian system. He is content to take life in his stride, confining his efforts to causing confusion in the minds of the officers – especially in regard to himself. He makes no pre-meditated and consistent attempt to hamstring the war effort, although in minor matters he succeeds in doing so, nor does his existence pose any serious threat to it. He is certainly not the conscious saboteur some Communist critics claimed him to be.

Naturally the Marxists thought or liked to think that Švejk was an international type, because they affected to believe that the 'little man' was oppressed in all capitalist states and only free when living under Communist rule. And Soviet thinking assumes that all wars except their own are unjust, so that their war against Finland in 1939, a nation of 'little men' if you like, was a 'just' war. In all armies and indeed in all countries there is a place for Švejks, but they would obviously have a securer existence in the capitalist world than under the Soviet empire, where it would be an act of treason to describe the Soviet army as anything else than an army of heroes or to suggest that the Soviet command was stupid. It is hard to imagine what would have been Hašek's fate today if he had spoken of the Soviet General Staff in the same ribald terms as he did of the Tsarist Russian.* Thus a true contemporary *Švejk* could not appear in print today in the Soviet Union, except in *samizdat*.

Is Švejk a 'dodger' and, if so, is he a 'dodger' on principle or of necessity? Of course a certain amount of 'dodging' activity goes on in all armies, but if Švejk 'dodges' he is clever enough

---

* He went around saying that 'if he put a finger up his arse he could direct the front better than the whole Russian general staff'.

to do so under the cover of protestations of patriotic enthusiasm and devotion to the Emperor. His creator, Hašek, was much more of a 'dodger' in civilian life. In the army he initially tried 'dodging' but later settled down, after which he certainly did not dodge dangerous expeditions, in fact he volunteered for one and was decorated for his courage in undertaking it. Švejk innocently 'dodges' or 'opts out' by getting himself into trouble, but we are never quite sure whether there is not method in his 'innocence'.

Many of these questions need never have been asked, if Hašek had lived longer and could have answered them for us. What is so strange is that he appears never to have discussed the meaning of his book with any of his drinking companions and friends at Lipnice, while he was writing it. Even Jarmila, to whom he read at least the first chapter of the book when he was taking it to the printer, tells us nothing about it, although she said that through reading it she 'learned to admire for his art the man she had once loved for his joy in life'.[1] This suggests that he was not writing because he had a message which he was bursting to unload on the world, but was making the fullest use of all the comic experiences which he had witnessed or heard about from others, and hugely enjoying the task of knitting them all together into his one and only novel.

Max Brod was the first to compare Hašek to Cervantes, and the German translator, Greta Reiner, followed him in this. Willy Haas called Švejk 'Sancho Panza without Don Quixote'. Hans Reimann wrote: 'Švejk, this clown of God, Sancho Panza and Don Quixote in one person, stands on the same heights as Rabelais, Shakespeare and Grimmelshausen [...]'[2] The same thought was echoed in *Zeitschrift für Bücherfreunde* a month or two later.[3] *Die Welt am Abend* too declared that Hašek had perhaps created a type which would live in world literature like Sancho Panza, Oblomov or Leporello.[4]

Were these eulogies hopelessly wide of the mark? Were the views of *Berliner Börsen-Courier*[5] or Kurt Tucholsky in *Weltbühne* more in line with the truth when they described these claims as nationalistic exaggeration? 'We are familiar with the efforts of small states – "Hungary consists only of the most celebrated artists" [...]' wrote Tucholsky.[6] But these critics seem to have been unaware that the official representatives or critics of this particular small state – Czechoslovakia – had played no part at all in any cult of Hašek, quite the contrary. It was German praise they were questioning, even if the Germans responsible for it – Max Brod, Willy Haas, Hans Reimann, Greta Reiner – at the time may have held Czechoslovak citizenship.

At first sight there would appear not to be much resemblance between *Don Quixote* and *The Good Soldier Švejk*. In *Don Quixote* it is the don who is mad and the world around him sane. In Hašek's novel Švejk finds himself in a world of fools and rogues, a mad world 'where the paragraph rules' and he has to act a part in order to get by. Švejk may be an idiot, he may have well-intentioned but impracticable ideas which do not work out, but he is not a prey to fantastic delusions like the Don.

It is true that when contrasted with Lukáš, who stands for conventional good sense, Švejk appears a fool. But compared with Dub, Biegler and other Austrian officers and officials he stands out as a model of good sense. This gives rise to ambiguities which the characters themselves have difficulty in resolving. In Cervantes' novel the Don is as much puzzled by Sancho as Lukáš is by Švejk. He says, 'Sometimes his simplicities are so shrewd that it gives me no small pleasure to consider whether it is simplicity or shrewdness that prevails.' Sancho boasts that he can tell 'many fine tales: yea, more than there are drops of water when it raineth'. Don Quixote says to him, 'If you tell your story that way, Sancho, and repeat everything you have to say twice over, you will not be done in two days. Tell it consequentially like an intelligent man or else be quiet.' This is just what Lukáš might have said to Švejk and Švejk might well have replied like Sancho: 'The way I am telling it is the way all stories are told in my country, and I don't know any other way of telling it.' (In fact Lukáš did say: 'If you were to go on talking until evening, the longer you went on the more rot you'd talk' (p. 661).) Don Quixote gets just as irritated with Sancho's repetitious proverbs as Lukáš does initially with Švejk's anecdotes, but he tolerates them while later Lukáš shows that he is much entertained by Švejk's repertoire. Moreover Švejk's habit of telling long stories is a part of his survival technique. He changes the subject so as to deflect away the anger of a superior or to disarm a listener. Sancho is very much of a natural: he is uneducated and can neither read nor write (although his rhetoric sometimes seems to belie this). Švejk is educated and knowledgeable, even if the experiences which he relates are as much based on Czech life and conditions in Bohemia as Sancho's observations are on local Spanish conditions. Both have a native shrewdness, but they could not be interchanged. Even if there were superficial resemblances between the Spanish and Austrian empires in Cervantes' time – both were ramshackle and heading for collapse – one cannot imagine Sancho in Švejk's place. He would have been lost when trying to deal with Austrian or Czech bureaucracy. Their idiocy could only be met by a simulated idiocy, of which Sancho Panza could hardly have been capable. Sancho could not exist without the Don, whereas Švejk stands almost alone.

Sancho is the slave of his appetitites – food, drink and sleep. His folly derives from his inability to control them. He is on the way to being a Baloun but falls short of it. Švejk is the opposite – he contributes out of his own purse to increase the lunch-portions he brings to Lukáš. Sancho is a coward and as he admits himself, has something of the rogue in him. 'True it is that I am somewhat malicious and have certain knavish glimpses: but all is covered and hid under the large cloak of my simplicity, always natural to me, but never artificial.' In Cervantes' novel the Don's madness is infectious and Sancho catches it from his master. Švejk, on the other hand, although claiming to be happiest of all in a lunatic asylum, is not mentally affected by the madness around him, wherever it happens to manifest itself.

The aims of the two writers were of course entirely different, as were the ages when they wrote. Cervantes accepted the counter-reformation and the spirit of the times. Apart from providing entertaining reading matter for the public, he wanted to parody the stories of chivalry on which the public were being fed. Hašek parodies the nonsense which is being written and spoken by the authorities in Austria but he goes further; he parodies the Monarchy itself, its army and the unnecessary war it has provoked. As a result, his novel is avowedly tendentious in a way in which *Don Quixote* is not.

Both the books are rich in characters and paint a lively picture of the country and the age. Cervantes' canvas has greater sweep, freer movement and a vaster range of interesting types drawn from all classes and from all over Spain. Švejk spends much of his time in prisons or trains, which is a limiting factor. Both books are epics, but *Don Quixote* is essentially an adventure story, while *The Good Soldier Švejk* is a novel of character. The sustained comic writing which rings the changes on burlesque parody and high comedy is a feature common to both books, as well as the underlying idea that madmen can at times talk lucidly and sane men act for most of the time madly.

There is some evidence that Hašek, who did little serious reading, had at least read *The Pickwick Papers*. Indeed the Pickwick Club may well have served as some sort of model for his 'Party of Moderate Progress within the Bounds of the Law'. Hašek had many qualities in common with Dickens – his human interest in everyday people, his sympathy for the poorer classes (shown more in his short stories than in his novel), his love of hyperbole and the grotesque; but he lacked Dickens' great qualities as a narrator and writer – his masterly character-drawing and that deeper and broader humanity, that absence of *Schadenfreude* which ilumines every scene and every character in Dickens' books. Hašek shares with Dickens his love of the grotesque, but not his penchant for melodrama and sentimentality. Some of the episodes in *The Good Soldier Švejk* are much funnier than those in *The Pickwick Papers*, but they are not told anything like as well. In genre painting Hašek can produce nothing to compare with Dickens' description of the Fleet. In this the English novelist, even as a beginner, shows himself to be Hašek's master in realism and commitment to social reform.

Fučík compared Švejk to Sam Weller, with whom he has some superficial resemblances, but who is fundamentally a very different character. Although Sam occasionally makes mistakes, he is a very competent servant, always on the look-out for some way of benefitting his master, and always rising to the occasion. He is certainly not 'the disaster' which Švejk often proves to be to those he serves. It is true that Sam always has his aphorisms to point a moral or suit the occasion, but they are generally trite and predictable, verging upon the tiresome – very different from Švejk's 'double-talk', which is usually unpredictable and intriguing. Sam's self-assurance and optimism stem from the confidence of a free man, whilst Švejk's caution and ambiguity betray him as coming from a part of Europe where serfdom had only been abolished less than a century before and national independence lost. But there are certain resemblances between the two books, which arise from their having both appeared in periodical instalments. Neither of the authors had quite thought out the story when they began, and, as the books proceed, the characters of both Pickwick and Švejk turn out to be rather different from what they appeared at the beginning. In *The Pickwick Papers* Mr Pickwick has always been the main comic character until Sam Weller appears. From that moment on he becomes a more serious and staid character.

It would be making too much of the character of Švejk or the literary stature of Hašek to compare the Good Soldier with Falstaff, and as far as I know, no one has yet seriously tried to do so. They have indeed even less in common. Švejk is no coward. There is no indication that he ever 'preserved his stinking skin from the Austro-Hungarian army' as Arne Novák suggested. The position of an orderly, which he had never sought, protects him from danger, and so he has no opportunity to test his courage. But he is capable of making sacrifices for his company commander and we have every reason to believe that, unlike his creator, he would follow him through thick and thin to the death. He is no braggart or liar like Falstaff. Drinking, eating or wenching seem to mean little to him. Indeed in this respect Falstaff has to a limited extent more in common with Švejk's creator than Švejk himself. On the other hand, although Švejk is able to confuse police officials and doctors, he is on a different plane of ingenuity, wit and eloquence from the fat knight, who is a ready match for someone so exalted as the Lord Chief Justice. One of the few qualities Falstaff and Švejk have in common is their cynical attitude to 'honour' on the battlefield. But even here in the case of Švejk it is tempered by his devotion to duty and his loyalty to his company commander, which is of a very different kind to Falstaff's devotion to Prince Hal. Švejk does not say, like Falstaff 'I like not this grinning honour.' In fact he says that it is fun to be a corpse!

It is easy with Max Brod to speak of Hašek's work in the same breath as that of Rabelais, but harder to justify the resemblance. There is a barrier between two epochs and two civilisations or systems, one gloriously uninhibited – the renaissance – the other, even in the twentieth century, still restrained by taboos, so that the gargantuan belly-laugh has declined into a sly snigger. Hašek was only too conscious of the discipline which convention imposed on him – his 'Epilogue to Part I' shows that – so that his humour is always kept within bounds, even in its most so-called 'Rabelaisian' parts. There is much to be said for the view of the Russian critic Bakhtin[7] that the grotesque with all its ribaldry and licentiousness was accepted as a natural and permissible facet of humour and merriment up to the renaissance, and it was the seventeenth and eighteenth centuries which started to clip humour's wings. Hašek, if he resembles Rabelais at all, comes closest to him, not in the occasional vulgar incidents or anecdotes he introduces, but in those scenes which are in the tradition of the carnival spirit of the medieval and renaissance burlesque, like Chaplain Katz preaching in the garrison chapel. As Bakhtin shows, the profanation of the mass in ribald parodies of it accompanied by obscene antics was long a tradition at carnival time. But many of the funniest scenes in Hašek's book have little in common with Rabelais. I suppose the scene in Dr Grünstein's ward after the stomach-pumping (pp. 62–78) might be compared to a scene in *Pantagruel* (although I should prefer not to read it as written by Rabelais); but Švejk's interviews with the authorities, the muddle over the cyphers, Švejk's various encounters with Dub, Švejk and Vodička's visit to the Kákonyis are as far removed from the Rabelaisian spirit of the renaissance as could be imagined. Rabelais was not only a master of words, which Hašek never would have claimed to be, but he was steeped in literature and learning as well. Moreover he was immensely resourceful in his powers of description, whereas Hašek was surprisingly poor.

Both were of course masters of satire, irony and parody and both vented their sarcasm on Church prelates, but this was in the spirit of every age and in the long tradition of satire. Rabelais was more interested in the conversations and actions of his characters than the characters themselves, whereas Hašek liked to delineate character with a few strokes and managed it well. What was original in Hašek was that he was the first writer to make the reader laugh aloud about the absurdity of war, while others had concentrated on its heroic or harrowing aspects.

Another writer whom some recent critics have linked with Hašek is Franz Kafka. They were both born in Prague in 1883, and died within a year of each other, though in different places. But if one tries to carry the juxtaposition further, one finds that Kafka belonged to the German cultural circle which had very little to do with the Czech, because the separation between the two cultures and the people who owed allegiance to them was a phenomenon of the period. In Budějovice (Budweis) where there is a large old square, the Germans would drink beer in an inn at one end of it and the Czechs at their inn at the other. 'And never the twain did meet.'

Hašek, who had no interest in any literary circles whatsoever, and felt contempt for modern and experimental writers, would most certainly have avoided Kafka and felt no sympathy for his writing. Attempts have been made to prove that Kafka actually met Hašek at the gathering of Hašek's mock political party, but this cannot be confirmed and it is highly unlikely that any meaningful meeting between them ever took place, otherwise Max Brod, who thought highly of both, would have told us about it. He does not appear to have made an attempt to bring them together, but this was probably because Max Brod knew Hašek's books better than his circle, into which he would certainly not have fitted. He and Kafka were too serious to be bohemians.

A Czech artist once said to me, 'We Czechs cannot read Kafka. We have lived through the Protectorate.' But that friend still reads and enjoys *Švejk*. He meant, of course, that Kafka reminded him of suffering, while Hašek took his mind away from it. Kafka's novels take place in a twilight. Hašek's *Švejk* is in broad daylight. Kafka is symbolistic. Palivec, to quote Hašek's own words, 'in unrefined language [...] expresses in a simple and honest way the detestation the ordinary Czech feels for Byzantine methods' (p. 215). Kafka's characters accept the Byzantine methods, or rather, as the Soviet critic Bernshtein puts it, 'fall in with the rules of the game'.[8] Švejk does not: he disrupts them.

On the other hand the Prague Germans reacted differently from the Czechs to Kafka's writings. To them they are essentially Prague itself, though not the Prague of the Czechs. 'I cannot imagine how any man who was not born in Prague around 1890 or 1880 can understand him [Kafka]...' These were the words of the Prague German Jew Willy Haas, who also said that he read Kafka's books 'as one reads a completely familiar panorama of one's own youth, where one immediately recognises every hidden nook, every corner, every dusty corridor, every lascivious thought or act, every allusion however delicate and remote. Kafka certainly said everything we had to say and did not because we could not. This is for me his genius.'[9] For the Czechs, however, Prague was far from being the 'twilight city' with memories of the Ghetto.

Karel Košík in his penetrating essay 'Hašek and Kafka'[10] has imagined that when Švejk was being led from the Hradčany garrison gaol down over the Charles Bridge he might have met Josef K. as he was being led up to his death in the Strahov quarry. He assumes that neither would have noticed the other – Josef K. would be absorbed in studying the physiognomy of his companions and Švejk would be chatting comradely with his guards. He believes that the two writers presented two separate visions of the world which in reality complement each other. Kafka taught that man must experience all types of alienation to be human. Hašek showed man as irreducible to an object and 'transcending reification'. For him man was indestructible.

Bernshtein suggests that the difference between Josef K. and Švejk lies in the fact that the former is surprised by everything and the latter by nothing.[11] One certainly could not imagine Švejk a prey to Josef K.'s metaphysical torments, even if his sentiment, based on bitter experience of life, that 'No one anywhere has ever worried about a man being innocent', comes close to Kafka's.

NOTES

Chapter 1

1 F. X. Šalda, 'Jaroslav Durych essayista', *Šaldův Zápisník*, I, Prague 1928–9.
2 Hašek's life is told in detail in the author's biography of him, *The Bad Bohemian*, London, The Bodley Head, 1978. References to source material which are contained in this book are not repeated here.

Chapter 2

1 J. V. Polišenský, *Britain and Czechoslovakia*, Prague 1966, who quotes from John Harrison's, *The Historie of Bohemia 1619–20* and John Taylor's *Taylor His Travels from the City of London in England to the City of Prague in Bohemia 1620*.
2 Karl Bosl, *Handbuch der Geschichte der Böhmischen Länder (Statistische Übersichten)*, Stuttgart 1968.
3 That this Battle of the Marchfeld had importance for Austria's national development is shown by the poet Grillparzer's patriotic drama on the subject *König Ottokars Glück und Ende*.
4 Hašek, after having joined the Bolsheviks, criticised the Czech historians for their blindness to the social revolutionary aspects of Hussitism. He called the Hussites 'the Czech Communists of the fifteenth century'. Hašek: 'Czech Communists of the Fifteenth Century'.
5 Hašek quotes the French historian Ernest Denis as saying that Josef wanted to 'create a state but created nationalities instead'. His policy of germanisation only served to stimulate national consciousness among the non-German peoples. (It is presumably *La Fin de l'indépendance Bohême* Hašek had in mind, but I have been unable to locate the passage.)
6 Metternich, whose estate was in Bohemia, helped the Czech movement for national revival as long as it was a purely cultural one. Czech animosity was mainly directed against his police chief von Sedlnitzky who, according to Hašek, demanded the alteration of texts even in theatre performances of Schiller's famous plays. The censorship was not only political but moral. One unfortunate dramatist was guilty of the incriminating words, 'Her breasts were milk-white and lush' and was immediately locked up until he changed it to 'Her front view was well developed.' (Hašek: 'Into the New Year')
7 On the eve of war there was such nervousness and excitement in Prague that the première of Smetana's opera *The Bartered Bride* which took place in 30 May 1866 was half empty.

8 Karel Kazbunda, 'Dvě Riegrova memoranda', *Zahraniční politika* ii 1925.
9 *Ibid.*
10 Graf Eduard Taaffe, *Politischer Nachlass* (ed. Dr Arthur Skedl), Vienna 1922.

Chapter 3

1 František Langer, *Byli a bylo*, Prague 1963.
2 Some of these are published in English in *The Red Commissar*, Lester and Orpen Dennys, Toronto, Heinemann, London and Dial, New York.
3 *Ibid.*
4 For further details see *The Bad Bohemian*, Chapter 8, and *The Red Commissar*.
5 Translated in *The Red Commissar*.
6 *Ibid.*
7 Radko Pytlík, *Toulavé house*, Prague 1971.
8 *Ibid.*
9 Golo Mann and Christian Schütze, *Das Beste aus dem Simplicissimus*. (No date or place of publication.)
10 'Zvilímkových politických satir', *Světozor* 35.1911.
11 See *The Red Commissar*.
12 *Ibid.*
13 *Ibid.*
14 *Ibid.*
15 *Ibid.*
16 *Ibid.*

Chapter 4

1 Zdena Ančík, *O Životě Jaroslava Haška*, Prague 1953.
2 Jarmila Hašková, 'Domovní prohlídka', *Drobné příběhy*, Havlíčkův Brod 1960.
3 Josef Lada, *Kronika mého života*, Prague 1954.
4 Aleksandra Lvova, 'Jaroslav Hašek', *Průboj* 24.1.1965.
5 Josef Lada, *Kronika*.
6 E. A. Longen, *Jaroslav Hašek*, Prague 1928.

Chapter 5

1 Jan Morávek, 'Jaroslav Hašek – dobrý voják Švejk', *Večerní české slovo* 1.9.1924 (and following articles in this series).

Chapter 6

1 Jan Morávek, *Jaroslav Hašek*.
2 *Ibid.*
3 Radko Pytlík, *Toulavé house*.
4 Jan Morávek, *Jaroslav Hašek*.
5 J. S. Lucas, *Austro-Hungarian Infantry 1914–18*, New Malden,

Surrey, Almark Publications 1973. The picture Hašek draws of the Austrian army is of course greatly distorted, even if some of what he says is no doubt based on personal experience. Mr Lucas of the Imperial War Museum has been most kind in pointing out to me what was not factual in Hašek's account and I have introduced corrections and reservations. But I am concerned here primarily with the picture Hašek drew of the Austro-Hungarian army rather than with the question whether it is true or not.

Chapter 7

1 Jarmila Hašková, 'Profil mrtvého druha', *Drobné příběhy*, Havlíčkův Brod 1960.
2 S. V. Nikolsky, 'Yaroslav Gashek', *Ocherki istorii cheshskoj literatury XIX–XX vekov*, Moscow 1963.
3 I. A. Bernshtein, *Cheshsky roman XX veka i puti realizma v evropeiskikh literaturakh*, Moscow 1979.
4 Nikola Georgiev, 'Parodie obsahu a parodie struktury, "Švejk" a anti-román', *Česká literatura* 4.1966.
5 *Die Abenteuer des braven Soldaten Schwejk* with introduction by Alfred Polgar, Köln-Berlin 1952.
6 Emanuel Frynta, *Hašek der Schöpfer des Schwejk*, Prague 1965.
7 Jarmila Hašková, 'Profil' ē František Langer, *Byli a bylo*.
8 Josef Lada, *Kronika mého života*.

Chapter 8

1 More detailed coverage of reactions in Czechoslovakia and Germany to *The Good Soldier Švejk* is contained in Pavel Petr, *Hašek's Schwejk in Deutschland*, Berlin 1963.
2 Max Brod, 'Švejk a jeho německé pojetí', *Literární noviny* 15.1931. See also his *Streitbares Leben*, Munich 1960.
3 Ivan Olbracht, *Rudé právo* 15 November 1921.
4 *Ibid.*
5 *Das Prager Tagblatt* 5 January 1923.
6 Julius Fučík, 'Pustý ostrov Švejk a universita', *Q* 1.1926. (Also *Stati o literatuře*, Prague 1951.)
7 Greta Reiner, 'Rote Fahne o Švejkovi', *Rudé právo – Dělnická besídka* 8 May 1927.
8 *Die Abenteuer des braven Soldaten Schwejk während des Weltkrieges* (trans. Greta Reiner), Prague 1926.
9 Karel Kreibich, 'Kniha dobrého vojáka Švejka', *Avantgarda* 6.1926.
10 F. C. Weiskopf, *Literarische Streifzüge*, Berlin 1956.
11 Willy Haas, 'Sancho Pansa ohne Don Quijote', *Die Literarische Welt* 12.11.1926.
12 J. O. Novotný, 'Rehabilitace Jaroslava Haška', *Cesta* 8.1927.
13 Jaroslav Durych, 'Český pomník, Dobrý voják Švejk', *Ejhle člověk*, Prague 1928.
14 Erwin Piscator, *Das politische Theater*, Berlin 1929.
15 John Willett, *The Theatre of Bertolt Brecht*, London 1959.

16 Max Brod, 'Švejk a jeho německé pojetí'.
17 Willy Haas, *Die Literarische Welt: Erinnerungen*, Munich 1958.
18 F. X. Šalda, 'O tzv. nesmrtelnosti díla básnického', *Studie o umění a básnících*, Prague 1948.
19 F. X. Šalda, 'Jaroslav Durych essayista', *Šaldův zápisník*, I, Prague 1928–9.
20 Kurt Konrad, 'Švejk není sám, Haškův Švejk v "D.35"', *Tvorba* 21.1935.
21 S. K. Neumann, *Válčení civilistovo*, Prague 1949.
22 Julius Fučík, 'Čehona a Švejk, dva typy z české literatury a života', *Milujeme svůj národ*, Prague 1954.
23 Greta Reiner, Introduction to the Fourth Edition of the German translation of *The Good Soldier Švejk*, Prague 1929.
24 Max Brod, 'Švejk a jeho německé pojetí'.
25 Kurt Konrad, 'Švejk a Oblomov', *Tvorba* 44.1935. (Pavel Petr quotes this in his book *Hašek's Švejk in Deutschland* (see note 1) but in Konrad's very diffuse article I cannot find any reference to 'revolutionary songs'.)
26 Bertolt Brecht, *Tagebucheintragungen* 27.5,1943.
27 *Taunusbote*, Bad Homburg 46.1959.
28 Max Brod, Letter to Olga Jeřábková 11.6.1958.
29 Arne Novák, *Stručné dějiny literatury české*, Olomouc 1946.
30 Jiří Opelík, 'Fučík jako kritický vykladač Haškova Švejka', *Česká literatura* 4.1954.
31 Radko Pytlík, *Toulavé house*.
32 *Die Abenteuer des braven Soldaten Schwejk* with introduction by Alfred Polgar, Köln-Berlin 1952.
33 Jiří Opelík, 'Fučík'.
34 Václav Černý, 'Král Ubu a pan Josef Švejk, jeho poddaný', *Host do domu* 12.1965 (6).

Chapter 9

1 Jarmila Hašková, 'Jaroslav Hašek', *Lidský profil Jaroslav Haška, korespondence a dokumenty* (ed. Radko Pytlík), Prague 1979.
2 Hans Reimann, *Das Stachelschwein* 2.1927.
3 Erik-Ernst Schwabach, 'Neue Bücher und Bilder', *Zeitschrift für Bücherfreunde, Neue Folge* 4 (July–August) 1927.
4 *Die Welt am Abend*, Berlin, quoted in Jan Münzer, 'Švejk v Německu', *Prítomnost* 8.1928.
5 *Berliner Börsen-Courier*, quoted in Münzer.
6 Ignaz Wrobel (Kurt Tucholsky), 'Herr Schwejk', *Weltbühne*, 8.6.1926.
7 Mihail Bakhtin, *Rabelais and His World*, Cambridge, Mass. and London 1968.
8 Bernshtein, *Cheshsky roman XX veka i puti realizma v evropeiskikh literaturakh*, Moscow 1979.
9 Willy Haas, *Die Literarische Welt*, Munich 1960.
10 Karel Košík, 'Hašek and Kafka', *Telos* 23.1975.
11 Bernshtein, *Cheshsky roman*.

APPENDIX 1

Hašek's contribution to newspapers and journals

If we confine ourselves to the study of those of Hašek's short stories and feuilletons which have been recently reissued, we have rather more than a thousand to consider. They originally appeared in a wide range of newspapers and magazines from Prague dailies like *National Policy* and *The National Newspaper* (the leading bourgeois papers), *The People's Right* (Social Democrat), *The Czech Word* (National Social) and *Revolutionary Youth, New Revolutionary Youth, Pauper* and *Commune* (Anarchist). *National Policy* had been founded as the organ of the Old Czechs, but managed to survive that party's collapse to become a widely read independent daily. *The National Newspaper* was the oldest established Prague daily (it was founded in 1861) and had by far the largest circulation. By Hašek's day it had become the organ of the important Young Czech Party and Dr Kramář. There were two groups of Anarchists – Anarcho-Syndicalists and Anarcho-Communists. Hašek identified himself for a time with the former and contributed to their ephemeral publications, but not to the journals of the latter like *The New Cult*, which was edited by the poet S. K. Neumann. This was of high quality and has its place in Czech literary history.

The range of magazines which published Hašek's articles was even wider, compromising a family illustrated like *Horizon* (comparable to the *Illustrated London News*), the satirical *Humorous Sheets*, literary reviews of old tradition like *Golden Prague* (once called *Lumír*), more light-weight productions like *Merry Prague* and cheap gutter press like *Caricatures, The Good Joker* and *Stinging Nettle*. Some of these 'rags' were run by the political parties – *Caricatures* by the National Socials.

In Russia Hašek wrote articles and stories for the Czech colony's paper in Kiev, *Čechoslovan*. Then, after deserting to the Bolsheviks, he started writing for Czech Communist papers in Russia (*Pioneer*) and later for Russian (*Our Path* and *Red Arrow*). On his return from Russia to Prague and up to his death he published in *Tribune* (a non-party daily), *Czech Word* or *Evening Czech Word* (National Socialist) and *Red Right* (Communist). He also contributed from time to time to *Kalendáře* (annuals), but did not publish a single article in the Social Democratic Party press.

Throughout his life Hašek did not discriminate between the various party organs, contributing to almost any of them which were prepared to accept his material, except the Catholic press. He had no scruples about writing for the major bourgeois dailies. It is true that after 1908 he said he would not contribute any more to *National Policy*, the most conservative of them, but

Appendix 1

even then he gave as his reason the way the humorous column was conducted, not the paper's politics, and failed to keep his word.

It was not until 1912 that any of his stories appeared in book form. In that year the first collection was published in Prague under the title *The Good Soldier Švejk and Other Strange Stories*. It contained the first *Švejk* stories and several others about military life. *The Tribulations of Mr That-Time*, which comprised a further selection of stories followed in the same year. In 1913 came *The Tourists' Guide and Other Satires from Home* and in 1915 *My Trade with Dogs and Other Comic Sketches*.

From 1916 onwards Hašek transferred his literary activities to Russia. In Kiev he contributed short stories and political articles to the Czech Legion's paper *Čechoslovan* until February 1918, when he deserted to the Bolsheviks and started contributing to Bolshevik papers like *Pioneer* (Czech), *Our Path* (Russian) and others. He was also engaged in editing and publishing papers and pamphlets for returning prisoners-of-war or exiles in various languages.

On his return to Prague at the end of 1920 he resumed his literary activities and *Two Dozen Stories* was published in that same year. In the following year came *Pepíček Nový and Other Stories* and *Three Men and a Shark and Other Edifying Stories*. The next year (1922) there was a reissue of *The Good Soldier Švejk Before the War and Other Strange Stories* and a further collection of nine stories which Hašek himself selected was published under the title *The Peace Conference and Other Comic Sketches*.

Hašek died on 3 January 1923, four months before his fortieth birthday. A year later Dr Antonín Dolenský, the Head Librarian in the National Museum, started to collect and publish a large number of his stories in an edition of 16 volumes. It was advertised as the 'first series' of Hašek's collected works, but after the last volume had appeared in 1929 no further volumes were published: 433 stories in all appeared in this edition.

It was not until 1955 (seven years after the Prague *coup d'état*) that the Czechoslovak State Publishing House began to publish a revised and more complete collection under the editorship of Zdena Ančík, a Communist journalist who, after 1948, became an official in the Ministry of Culture. The original programme, which appears by now to have been completed as far as the short stories are concerned, was as follows:

Volume I	1955	*Sketches, Short Stories and 'Humoresques from' Travels* (112)
Volume II	1958	*Murderer and Thief Before the Court* (91 stories of social satire)
Volume III	1961	*Mr Šafránek's Legacy* (78 'humoresques' or humorous sketches)
Volume IV	1962	*A Traitor to the Fatherland at Chotěboře* (80 stories about little men and bureaucrats)
Volume V	1961	*Purple Thunder* (73 stories on the Church and the nobility)
Volume VI	1961	*The Tribulations of Mr That-Time* (45 stories of love and married life)
Volume VII	1960	*On Children and Animals* (68 stories)

203

Volume VIII	1964	*From the Gallery of Caricatures* (104 stories about politicians and politics)
Volume IX	1963	*The History of the Party of Moderate Progress Within the Bounds of the Law* (82 stories about the Party and its members)
Volume X	1957	*The Good Soldier Švejk Before the War and Other Strange Stories* (77 stories of an anti-militarist tendency)
Volume XI	1972	*Cries of May* (51 miscellaneous stories in addition to the poems which provide the title)
Volume XII	1973	*Prague by Day and Night* (Changed to *The Entertaining and Edifying Corner*) (17 stories and various short pre-war press contributions)
Volumes XIII–XIV	1973	*The Good Soldier Švejk in Captivity* (The second version of *Švejk* and 67 articles and humoresques written in Kiev during the war)
Volume XV	1966	*In Soviet Russia* (Changed later to *The Commandant of Bugulma*) (47 stories and articles published in the Bolshevist press in Russia or in the Prague press after Hašek's return)
Volume XVI	1968	*My Confessions* (64 stories published in Prague after the war)
Volumes XVII–XVIII		*The Good Soldier Švejk and His Fortunes in the World War* (Various new editions of the novel have been published since but not in this series)
Volume XIX		*Life and Works of Jaroslav Hašek* (not yet published in the series)

The Communist editors of the new series accused Dolenský of having deliberately suppressed any of Hašek's writings which did not suit the political views of the *bourgeoisie* at the time. They in their turn have been criticised for shortcomings in their selection and arrangement of Hašek's works. Their edition seems originally to have been planned on the chronological principle. Thus the first volume contains the very early stories which Hašek had written in his teens and during his tramps all over Austria-Hungary. But then the editors switched to another principle, that of collecting and publishing stories with related subject matter (Volume II deals with criminals, Volume VII with children and animals and Volume X with army life). The disadvantage of this arrangement was that the reader was faced with a formidable number of stories with monotonously similar themes. As a result of criticisms to this effect later volumes were again arranged chronologically.

Appendix 1

In fact Dolenský's edition had some advantages over the more recent one. The average number of stories in each of his 16 volumes is only 21, whereas the first volume of the new series contains as many as 118, the second 91 and the eighth 104! To expose the readers to such an abundance of stories, most of which are only 2–3 pages in length, written when the writer was very immature, was to say the least, a tax on their endurance. The publishers' original aim seems to have been to cram as many stories as possible into each volume.

Ančík admitted that his task as editor was no easy one. Hašek himself had prepared for publication eight volumes of his stories but no more. The manuscripts were lost and the work of identifying and collecting stories which were scattered in a wide number of small publications and signed with a whole variety of pseudonyms – mostly names of living people – was extraordinarily difficult. In fact it cannot be proven that all the stories which Ančík included are Hašek's own. The decision to assign them to his authorship was in many cases taken on subjective grounds (presumed similarity of style or likelihood of subject) or sometimes on the advice of those of Hašek's contemporaries who had survived.

Nor can we be certain even now that all Hašek's writings have been published or that the most recent editors have not committed the sin of which they accuse Dolenský. Hašek was a mercurial and irresponsible character, and among the 1,200 stories which are attributed to his authorship there must certainly have been some which would be considered unsuitable by the present régime and likely to distort the picture it is trying to paint of him as a dedicated Communist. And are we quite sure we have all the stories and articles he wrote in Russia? Have the Soviet authorities really given the Czechs all the manuscripts found there? In any case the latest collection of Hašek's works admittedly includes only some 80 per cent of what is reputed to be his total output.

At present very few of Hašek's stories have been translated into English, or indeed into any Western language, but it is to be hoped that with time more will become available.

APPENDIX 2

Original Czech Titles of Hašek's Stories and Feuilletons mentioned in this book

A English title	B Original Czech title	C Volume in which it is to be found	D Page in text of this book
About the Activities of the Social Democrat Deputies Folber, Klička, Biňovec, Remeš and Jaroš in the *Reichsrat* in the *couloirs* and outside Parliament	Z činnosti sociálně demokratických poslanců Folbra, Kličky, Biňovce, Remeše a Jaroše na říšské radě, v kuloarech i mimo parlament	VIII	63
Above Lake Balaton	Nad jezerem Blatenským	I	59
Abstinents' New Year's Eve, The	Silvestr abstinentů	IV	82
Adventures of Václav Pejs, The	Dobrodružství Václava Pejse	IV	82
Adventures of Government Counsellor and School Inspector Kalous, The	Dobrodružství vládního rady a školního inspektora Kalouse	VII	90
Alarm Signal, The	Poplašný signál	VII	90
Albanian Throne, The	Albánský trůn	X	74, 83
And He Shook off the Dust from His Shoes	I vyklepal prach z obuvi své . . .	XV	72
Apostolic Activity of Three Members of the Party As Reflected in Letters to the Executive Committee, The	Apoštolská činnost tří členů strany zračící se v dopisech na výkonný výbor	IX	65
At the Divinity Lesson	V hodině náboženství	V	79

206

A English title	B Original Czech title	C Volume in which it is to be found	D Page in text of this book
Expedition of Šejba the Burglar, The	Výprava zloděje Šejby	II	87
First Day after the Coronation, The	První den po korunovací	X	74, 83
For Olga Fastrová	Za Olgou Fastrovou	XVI	71
Fortunes of Mr Hurt, The	Osudy pana Hurta	XIII–XIV	66, 68
From the Old Pharmacy	Ze staré drogerie	IV	61
Galician Landscape with Wolves	Krajina z Haliče s vlky	I	59
Good Soldier Švejk Is Cashiered, The	Superarbitrační řízení s dobrým vojákem Švejkem	X	100–101
Good Soldier Švejk Learns How to Handle Gun-Cotton, The	Dobrý voják Švejk učí se zacházet se střelnou bavlnou	X	101–102
Good Soldier Švejk Obtains Wine for the Mass, The	Dobrý voják Švejk opatřuje mešní víno	X	99–100
Good Soldier Švejk Operates in Aeroplanes, The	Dobrý voják Švejk působí u aeroplánů	X	102
Gypsy's Funeral, The	Cikánský pohřeb	I	59
History of the Party of Moderate Progress within the Bounds of the Law	Dějiny strany mírného pokroku v mezích zákona	IX	11, 64–66
Honest Finder, An	Poctivý nálezce	XVI	71
Hořice District Police Chief, The	Hořický okresní hejtman	XIII–XIV	67
How I Left the National Social Party	Jak jsem vystoupil ze strany nár. sociální	VIII	57
How I Met the Author of My Obituary	Jak jsem se setkal s autorem svého nekrologu	XVI	70

How in the Parish of Cikánov Brothel Keepers Joined the Organisation of the Christian Social Party	Jak vstoupili v obci Cikánově bordeláři do křest'anskosociální organisace	V	79
How My Wife Writes *Feuilletons*	Jak píše má žena fejetony	VI	58
Idyll from a Wine Cellar	Idyla z vinárny	XVI	71
Idyll from the Almshouse at Žižkov, An	Idyla z chudobince na Žižkově	II	82
In the Mountains on the Romanian Side	V horách na Rumunské straně	I	59
In the Reserve (poem)	V reservě	XIII–XIV	156
In the Tracks of the State Police in Prague	Po stopách státní policie v Praze	XIII–XIV	34
Into the New Year	Do nového roku	XIII–XIV	198
Intrepid Catholic Grandfather Šafler on Election Day, The	Neohrožený katolík dědeček Šafler v den voleb	V	79
Judicial Reform of State Counsellor Zákon, The	Soudní reforma pana dvorního rady Zákona	III	87
Justice and the Lesser Bodily Needs	Malá tělesná potřeba a justice	X	88
Justice Will Prevail	Spravedlnost zvítězí	X	85
King of the Romanians Goes after Bears, The	Král Rumunů jede na medvědy	I	83
Little Soul of Jaroslav Hašek Tells Its Story, The	Dušička Jaroslava Haška vypravuje	XVI	70
Money Sent by Telegram	Peníze telegraficky poukázané	XVI	71
Mr Gloatz, Fighter for the Rights of the People	Pan Gloatz, bojovník za práva lidu	V	78
Mr Kalous in the Rôle of Detective	Pan Kalous detektivem	X	84–5
My Confession	Moje zpověď'	XVI	70

English title	Original Czech title	Volume in which it is to be found	Page in text of this book
My Trade with Dogs (see Cynological Institute, The)	Můj obchod se psy	III	88
Official Zeal of Mr Štěpán Brych	Úřední horlivost pana Štěpána Brycha,		
Toll-keeper on the Prague Bridge, The	vybérčího na pražském mostě	I	59
Oh, Dunajec, You White Water	Oj, Dunajec, biała wóda	II	85
Old Man Jančar	Stařeček Jančar		
On Reading through Old Newspapers	Nad starými novinami	XIII–XIV	46, 48
Peace to His Ashes!	Pokoj jeho popelu!	IV	89
Preface by the Author	Předmluva od autora	XVI	72
Psychiatric Enigma, A	Psychiatrická záhada	III	10, 20
Punishment – Its Aim and Motive	Účel a důvod trestu	V	80
Reign of Francis Joseph, The	Panování Františka Josefa	XIII–XIV	83
Republican Programme in Bohemia, The	Republikánský program v Čechách	XIII–XIV	50
Ruler Who Will Sit down on Czech Bayonets, The	Panovník, který se posadí na české bajonety	XIII–XIV	15, 83
Sad Fate of Peter Hříbal, The	Smutný osud Petra Hříbala	VIII	63
Sad Fate of the Station Mission, The	Smutný osud nádražní misie	II	83
Saved	Zachráněn	II	87
School Excursion, The	Školní výlet	VII	90
School for the State Police, The	Škola pro státní policii	XIII–XIV	41, 84
Second and Third Main Prize, The	Druhá a třetí hlavní výhra	VII	89

Appendix 2

A English title	B Original Czech title	C Volume in which it is to be found	D Page in text of this book
Wanted a Murderer!	Hledá se vrah	x	84
What Every Czech Should Know about His Country	Co má každý Čech věděti o své vlasti	xiii–xiv	24
Where Deputy Klofáč Gets His Money from	Kde bere poslanec Klofáč peníze	viii	62
Why Are We Being Sent to France?	Proč se jede do Francie?	xiii–xiv	68
Young Emperor and the Cat, The	Mladý císař a kočka	x	83

APPENDIX 3

The original Czech names of newspapers and journals mentioned in the book

Caricatures	*Karikatury*
Commune	*Komuna*
Czech Word, The	*České slovo*
Evening Czech Word, The	*Večérní české slovo*
Golden Prague	*Zlatá Praha*
Good Joker, The	*Dobrá kopa*
Horizon	*Světozor*
Humorous Sheets	*Humoristické listy*
Merry Prague	*Veselá Praha*
National Newspaper, The	*Národní listy*
National Policy	*Národní politika*
New Revolutionary Youth	*Nová omladina*
Our Path	*Nash put' (Russian)*
Pauper	*Chud'as*
People's Newspaper	*Lidové noviny*
People's Right, The	*Právo lidu*
Pioneer	*Průkopník*
Red Arrow	*Krasny strelok (Russian)*
Red Right	*Rudé právo*
Revolutionary Youth	*Omladina*
Stinging Nettles	*Kopřivy*
Tribune	*Tribuna*
Young Currents	*Mladé proudy*

BIBLIOGRAPHY
Books and articles on Hašek and Švejk

Ančík, Zdena, *A živolě Jaroslava Haška*, Československý spisovatel, Prague 1953

Brod, Max, *Prager Sternenhimmel*, Paul Szolnay, Vienna and Hamburg 1966

Durych, Jaroslav, *Ejhle člověk! Český pomník*, Prague 1928

Frynta, Emanuel, *Hašek, the Creator of Švejk*, Prague 1965

Hájek, Ladislav, *Z mých vzpomínek na Jaroslava Haška*, Čechie, Prague 1925

Hampl, František, *Nejznámější absolvent Českoslovanské – Jaroslav Hašek*, Střední ekonomická škola, Prague 1972

Hašková, Jarmila, *Drobné příběhy*, Krajské nakladatelství, Havlíčkův Brod 1960

Janouch, Gustav, *Jaroslav Hašek, der Vater des Braven Soldaten Schwejk*, Berne and Munich 1966

Kalaš, Josef, *Jaroslav Hašek ve fotografii*, Československý spisovatel, Prague 1959

Křížek, Jaroslav, *Jaroslav Hašek v revolučním Rusku*, Naše vojsko, Prague 1957

Lada, Josef, *Kronika mého života*, Československý spisovatel, Prague 1954

Lada, Josef, *Můj přítel Švejk*, Svoboda, Prague 1969

Langer, František, *Byli a bylo*, Československý spisovatel, Prague 1963

Longen, E. A., *Jaroslav Hašek*, E. Beaufort, Prague 1928

Lvova, Alexandra, *Jaroslav Hašek ve vzpomínkách své ženy*, Průboj, Prague 24.1.1965

Menger, Václav, *Lidský profil Jaroslava Haška*, Koliandr, Prague 1946

Novák, Arne, *Stručné dějiny literatury české*, Promberger, Olomouc 1946

Opočenský, Gustav R., *Čtvrt století s Jaroslavem Haškem*, J. Steinbrener, národní správa, Vimperk 1948

Parrott, Cecil, *The Bad Bohemian. A Life of Jaroslav Hašek*. The Bodley Head, London, Sydney and Toronto 1978

Petr, Pavel, *Hašeks 'Schwejk' in Deutschland*, Rütten und Loening, Berlin 1963

Pletka, Václav, *Písničky Josefa Švejka*, Supraphon, Prague 1968

Pytlík, Radko, *Jaroslav Hašek*, Československý spisovatel, Prague 1962

Toulavé house, Mladá fronta, Prague 1971

Lidský profil Jaroslava Haška, Československý spisovatel, Prague 1979

Pytlík, Radko and Miroslav Laiske, *Bibliografie Jaroslava Haška*, Státní pedagogické nakladatelství, Prague 1960

Bibliography

Sauer, František, *Franta Habán ze Žižkova*, Nakladatelství politické literatury, Prage 1965

Sauer, Franta and Ivan Suk, *In memoriam Jaroslava Haška*, Družstevní nakladatelství, Prague 1924

Stejskal, Vladimír, *Hašek na Lipnici*, Krajské nakladatelstvi, Havlíčkův Brod 1954

Štěpánek, Kliment, *Vzpomínky na poslední léta Jaroslava Haška*, Krajské nakladatelství, Havlíčkův Brod 1960

Warausová, Vilma, *Přátelé Haškovi a lidé kolem nich*, Krajské nakladatelství, Havlíčkův Brod 1965

INDEX

Index

Index

Index

Lightning Source UK Ltd.
Milton Keynes UK
UKOW02f1031310716

279546UK00001B/20/P